PENGUIN BUSINESS
SUSTAINABLE SUSTAINABILITY

Rajeev Peshawaria is the Chief Executive Officer (CEO) of Stewardship Asia Centre (SAC) in Singapore and Founder President of the Leadership Energy Consulting (LEC) Company in Seattle, WA, USA.

Author of the Wall Street Journal and Amazon bestseller *Open Source Leadership* (McGraw Hill), *Too Many Bosses, Too Few Leaders* (Simon & Schuster), co-author of *Be the Change* (McGraw Hill) and a regular writer for Forbes, he constantly challenges conventional wisdom on leadership, management, stewardship, sustainability and corporate governance.

Before joining SAC and starting LEC, he was CEO of the Iclif Leadership and Governance Centre. Formerly, he has been Chief Learning Officer of Coca-Cola and Morgan Stanley and has held senior positions at American Express, HSBC and Goldman Sachs. At Goldman, Rajeev helped found Pine Street—the firm's acclaimed leadership academy—and headed Pine Street for Europe and Asia. In his early career, he was a banker and currency trader.

A high-energy inspirational speaker, Rajeev provides speaking, coaching, consulting and advisory services to corporate and public sector clients globally and has also served as guest faculty at leading business schools. He is a sought-after international speaker and has been widely featured in international media platforms such as CNN, Bloomberg TV & Radio, National Public Radio (NPR), *Harvard Business Review*, CNBC, *Fast Company*, *Leader to Leader*, *American Management Association (AMA) magazine*, *Leadership Excellence magazine*, *The Times of India*, *The Straits Times*, *The Business Times* and many more.

In 2014 and 2017, he was named one of Top 100 Global Thought Leaders for Trustworthy Business by 'Trust Across America'.

ADVANCE PRAISE FOR *SUSTAINABLE SUSTAINABILITY*

'The greatest danger to our planet is the belief that someone else will save it. In this book, Rajeev describes a higher form of leadership, one in which leaders see themselves as stewards of the environment and humanity. It is a must-read for anyone who cares.'

—Robert Swan, Officer of the Order of the
British Empire, Record-breaking Polar Explorer
and Environmental Campaigner

'This is not a crisis of climate change, inequality or food security. Many will argue that this is a crisis of greed, apathy and selfishness. *Sustainable Sustainability* shines light, with some practical examples, on what it takes to be a leader in today's world.'

—Paul Polman, Former CEO, Unilever
Author, *Net Positive*

'Rajeev sees things with great clarity, comes up with persuasive insights, and shares these with conviction and simplicity. Steward leadership is an important part of the solution to the world's biggest problems, and one that seems so obvious once Rajeev brings it to life—as he does so beautifully in this book.'

—Elaine Yew, Senior Partner and Global Co-Head, Family
Business & Family Office
Asia Lead on Board and CEO Succession, Egon Zehnder

'*Sustainable Sustainability* is a must-read for anyone interested in turning a vision into meaningful action. Rajeev provides a compelling argument for the need for genuine stewardship and offers practical steps for businesses to take. The recommendations are backed by extensive research and inspiring real-world examples—making it all real.'

—Ahmed Mazhari, President, Microsoft Asia

'The need for courageous and bold leadership is essential if businesses are truly to become a force for good. This book shows how these leaders must be willing to take risks, challenge the status quo and engage in long-term actions on the way to the sustainable, inclusive prosperity we so badly need.'

—André Hoffmann, Vice Chairman, Hoffmann-La Roche

'As we stand at the crossroads of progress in addressing environmental and social challenges, *Sustainable Sustainability* reinforces the urgent need for a new kind of leadership—steward leadership—and urges us to make a lasting impact. Based on extensive global research, Rajeev eloquently provides a cogent guide for those committed to shaping a brighter tomorrow for generations to come.'

—Keiko Honda, Former CEO and EVP, Multilateral Investment Guarantee Agency, World Bank Group
Adjunct Senior Research Scholar, School of International and Public Affairs, Colombia University

'Our environmental and social challenges require genuine and proactive efforts from stakeholders. But when challenges are public in nature and many parties need to be involved, it often ends up in coordination failure. ESG disclosure and incentive frameworks are necessary, but not sufficient, to tackle these challenges, which will only intensify over time.

Sustainable Sustainability provides light at the end of the tunnel. It focuses on stewardship values of leaders and clearly shows how to translate them into practice. Convergence of stewardship values among leaders will not only solve the coordination failure, but also produce sustainability in substance that is long lasting and collectively commensurate to the magnitude of our challenges.'

—Veerathai Santiprabhob,
Former Governor, Bank of Thailand
Secretary-General and Chairman of the Executive Board,
Mae Fah Luang Foundation under Royal Patronage

'Rajeev Peshawaria argues convincingly that we need to replace the "G" in ESG with "L" for Leadership, specifically, Steward Leadership. While his insightful discussion is backed by nine real-world case studies, he does not stop at case analysis alone. After explaining the "Steward Leadership Compass" concept, he presents a detailed questionnaire that companies can use to assess where they are on their journey to become champions of sustainability. This is a must-read for every top executive who believes that it is their responsibility to address environmental and social issues through their business.'

—Ilian Mihov, Former Dean, INSEAD
Visiting Scholar, Stanford

'There is often a gap between word and deed. The purpose of this excellent book is to close that gap on sustainability.'

—Tommy Koh, Ambassador-at-large,
Ministry of Foreign Affairs, Singapore

'Ah, the magic of an author who is steeped in effective pedagogy! In *Sustainable Sustainability*, Rajeev Peshawaria provides theoretical concepts and shares data and real-world illustrations to deepen the readers' understanding, but he doesn't stop there. He has created a practical assessment tool to determine where your organization sits in its journey to becoming an exemplar in sustainable sustainability, and action ideas for how you, as a leader, can take it there. So this is not just a book but also a course and a guide for action and results. Obligatory reading for managers and executives for every organization.'

—Melanie Barnett, Executive Director, Secretary and Treasurer,
UNICON International University Consortium

'This thought-provoking book challenges conventional wisdom from the word go. It provides great insights on not only the gravity of problems we face today but also what differentiates the real ESG champions from others. As a CEO, I personally subscribe to the steward leadership concept and feel that Rajeev hits the nail on the head when he asserts that only genuine passion and purpose of the leader and the organization can make the difference. I will certainly use this book and the principles within to foster true steward leadership in our organization.'

—Hina Nagarajan, Committee member,
Diageo Global Executive
President, Diageo India

'Rajeev's *Sustainable Sustainability* addresses the momentous and fundamental question of what creates true steward leadership. Illustrated with many cases and examples from across organizations, cultures, regions and issues, this wonderfully readable volume will guide many, from leaders to observers, towards a deeper understanding of how to move towards the long-term, holistic, positive social impact that we all need and long for. The four dimensions of interdependence, long-term orientation, ownership mentality and creative resilience, while leaving much space to an organization's own identity, give the basis of a toolkit towards successful and impactful stewardship. Thank you, Rajeev, for this important addition to our understanding of what drives true sustainability.'

—Didier Cossin,
Chaired Professor of Governance and Finance, IMD
Founder and Director, IMD Global Board Center

'Peshawaria raises a powerful point about the need to transition from ESG to ESL. There is great wisdom in the concept of steward leadership and creative resilience. While this may feel like a small change, it is anything but. This is exactly where the catalyst to drive lasting behaviour change and results in our pressing environmental and social issues will be found. It is all about leaders that take on the challenges ahead.'

—Salman Amin,
CEO, Pladis Global

'Good governance has always been about adhering to the spirit of the law, not only to the letter of the law. The book *Sustainable Sustainability* introduces the concept of "steward leaders" that combine governance in practice, ecosystem building and transformational leadership with persistence for a collective better future. It focuses on the consistent application of values, through testing times. Rajeev has delivered a set of compelling and diverse cases that challenge the widely accepted approach of evaluating the performance of companies and their executives, focusing on values articulated and practised, putting culture in action, with evidence of integrity.'

—Christine Chow,
Board Member,
International Corporate Governance Network (ICGN)
Sustainable and ESG Investment Woman of the Year,
Women in Investment Award (2022)
Managing Director and Head of Active Ownership, Credit Suisse
Asset Management, a UBS Group company

'Stewardship is the overarching business philosophy of creating and preserving value, over the long term, for all stakeholders. In this compelling book, Rajeev does a fantastic job of highlighting the importance of steward leadership as a core attribute for boards and senior management teams to navigate, and thrive, in today's business environment. Rajeev defines steward leadership as "the genuine desire and persistence to create a collective better future"—every word in that sentence is relevant and impactful; and serves as a strong call-to-action for companies. Very helpfully, the book shines the spotlight on progressive companies that have evolved past the moral imperative and are realizing the tangible financial and non-financial business benefits of steward leadership. These case studies can help inspire companies and help raise the collective consciousness of the business communities around the world. Very timely book indeed.'

—Shai Ganu, MD and Global Leader,
Executive Compensation & Board Advisory Business
Global Governing Board member, Climate Governance Initiative

'Steward leadership demands that one should rise above self-interest—to do what is right for the greater good. As the challenges facing us grow ever more urgent and complex, Rajeev's timely book serves as a compass for anyone who aspires to lead with compassion, courage, and conviction to create a brighter and more sustainable future for all.'

—Desmond Kuek,
CEO, Temasek Trust

'*Sustainable Sustainability* is a very timely addition to the myriad content on this subject coming out around the world. Rajeev makes a powerful case for the age-old maxim of "doing the right thing" rather than "doing things right". The battle for a sustainable world can only be won in the hearts and minds of leaders across commercial and non-commercial organizations, governments, regulators, and social bodies, since, as Rajeev correctly says, innovation cannot be legislated. In Part 2 we see great examples of responsible sustainability in action. The methodology to assess an organization's culture and DNA in Part 3 is a very useful checklist for us to get this right. The concept of steward leadership is powerful. It is a great ready reckoner for any leader aspiring to go from good to great. A great read to wake up the world to this critical priority for our planet.'

—Sanjeeb Chaudhuri,
Chairman, IDFC First Bank
Former CEO, Citibank EMEA
Former Group Head, Standard Chartered Bank

Sustainable Sustainability

Why ESG is Not Enough

Rajeev Peshawaria
CEO, Stewardship Asia Centre

With contributing chapters by Arnoud De Meyer and Vinika Rao,
and case studies and research compiled by the SAC Research Team:
Abigail Chan, Bee Lin Ang, Annisah Smith, Jane Ang, Sandhya Haridas,
Cherine Ang, Jau Loong Chow and Sunil Puri

PENGUIN
BUSINESS
An imprint of Penguin Random House

PENGUIN BUSINESS

USA | Canada | UK | Ireland | Australia
New Zealand | India | South Africa | China | Southeast Asia

Penguin Business is part of the Penguin Random House group of companies
whose addresses can be found at global.penguinrandomhouse.com

Published by Penguin Random House SEA Pte Ltd
9, Changi South Street 3, Level 08-01,
Singapore 486361

First published in Penguin Business by Penguin Random House SEA 2023

ISBN 9789815144574

Typeset in Garamond by MAP Systems, Bengaluru, India

www.penguin.sg

To Alara and her generation

Contents

Foreword by Sanjay Sarma

We are in a time of rapid change. June 2023 was the hottest month in recorded history[1] and at the time of writing, July 2023, the current month is on course to be hotter still[2]. This news comes on the heels of distressing news about the decade—the eight previous years have been reported to be the eight warmest recorded[3]. Meanwhile, as the world emerges haltingly from the pandemic, the global labour market finds itself in a time of unprecedented uncertainty with the rise of generative AI. Language—a defining connective tissue of humanity—finds itself automated. And more automation is on the horizon with automated computer programming, robotics, autonomy and IoT. All this while we witness tectonic geopolitical changes across Europe and Asia.

In this era, externalities have become existential. Regulations, Pigouvian taxes, subsidies, incentives, permit trading, reduced transaction costs, efficient markets—these are the supposed panaceas intended to stave off the tragedy of the commons. But as a mechanical engineer, I understand dynamics and the importance of reaction speed. We are today a far cry from the unhurried, halcyon times where these ideas might have worked and we have not yet arrived at the kinetic state where our regulations and policies can keep pace with the changes.

This particularly applies to environmental, social and governance or ESG, considerations, which have become ubiquitous in assessing companies for investment. ESG is fine but as ratings, frameworks and standards struggle to capture the precision and specificity required, a vast grey area remains. Within that grey area lurk practices that range from cynical greenwashing to dismissive check-boxing, particularly on the E and S fronts. And the G of ESG has not had a particularly good decade; a cavalcade of individual and corporate malfeasances reminds us that the planet and humanity, cannot be left to the system per se.

Systems exist to help humans, not to absolve us of responsibility. This, says Rajeev Peshawaria, is the reason why our definition of leadership must evolve to incorporate *stewardship*—beyond the traditional model of profit-driven leadership. The leader must therefore embody the values of ESG, rather than simply using ESG passively as a set of guideposts; such leaders transcend mere governance and embrace the tenets of ESL—where 'L' stands for Leadership, specifically, 'steward leadership'. In this timely and inspiring three-part book, Rajeev focuses the first part on the rationale for doing well by doing good. In the second part, he presents a series of vivid examples, ranging from inspiring to sobering, of steward leadership and poor leadership. The third part of the book addresses the practice of steward leadership. Rajeev presents metrics that make stewardship more real in Chapter 13. Two essays follow. Sometimes it takes a village, as the expression goes and Arnoud De Meyer describes leadership in ecosystems. Vinika Rao addresses (and challenges) leadership in the area of diversity, equity and inclusion in these fraught times.

It is lonely at the top, it is said. It can be especially lonely when the leader yearns to make a difference, which, as the book posits, requires the leader to *be* different. This book is a must-read because it provides every leader with the tools, the examples and the perspectives needed to create change that leaves a positive legacy—on the organization and on the planet. Peter Drucker once said, 'Whenever you see a successful business, someone once made a courageous decision.' The same can be said about ESG or more specifically, about ESL. This book is truly about that someone—aka you.

Sanjay Sarma
CEO, President and Dean, Asia School of Business
Professor of mechanical engineering,
Massachusetts Institute of Technology

Foreword by Rebecca Fatima Sta. Maria

Not a day goes by when we are not confronted by the existential challenge of climate change and the question, 'What are *you* doing about it?' In this book, Rajeev Peshawaria gets us thinking about each of our roles in managing this challenge. And his rationale for doing this? He sums it thus: 'The good news is that *everyone* is talking about ESG. The bad news is that everyone is *talking* about ESG.'

He challenges the reader to think of ESG beyond regulatory requirements and compliance and to instead focus on genuinely 'doing well by doing good', espousing a 'values-based revolution'.

In his typical no-holds-barred style, he uses case studies to make his point, illustrating failures (Enron, Boeing 737 Max, Volkswagen Dieselgate, Theranos) with the counterpoint of companies that got it right (Faber-Castell, Mae Fah Luang Foundation, the Tata Group, Mars, Incorporated, Farm Fresh, APRIL Group, Unilever) by successfully embedding environmental and social sustainability in their strategy, execution and culture. The latter set of companies also illustrate stewardship values of interdependence, long-term view, ownership mentality and creative resilience.

This book is a reflection of Rajeev's passion and belief in steward leadership, i.e., the genuine desire and persistence to create a collective better future, which then creates value by integrating the needs of stakeholders, society, future generations and the environment. In a word, stewardship. Yes, he does provide a theoretical framework, based on stewardship, to further the discussion on ESG. But to be sure, this is not an idealistic, ideological treatise on sustainability and leadership.

Neither is it a didactic, 'let-me-tell-you-how-to-do-it' tome. It is well-researched, thought through and thought-provoking.

Rebecca Fatima Sta. Maria
Executive Director, Asia Pacific Economic
Cooperation (APEC) Secretariat

Acknowledgements

This book would not be possible without the amazing teamwork and passion of my colleagues at Stewardship Asia Centre. I will be thankful to them forever for challenging, debating, tirelessly testing and tweaking—for months—before we settled on the Steward Leadership Compass model as presented in Part One. The thinking on stewardship had started long before I arrived on the scene in 2020. My predecessor Ong Boon Hwee, along with his two co-authors Didier Cossin and Mark Goyder, had already laid a strong foundation for stewardship thought and action. It was my pleasure to continue building the house they started.

Sustainable Sustainability is more than just a book. In fact, it is the culmination of everything we have built and launched over the last three years.

We started with building the Steward Leadership Compass. This was to codify why and how the best champions of environmental and social sustainability succeed in marrying purpose with profit. Then we created the Steward Leadership Quotient to enable organizations to measure the strength of their steward leadership culture. Next, we built and launched a whole executive education curriculum for senior business leaders and board directors. Joanna Soh, Yancy Toh, Annisah Smith, Cherine Ang, Keng Boon Ng, Jau Loong Chow and others worked hard over the next three years to bring everything to fruition.

Next, we created the Steward Leadership 25 (SL25) programme to recognize the twenty-five best stories of steward leadership—doing well by doing good—in business within the Asia-Pacific region. Our annual Steward Leadership Summit followed next. Veena Nair, Luke Phang, Annisah Smith, Jane Ang and others brought these to life. Thanks also to our SL25 partners INSEAD Hoffmann Global Institute for Business and Society, WTW and The Straits Times, all of whom signed up to co-launch SL25 with us without any hesitation.

Finally, to enable the global community in sharing their innovative ideas to save planet Earth and humanity, we built stewardshipcommons.com—a global, crowdsourced content and community hub for all things related to stewardship, sustainability, responsible investing and ESG. I cannot thank Han Siong Yap, Shaggy Herur and Bee Lin Ang enough for making this dream a reality.

It was only after testing and practically applying all of the above that we brought everything together in this book.

My sincere thanks to Arnoud De Meyer and Vinika Rao for agreeing to contribute a chapter each for Part Three. Their thought leadership added new dimensions to make the book complete.

A special thanks to my friend Sachin Goel for giving me the idea of the title. I was explaining to him what we do and he said, 'Rajeev, it sounds to me that you are trying to make sustainability itself sustainable.' That's how the working title *Making Sustainability Sustainable* was born. Eventually, thanks to Nora Nazarene Abu Bakar, my publisher at Penguin Random House, the title became even more memorable with *Sustainable Sustainability*.

Finally, a huge thanks to Abigail Chan and Sunil Puri. Abigail's passion for the book, eye for detail, amazing research and expert editing made this book what it eventually became. Sunil joined the party towards the end and was extremely helpful in reviewing the first few drafts of the manuscript with a fresh pair of eyes.

Many others helped along the way and it would be challenging to name all of them here. Thank you!

Introduction

With all the buzz around environmental and social sustainability of late, it is hard to get through the day without seeing at least one headline related to the business world's response to today's existential challenges. Urgent calls for action on climate change, socioeconomic inequality and cyber vulnerability have spawned a new sector for the asset management industry, with the emergence of Environmental, Social and Governance (ESG) funds. There are lawyers, consultants, bankers and numerous other professionals specializing in the theme and ESG is now considered an industry in its own right. This fast-growing investment sector is expected to see assets under management reach $50 trillion by 2025[4], almost twice the projected United States GDP[5].

Everyone and every organization, seems to be saying or doing something about the environment and society. According to a London School of Economics and Political Science commentary in February 2023, twenty-seven countries have enacted net-zero legislation and this number is growing. In science, innovations targeting renewable energy, social inclusion and cybercrime have grown by leaps and bounds, supported by investment capital and, to a degree, regulation.

At first glance, you might agree that all of this is great news. After all, unless all of humanity collaborates across boundaries, we are unlikely to overcome these challenges. But the reality behind the buzz is not as encouraging as it sounds. Rampant greenwashing aside, the extent to which the ESG industry and this huge capital allocation are positively impacting the environment and society remains questionable. Greenhouse gases are at an all-time high, the rate of species extinction is 10,000 times the normal rate, the richest 1 per cent in the world have more than double the wealth of 6.9 billion people and a cyber-attack is recorded every 39 seconds, with 43 per cent targeting small businesses. (See table at the end of this introduction for more on the current state of affairs.)

In my public speaking assignments, I have been asking people all over the world if they think current solutions will be enough to save planet Earth and humanity from the enormity of challenges we face today. We also asked 10,000 respondents the same question as part of a global survey we conducted in 2023. Overwhelmingly, the answer is a big no. Despite significant efforts currently underway, most people agree that something is missing.

In this book, we argue that all current efforts, based largely on a system that incentivizes good behaviour, regulates against bad behaviour and rewards or punishes based on the myriad of measurement and reporting frameworks (e.g., scope measures for greenhouse gas emissions) are inadequate. We base our argument on the following observations:

1. Overreliance on incentives based on formulaic measurements can cause bad behaviour like greenwashing and other types of fraud.
2. Regulation may prevent further harm but does not maximize good. Just because someone is law-abiding and refrains from indulging in bad behaviour does not make them a good, responsible person.
3. We need massive innovation to defeat climate change and socioeconomic activity. Regulation does not spur innovation—innovation cannot be legislated.
4. Shareholder-centric free market capitalism and the 'invisible hand' may have worked during economist Adam Smith's 18th century, but it does not scale in today's world of eight billion people.

So, what is the solution? In Part One, using data from our global research, we provide extensive evidence to support the above observations and strongly posit that the missing link is genuine stewardship intent to 'do well by doing good'. Rather than just rules, regulations and incentives, we need a values-based revolution to overcome today's challenges. We will win as humans if the desire to address environmental and social challenges is intrinsically driven and 100 per cent genuine, not virtue signalling or grudging adherence to the lowest regulatory measure. We also present a step-by-step playbook for businesses to take ownership and thrive by addressing the very challenges that are threatening our existence today. And the good news is that it is possible.

In Part Two, we narrate several stories of companies that have been good stewards of planet Earth and society and have consistently done well by doing good over long periods of time. We also provide a few stories of bad behaviour and the disastrous consequences it caused.

In Part Three, we present a way to assess an organization's culture and DNA to determine its readiness to do well by doing good. Following this are two chapters contributed by Professors Arnoud De Meyer (Chairman of Stewardship Asia Centre, Former President of Singapore Management University, Director of the Judge Business School of the University of Cambridge and founding Dean of INSEAD's Asia Campus in Singapore) and Vinika Rao (Executive Director, Emerging Markets Institute & Gender Initiative, INSEAD; Director, Hoffmann Global Institute for Business and Society, Asia). These chapters show how a stewardship approach can turbocharge business ecosystem collaboration and diversity, equity and inclusion (DEI) efforts. We finally end Part Three with data collected from our global survey spanning twenty-five countries.

I hope you will enjoy reading *Sustainable Sustainability* as much as my team and I have enjoyed writing it. I hope you will immerse yourself in the stories throughout the book and find the inspiration and some tangible ideas to make a difference. And as you re-imagine your journey ahead as a steward leader, I hope you will inspire others to join you. Good luck!

The challenges we face today are stark to say the least. Consider just a few facts.

1.	Millions of people are fleeing their homes to avoid the impacts of droughts, extreme weather events and floods. The International Organization for Migration estimates that up to 200 million people could be displaced by climate change by 2050. Around 50 per cent of all carbon emissions are emitted by the richest 10 per cent of the world's population. Yet, global warming is making climate change refugees some of the world's poorest[6].
2.	We are using more of Earth's resources than she can renew. If we carry on using Earth's resources at our current rate of consumption, we would need 1.7 planets to support the demand of Earth's ecosystems[7].
3.	More than 1 million species face extinction. While the expected rate of species extinction is usually around 5 species a year, we are currently losing up to 10,000 times the normal rate—this means that dozens of species go extinct every single day. This loss of biodiversity reduces water quality and food security and results in a loss of natural pest control as predators like frogs and spiders become extinct[8].
4.	Many leaders still are not taking climate change seriously. The world has been aware of it for at least five decades now. Yet, many ignore the facts. Although the Paris Agreement was signed in 2015, none of the world's major economies are on track to keep global warming below 1.5 degrees above pre-industrial levels[9].
5.	Almost half the world's population lives on less than $5.50 a day, according to World Bank estimates[10].
6.	The world's richest twenty-two men have more money than all the women in Africa. Globally, women and girls put in 12.5 billion hours of unpaid work every day[11].

7.	Since the Covid-19 pandemic, the FBI has reported an increase of 300 per cent in reported cybercrimes.
8.	Four million files are stolen every day. That is forty-four files every second.
9.	Cybercrime is quickly becoming more profitable than the illegal drug trade[12].

Part One

Stewardship and Steward Leadership

Chapter 1

From ESG to ESL

The good news is that much of the world is slowly but surely recognizing that we need to act urgently to save planet Earth and humanity. It is widely acknowledged and understood that all sections of society—governments, regulators, businesses and civil society—must collaborate to have meaningful impact on 21st-century challenges like climate change, environmental degradation, socioeconomic inequality and cyber vulnerability. The challenges are too big for any entity to address singly. We now know that we need cross-border and cross-sector collaboration on an unprecedented scale. Thankfully, humanity has shown that when faced with grim threats, it can act quickly and in unison. When Covid-19 brought human life to a halt in 2020, we understood that no one could be safe until everyone was safe. We created vaccines in record time and distributed them around the world. So, we *can* act with urgency and in unison to do the right things when faced with imminent existential threats.

But are we capable of the same urgency and unison when the threat is not perceived as pressing or extensive? Will we be able to act in time to save ourselves from climate change and socioeconomic inequality? Critics think that it is unlikely because the current shareholder-centric model of capitalism drives profits and growth while ignoring negative consequences to people and planet. They argue that we need a more inclusive and humane form of capitalism that focuses not only on shareholders but on other stakeholders and society at large as well.

Consequently, governments, regulators, multilateral agencies and the private sector have come together in the recent decades to create mechanisms encouraging businesses to act more responsibly towards the environment and society. The United Nations Global Compact (UNGC), Sustainable Development Goals (SDGs), Principles of Responsible Investing (PRI), Global Reporting Initiative (GRI), stewardship codes for responsible investing, Carbon Disclosure Project (CDP), Sustainability Accounting Standards Board (SASB), Task Force on Climate-related Financial Disclosures (TCFD), World Development Indicators (WDI) and the Environmental, Social and Governance (ESG) framework are just some of the many examples.

But will our current efforts be enough?

No, because of one huge problem. All the above mechanisms use the same system that created the irresponsible behaviour within the shareholder-centric model of capitalism in the first place:

Let us first take a detour to understand how shareholder-centric capitalism has fared over the last 200 years, then make the case as to why the *Incentivize → Regulate → Measure → Reward or Punish* system will not scale in the 21st-century world with over eight billion people.

The basic philosophy of shareholder-centric or free-market capitalism is as follows:

If businesses work with the sole aim of maximizing profits while following the rule of law and avoiding deception or fraud, societal needs will be automatically taken care of. This will happen in two ways:

1. To make a profit, a business will need to provide goods and services that society needs. By providing such goods and services, businesses first fulfil a societal need, then make a profit. It is a win-win situation.
2. By making profits, businesses pay taxes. Governments are meant to use taxpayer money to provide those goods and services that businesses do not provide e.g., social

security, universal healthcare, education for all, defence and public safety.

Based on the above philosophy, the *Incentivize* → *Regulate* → *Measure* → *Reward or Punish* system is expected to marry shareholders' need for profits with the needs of people and the planet.

Incentivize: Management teams and employees in the business world are incentivized to achieve goals that maximize profits and minimize costs.

Regulate: Regulators frame laws to make sure management and employees play within the rules of the game and do not engage in deception or fraud while pursuing their goals.

Measure: Performance is measured against pre-determined goals. Typically, the two types of goals are: (i) Maximizing profits and minimizing costs and (ii) Regulatory compliance.

Reward or Punish: Based on performance measurement against stated objectives, rewards—in the form of bonuses, promotions or dividends—are declared and those found violating or not complying with the laws of the land are punished. Or so goes the theory.

The theory, as first conceived by Adam Smith in the 18th century, was mostly sound. In his first book, *The Theory of Moral Sentiments*, he proposed the idea of an invisible hand—the tendency of free markets to regulate themselves using competition, supply and demand and self-interest. Later, he articulated the now-famous three natural laws of economics:

1. Law of self-interest: People work for their own good.
2. Law of competition: Competition forces people to make a better product for a lower price.
3. Law of supply and demand: Enough goods will be produced at the lowest price to meet the demand in a market economy.

With some exceptions, the theory worked for much of the 20th century. With the collapse of socialist and communist models, free-market capitalism—despite some inherent problems—was declared the best form of economic development. The free-market capitalism model was so successful that, in 1970, economist Milton

Friedman famously declared in his *New York Times* op-ed: 'There is one and only one social responsibility of business—to use its resources and engage in activities designed to increase its profits so long as it stays within the rules of the game, which is to say, engages in open and free competition without deception or fraud.'[13]

However, towards the end of the 20th century, a few things began to challenge Adam Smith's theory and Milton Friedman's claim:

- Global population growth accelerated considerably, putting a huge strain on Earth's natural resources.
- The havoc caused by climate change began to further exasperate the strain on resources.
- Businesses' single-minded quest for profit maximization clashed with the need for responsible behaviour towards the environment and society.
- Growth became even more lopsided with the rich getting richer and the poor getting poorer, causing social unrest in many parts of the globe.
- The misuse of technology and personal data led to the death of privacy, misinformation and rampant manipulation of behaviour.

And so, the call for a more inclusive form of capitalism grew louder. It was time to challenge Milton Friedman and fine-tune Adam Smith's theories. And this was when frameworks such as UNGC, SDGs, PRI, GRI, CDP, SASB, ESG, etc. started to appear.

The rise and rise of ESG

Of them all, the ESG framework seems to have emerged as the frontrunner to drive businesses towards addressing the existential challenges we refer to throughout this book. While ESG as a framework has succeeded in bringing the conversation to the forefront, as stated earlier, it is using the same *Incentivize* → *Regulate* → *Measure* → *Reward or Punish* system to do so. This has created both confusion and misuse. Confusion abounds because there are already more than 600 ESG rating frameworks in practice[14]. And because the ESG framework incentivizes meeting, measuring and rewarding specific markers related to the environmental and social pillars (e.g., carbon emissions and diversity and inclusion), it leads to rampant misuse ranging from box-ticking to window-dressing and outright greenwashing (more on that later). Is there a better, more comprehensive solution? To attempt answering this question, let us begin with a brief history of ESG. Once we understand the origins and the current state of play, we will identify what is working and what is not and propose a solution that might be better suited for today's reality.

ESG history in brief

Elizabeth Pollman is a Professor of law and the Co-Director of the Institute of Law and Economics at the University of Pennsylvania Carey Law School. In her research paper titled 'The Making and Meaning of ESG', she describes the ESG conundrum as follows:

'Does ESG refer to "three criteria to evaluate a company's sustainability performance"? Is it a "set of standards for a company's operations that socially conscious investors use to screen potential investments"? Does it "put . . . money to work with companies that strive to make the world a better place"? Or perhaps more broadly is it a new term or synonym for "corporate social responsibility" (CSR) or its cousin "sustainability"? Could the answer be that ESG simultaneously refers to all of the above?'[15]

In addition to the above confusion, there is another issue that I highlighted at a conference in late 2022. I was one of four panellists in a discussion about ESG. At the end of the discussion, each panellist was asked to give a closing statement in twenty seconds or less. Here is how I summed up the current state of play:

'The good news is that *everyone* is talking about ESG.
The bad news is that everyone is *talking* about ESG.'

To trace how the ESG movement began and where we are now, I will draw on Pollman's excellent paper over the next few paragraphs.

The origins of the term ESG date back to the 1990s when Kofi Annan, then-Secretary-General of the United Nations, started engaging with the corporate sector to address some of society's pressing problems. In a 1999 speech at the World Economic Forum, he said:

'Globalization is a fact of life. But I believe we have underestimated its fragility. The problem is this—the spread of markets outpaces the ability of societies and other political systems to adjust to them, let alone to guide the course they take. History teaches us that such an imbalance between the economic, social and political realms can never be sustained for very long. The industrialized countries learned that lesson in their bitter and costly encounter with the Great Depression. In order to restore social harmony and political stability, they adopted social safety nets and other measures designed to limit economic volatility and compensate the victims of market failures. Our challenge today is to devise a similar compact on the global scale, to underpin the new global economy.'[16]

The speech became a precursor to the formation in 2000 of the UN Global Compact, a voluntary initiative based on CEO commitments to support UN sustainability goals. It outlines ten principles on human rights, labour, environment and anti-corruption. As the compact grew in its acceptance among the corporate world, in 2004, Annan wrote to the CEOs of the world's fifty-five leading financial institutions to join an initiative titled *Who Cares Wins*. This effort included a report with the same title wherein the term ESG was first used. The report described how to better integrate environmental, social and corporate governance issues in investment decisions, asset management, securities brokerage services and associated research functions.

The report cited the business case for good management of ESG issues contributing to shareholder value creation. It explained that companies with strong track records of environmental and social responsibility could increase shareholder value by better managing environmental and social risks. It further explained why Governance was added to 'E' and 'S':

'Sound corporate governance and risk management systems are crucial pre-requisites to successfully implementing policies and measures to address environmental and social challenges. This is why we have chosen to use the term "environmental, social and governance issues" throughout this report, as a way of highlighting the fact that these three areas are closely interlinked.'[17]

So, the ESG framework began as an investment evaluation and risk management tool. Purposely, the initial coining of the term and the framework did not specify details of what to include or exclude under E, S or G while evaluating investment decisions. It noted that ESG issues differ across regions and sections. While it gave some examples under each of the three elements, the report left it to individual researchers and organizations to determine the factors important to them. This flexibility might have been responsible for the framework's meteoric rise. In the years immediately following the *Who Cares Wins* report, less than 1 per cent of earnings calls used the term ESG. However, by 2021, it was mentioned in nearly one-fifth of earnings calls. A survey found that 72 per cent of institutional investors implemented ESG factors.

Besides being used for investment evaluation and risk management, ESG has of late also come to be seen as 'a step to a better world'. For example, the PRI framework recognizes the social angle, declaring, 'We also recognize that applying these Principles may better align investors with broader objectives of society.' It is now common to see the terms sustainability, ESG and CSR being used synonymously. In some circles, ESG is also characterized as a preference. As consumer and customer preferences change towards smarter, greener, healthier and sustainable products and services, investors and board members increasingly use the ESG framework to develop their own voting and investing preferences.

The current state of play

While the flexibility of the ESG framework has helped provide an overarching language and framework to address environmental and social challenges through business, it has also given rise to several problems.

One issue is the dissimilarity between E, S and G. While E and S are existential challenges that need to be addressed, G is one of the mechanisms to do so. In this sense, E and S are outcomes or goals, while G is a means to achieve them. Does it make sense to bundle them all together when they are so different?

Among other issues, the bundling facilitates greenwashing. ESG rating frameworks try to employ sophisticated individual measurements for E, S and G factors. Therefore, disproportionately positive progress in one of the three factors could help to hide the harmful effects of the business in other areas. For example, Tesla is included in many ESG-labelled funds, but observers point to potentially problematic S issues for the company relating to racial and sexual discrimination and child labour usage. Pollman also notes that ironically, Tesla CEO Elon Musk makes a counter point: 'Exxon is rated top ten best in world for environment, social & governance (ESG) by S&P 500, while Tesla didn't make the list! ESG is a scam. It has been weaponized by phony social justice warriors.'

As one commissioner from the US Securities and Exchange Commission observed, 'One person's eco-friendly windmill is another person's bird killer.'

We are thankful to Kofi Annan and his team for establishing a common language to discuss the biggest challenges in human history. The term ESG has succeeded in focusing the business world's attention on doing well by doing good. However, one big problem remains—the overreliance on G to address E and S challenges. *Will G, in its current form of practice, be enough to solve for E and S?* As stated earlier, the ESG framework and G in particular, relies heavily on rules, regulations, extrinsic incentives and measurement as captured by the *Incentivize → Regulate → Measure → Reward or Punish* system. Such carrot-and-stick approaches are indeed required, but will they be enough to drive the extent of positive action needed to address climate change and income inequality? And how do we prevent misuse? To answer these questions, let us look at three recent stories. Below, I provide just a quick overview of the stories. Part Two of the book chronicles each of them in detail.

1. Boeing 737 Max

As is now clear from the investigations and the $2.5 billion plea agreement that it made, Boeing—a company once known for its singular focus on safety and quality engineering—lost its way while designing and producing the 737 Max[18]. Under pressure from customers to produce a fuel-efficient aircraft quickly, Boeing seems to have compromised its storied engineering excellence, cut corners and withheld information from regulators to get the Max approved.

When the first Max crashed in Indonesia, the company responded by absolving itself of all responsibility and shifted blame to the airline. Sadly, it took another crash within five months for the truth to emerge.

How is it that both the company's Board of Directors and the aviation regulators failed to prevent the disasters from happening? Could the incentive system—minimizing costs and maximizing profits in this case—and regulatory loopholes be responsible for 346 deaths in five months?

More importantly, how can Boeing restore customer and regulator confidence going forward? What does it need to focus on?

2. Volkswagen Dieselgate scandal

In 2015, the US Environmental Protection Agency (EPA) found Volkswagen guilty of cheating on emissions tests. In the early 2000s, the EPA had tightened regulations on nitrogen oxide emissions. Instead of finding solutions to comply, it installed software (defeat devices) in their cars that would report lower emissions during inspections and lab tests. While the cars passed the tests in the labs, their emissions were five to thirty-five times more than EPA's permissible limits on the road.

This would not be the first time VW had been found engaging in unethical behaviour[19]. According to an article published by NBC News on 23 September 2015, they were fined $120,000 for similar conduct in 1974[20]. In 1999, they developed a software for their Audi line to reduce engine noise at idle, which increased emissions. For their defeat device offences in 2015, they paid a fine of $2.8 billion and a total cost—including recall—of €30 billion worldwide[21].

Again, was it financial pressure and market competition that motivated such unethical behaviour? Why were regulations not an effective driver of good behaviour?

3. Theranos: A case of purpose-washing?

In 2022, Elizabeth Holmes, the charismatic founder of the biotech unicorn Theranos was sentenced to over eleven years in prison for misleading investors and regulators about their product[22]. Holmes dropped out of Stanford to create new technology that would forever change the way blood tests were conducted. Instead of drawing vials of blood using a long needle, Theranos machines would conduct multiple blood tests from just a few drops of blood drawn from a finger prick. Blood tests would be cheaper, faster and more accessible.

But when the technology did not work, instead of admitting it to the regulators and investors, she chose to mislead them. Blinded by her purpose, she continued to defraud customers, patients, her investors and the regulators until a whistle-blower collaborated with a *Wall Street Journal* investigative reporter to bring the story to light.

At its peak, Theranos was valued at $9 billion[23]. Despite repeated red flags, Theranos' board took no action.

While Holmes probably started with all the right intentions, what went wrong, when and why?

The 'G' problem

What was common in the three stories? I usually ask this question in my seminars and most people say that it was poor corporate governance and a complete failure of compliance. If this is the case, then we have a huge problem because boards spend a majority of their time on risk management and regulatory compliance. A few years ago, my colleagues and I at the Iclif Leadership and Governance Centre (now part of the Asia School of Business—a collaboration between MIT Sloan and the Central Bank of Malaysia) surveyed board directors across the ASEAN region. We wanted to know what activities corporate boards spend most of their time on. Here is what we learned:

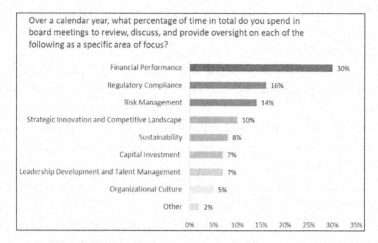

Figure 1: Percentage of time board directors spend in board meetings discussing specific areas of focus.

Reproduced with permission from the Iclif Leadership and Governance Centre, 2018.

According to this survey, 60 per cent of the board's time is spent between financial performance, regulatory compliance and risk management. Given the burden of fiduciary and legal duties on individual board members, it is not surprising to see the mix.

We also asked respondents to share their opinion about the adequacy of time spent on each focus area as shown in the figure below:

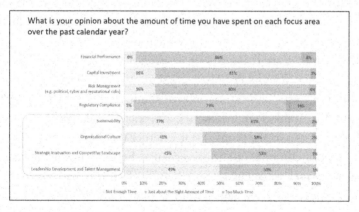

Figure 2: Amount of time board directors spend on each focus area over the past calendar year. Reproduced with permission from the Iclif Leadership and Governance Centre, 2018.

Not surprisingly, sustainability, culture, strategic innovation and leadership/talent issues were reported as ones on which they were not spending enough time.

From my experience working with boards globally, I find that the ratio of time allocation does not change much across geographies as compared to the ASEAN data above. Barring a few exceptions, the charts above can represent a typical board anywhere in the world. Since Covid, there has been some increased focus on environmental and social sustainability in boardrooms, but the G of ESG still largely comprises providing financial oversight, ensuring regulatory compliance and managing risk. So, if a majority of time is spent on providing oversight and compliance, which is nothing but *Incentivize → Regulate → Measure → Reward or Punish*, how do boards miss fiascos like Boeing's 737 Max, VW's Dieselgate and Theranos?

And even if boards were more effective in preventing scandals, would that help in adequately addressing our existential challenges? Let's assume every company and every individual fully follows the letter of the law when it comes to environmental and social responsibility. Would that result in humanity overcoming climate change and socioeconomic inequality? Many management experts argue that incentives and deterrents drive behaviour. So, they insist that organizations and governments must provide the right incentives and deterrents. Incentives can be rewards for good behaviour such as tax breaks for going green. Deterrents can be in the form of strict laws to book bad actors, like penalties and imprisonment for creating pollution or wilfully deceiving investors and regulators.

The point we are making is this—even if the *Incentivize → Regulate → Measure → Reward or Punish* system worked perfectly without ·confusion or misuse, the stories above allude to the fact that it will be inadequate to address environmental and social challenges.

Coming back to the point about whether the three stories were the result of poor compliance and governance, here is what Andy Fastow, the former Chief Financial Officer (CFO) of Enron, had to say:

'Many people believe Enron was a failure of compliance. I disagree. What Enron was . . . was a culture failure. It was a culture of loopholes where the principles didn't matter, only technical adherence to the rules.'

As reported on the website of the University of Calgary[24], Fastow said this while speaking at the Canadian Centre for Advanced Leadership in Business in 2019. Holding up in one hand a CFO-of-the-year trophy given to him by *CFO Magazine* during the heydays of Enron and his prison card in the other, he added:

'How is it possible to be the CFO of the year and commit the greatest corporate fraud in American history for doing the same deals? . . . Every single deal I did was approved by Enron's accountants, by the outside auditors, by Enron's attorneys, by Enron's outside attorneys, by the bank's attorneys when appropriate and by Enron's Board of Directors.'

If Fastow is right about the failure of culture, principles and values, then we clearly have a big problem—a G problem! While we need rules, regulations and compliance, there is no guarantee that bad behaviour will be eliminated from society. There is even less guarantee that adequate good behaviour—the amount and extent of proactive action required to save the planet—will occur. What good regulation and governance do is this: They provide a baseline for good behaviour. 'Thou shall be punished for breaking the law'. But it does not ensure good behaviour. Complying with the law may keep someone out of trouble, but it does not motivate them to do good. At best, it keeps them from doing harm. And as demonstrated in the cases of Fastow and his colleagues at Enron and all the great minds at Boeing, VW and Theranos, regulations did not even achieve that.

So, how should we further strengthen the business community's efforts to address our existential challenges? How should we ensure greenwashing and purpose-washing are minimized? More importantly, how should we motivate more business leaders to proactively choose *doing well by doing good*? To answer these questions, let's look at three more stories. As with the stories earlier, I summarize them below. Detailed narratives are in Part Two.

1. Faber-Castell: Over 260 years of doing well by doing good

German pencil maker Faber-Castell has a long history of placing sustainability at the core of its business strategy. Based on the belief that happy employees would work harder to make the business successful, Lothar von Faber, the company's fourth-generation leader, introduced employee benefits like health insurance forty years before they became the law in Germany. Later, he set up a savings bank and pension fund for employees, built housing for them, provided financial support for schools and established a day nursery for employees' children.

Each successive generation did the same and made addressing environmental and social issues central to strategy and execution. Count Anton-Wolfgang von Faber-Castell, the eighth-generation— and last—family member to helm the business was no exception. For example, even when the business was going through a challenging time in the 1980s, he invested heavily in sustainable forestry in Brazil[25]. The trees planted in Brazil would take twenty years to mature, but after that, all the wood needed for FC pencils would come from forests certified as sustainable by the Forest Stewardship Council.

Even while the family has since passed on the reins of the company to professional management, the family, the board and the management continue to grow the company profitably with sustainability at the heart of everything they do.

What has driven this ethos at Faber-Castell for over 260 years?

2. Doi Tung Development Project

Until 1987, the Doi Tung region in northern Thailand was a hotbed of crime. Opium plantations, human and drug trafficking, prostitution and other unlawful pursuits were the only means of livelihood for ethnic villagers of the region. There were no schools or hospitals nearby and villagers resorted to opium as medication to ease their pain. Heavily armed independent militia controlled the area and the once lush green region was almost barren because of indiscriminate deforestation.

All of this changed with the arrival of the Princess Mother and her deputy, Khun Chai. Thanks to their untiring efforts, today, not only is the region completely reforested, but it is also a shining example of community sustainability. Villagers now own and operate a profitable coffee and macadamia nuts production and export business, handicrafts, textiles, cafés and tourism. It has also become a living open university of the circular economy concept. 'Students' from around the world come to learn about environmental and social sustainability. As you will see in Part Two, it took a strong vision and even stronger execution to overcome considerable obstacles to transform the region from the crime-infested hellhole it once was into a thriving and peaceful hub of economic prosperity.

3. The Tata Group: 155 years of community-focused growth

'In a free enterprise, the community is not just another stakeholder in business, but is in fact the very purpose of its existence,' Jamsetji Tata, the founder of the Tata Group, said in the 1800s[26].

The UK-educated Jamsetji wanted to alleviate poverty in India and saw industrialization as the means to do so. In 1874, he established the Central India Spinning, Weaving and Manufacturing Company in Nagpur, which became his laboratory for technology and social welfare. Polluted water was a common cause of illness, so he installed a water filtration plant and arranged for sanitary huts. He then opened a grain depot and a dispensary, before introducing a provident fund and pension schemes for his employees. He also introduced a system of apprenticeship.

Each successive generation of the family built on the societal sustainability focus that Jamsetji established. Over 150 years, notable leaders such as Sir Dorabji Tata, J.R.D. Tata and Ratan Tata have expanded the business across several verticals including aviation, steel, energy, textiles, software and retailing. They did so while firmly abiding by the values of the founder. Like Faber-Castell and the Doi Tung Development Project, sustainability is at the core of the Tatas' strategy, execution and culture.

Today, the over $300-billion conglomerate continues to grow profitably in over 100 countries and 66 per cent of the share capital of Tata Sons—the holding company—is still owned by charitable trusts.

Let's ask the same question when I summarized the three negative stories earlier: What is common among the Faber-Castell, Doi Tung and Tata stories? What has motivated these three organizations to do well by doing good? Was it effective deterrents in the form of strict regulations? Was it incentives, measurement and rewards? Or was it something else? What was the single largest motivator here?

To the proponents of stiff regulations as the most important driver of behaviour, here is what I have to say:

1. As stated above, regulation sets the minimum standard of good behaviour. It does not drive behaviour beyond that standard. Doing no wrong does not mean doing enough good.

2. Regulation may preserve present value, but it does not enhance future value. To create the better future needed for our planet and society, we need innovative models that create shareholder value by addressing the very challenges that are threatening us. This requires action way beyond regulatory compliance as innovation cannot be legislated.

3. Regulation is reactive. New regulations are created when something has already gone wrong. So, they might prevent future wrongdoing, but do not undo the harm already caused. A case in point is the 2008 financial crisis. For all the people that had already suffered due to the predatory sub-prime lending, there was no recourse. We need a framework which prevents the wrongdoing from happening before regulations set in.

And to those that believe in 'what gets measured and rewarded gets done', I say, 'What gets measured and rewarded often gets misused.' And the misuse is not a new phenomenon. Steve Kerr, former Chief Learning Officer of General Electric and Goldman Sachs and professor at The Ohio State University, the University of Michigan and the University of Southern California, warned us about over reliance on incentives and measurement decades ago. In a 1975 article[27], which has since become an Academy of Management classic, he provided many examples:

In universities

Society hopes professors teach as much as possible to the best of their abilities, but they are rewarded almost exclusively for their research and publications. So, professors need to choose between teaching and research activities while allocating time. There are hardly any rewards for outstanding teaching. However, rewards abound for research and publications.

In sports

It is well known that a key to winning in basketball is effective passing. However, a college player who passes the ball instead of shooting accomplishes less impressive individual shooting scores and is almost never drafted by the pros. We hope for teamwork and passing, but we reward individual performance.

In business

In one health insurance company, a measurement system was established in claims processing. Two specific measures were used: (1) The number of complaints and (2) The processing speed. A claims processor who had fewer complaints and processed more claims per day was rewarded more than others. New hires quickly learned that overpayment was a better strategy than opting for a deeper investigation of doubtful cases. They followed the mantra: 'When in doubt, pay it out'; obviously causing avoidable overpayment. While hoping for superior customer service and speed, the company inadvertently rewarded undesirable behaviour.

In medicine

Theoretically, physicians can make one of two types of errors and intuitively, one seems as bad as the other. Doctors can pronounce patients sick when they are actually well (a type 1 error), thus causing them needless anxiety and expense, curtailment of enjoyable food and activities and even physical danger by subjecting them to needless medication and surgery. Alternately, a doctor can label a sick person well (a type 2 error) and thus avoid treating what may be a serious, even fatal, ailment. It might be natural to conclude that physicians seek to minimize both types of error. Such a conclusion would be wrong. It has been estimated that numerous Americans have been afflicted with physician-caused illnesses. This occurs when the doctor is approached by someone complaining of a few stray symptoms. The doctor classifies and organizes these symptoms, gives them a name and obligingly tells the patient what further symptoms may be expected. This information often acts as a self-fulfilling prophecy, with the result that from that day on, the patient, for all practical purposes, is sick.

Aptly titled 'On the Folly of Rewarding A, While Hoping for B', the article is as relevant today as it was when it was written forty-seven years ago. We still reward quarterly earnings while hoping for long-term growth and environmental sustainability, individual effort while hoping for teamwork and reporting good news—whether or not it is true, while hoping for candour.

The 2008 sub-prime mortgage crisis was caused by a similarly fouled-up incentive, measurement and reward system. More recent headlines about greenwashing and the misuse of the ESG framework such as 'Goldman Sachs Agrees to Pay $4 Million to SEC for ESG Violations'[28] and 'Amazon, IKEA and Apple Exaggerating Sustainability Claims—Can Technology Solve Greenwashing?'[29] provide ample proof that the rampant misuse is still alive and kicking.

The Spectrum of Environmental and Social Action

However, not everyone is bad. The ESG movement has certainly created some good players as well. We can map businesses on a spectrum of ESG behaviour as follows:

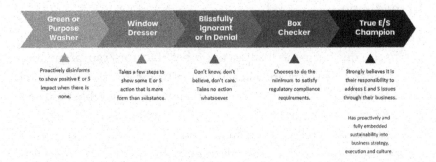

Figure 3: The E/S Action Spectrum. Source: Rajeev Peshawaria, Stewardship Asia Centre.

We see five types of players in today's market when it comes to their environmental and/or social action. On the extreme left of the figure above are the greenwashers and purpose-washers. Volkswagen's emissions scandal was the perfect example of proactive deception to show positive impact when there was none. And Theranos was a clear case of purpose-washing. Purpose has, of late, become the holy grail of doing well by doing good. We will come back to that a bit later. For now, let's stay with Theranos. One could argue that Elizabeth Holmes, the charismatic young founder, started out with a worthy purpose of creating wealth by making a positive S contribution. But it seems that when things started to go wrong, she chose fraud over truth. She convinced herself that the means justify the worthy end. Was she blinded by the so-called 'worthy purpose'? And as she and her partner Sunny Balwani continued to mislead investors and regulators, what was the board doing? You will read in Part Two that even when they were informed of the wrongdoing by whistle-blowers, the board chose to ignore the warnings. What does that say about governance? Did the board also suffer from purpose blindness? According to Erika Cheung, the Theranos employee who took a great personal risk to finally bring the Theranos fraud to light, they were suffering from FOMO—the fear of missing out. While in Singapore to speak at the inaugural Steward Leadership Summit[30] in November 2022, Cheung told the audience that 'they did not want to miss out on the next Amazon and make 60 times returns on their investment'. Whatever the real reason, governance certainly failed here not only in preventing fraud, but also in driving the right E and S behaviour.

Not far behind the greenwashers and the purpose-washers are the window-dressers. They take a few token steps to show E or S action, but it is more form than substance. A recent example is Innocent Drinks, a maker of smoothies and cold pressed juices wholly owned by the Coca-Cola Company. Given that they are a big user of single-use plastic, their TV advertisements, featuring cute cartoon characters singing songs about recycling and fixing the planet, were reported by Plastics Rebellion[31] and later banned by the American Standards Association. Next up on the continuum are the blissfully ignorant or in-denial organizations. They either fail to understand what is at stake or choose to remain in denial. One step better are the box checkers who do as much as the law requires and no more. They want to remain regulatory compliant, but do not take any proactive steps to do what they can for the planet or the people.

E/S champions

And finally, on the far-right ride are the true E and/or S champions. They strongly believe it is their responsibility to address E and S challenges through their business and have figured out how to fully embed sustainability both in strategy and execution. They do not wait for regulators to tell them what to do. They also do not wait for the government to provide them with green incentives. They are motivated to do well by doing good because of their own proactive volition. In the next chapter, we will describe these champions in a lot more detail. Going by their past records, the three stories discussed earlier—Faber-Castell, Tata and Doi Tung—belong in this category.

The next chapter explores what motivates true E/S champions most and how to create a similar culture within business organizations. We posit that while rules, regulations, measurements, compliance, reporting, incentives and cheaper capital are all important and required to ensure that harmful behaviour is minimized, they do not drive enough proactive positive behaviour needed to address our existential challenges. Unfortunately, the G of ESG focuses mainly on just these issues. What drives E/S champions most is not G but L—leadership. We must therefore upgrade ESG to ESL, where L is a higher form of leadership, which we will discuss in detail in the rest of Part One. In the chapters ahead, we will also substantiate the move to ESL with research data from twenty-five countries.

Chapter 2

A Higher Form of Personal Leadership

At a conference of 350 business and government leaders in November 2022, I told my audience the stories of Faber-Castell, Tata and the Doi Tung Development Project.

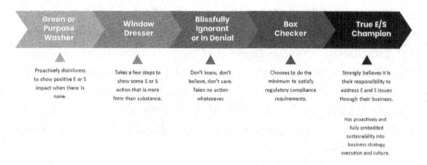

Green or Purpose Washer	Window Dresser	Blissfully Ignorant or In Denial	Box Checker	True E/S Champion
Proactively disinforms to show positive E or S impact when there is none.	Takes a few steps to show some E or S action that is more form than substance.	Don't know, don't believe, don't care. Takes no action whatsoever.	Chooses to do the minimum to satisfy regulatory compliance requirements.	Strongly believes it is their responsibility to address E and S issues through their business. Has proactively and fully embedded sustainability into business strategy, execution and culture.

Figure 4: The E/S Action Spectrum. Source: Rajeev Peshawaria, Stewardship Asia Centre.

Based on the stories, I introduced the E/S Action Spectrum and asked them a poll question:

What motivates true E/S champions most to create long-lasting positive impact on the environment and/or society? Choose one of the following options:

1. Measurement and reporting
2. Regulation and compliance
3. Tax and compensation incentives
4. Cheaper capital (e.g., from green finance)
5. Proactive, genuine leadership intent to do well by doing good

Here is how they responded:

Measurement and reporting	2.83 per cent
Regulation and compliance	3.77 per cent
Tax and compensation incentives	1.89 per cent
Cheaper capital (e.g., from green finance)	1.89 per cent
Proactive, genuine leadership intent to do well by doing good	89.62 per cent

This may not be a perfectly scientific method of data collection, but the one-sided nature of the results says something.

I have observed good and bad leadership in the corporate world for over thirty years. I have worked at five Fortune 500 companies as an employee and served over 100 as a leadership and corporate governance consultant. For my previous books, I conducted research in twenty-eight countries. Through all this experience, I have found that exceptional leaders—those that make a meaningful difference through their work—do so not because of extrinsic carrots and sticks but because of an intrinsic sense of values and purpose. Money and extrinsic rewards are important to them, but these are not their main motivators. So, the consensus within the result confirms my experience over three decades.

To ensure that the conference poll was not a one-off result, I decided to cast a wider net and ask people similar questions in twenty-five countries. Essentially, I wanted to uncover global perceptions about the motivation behind the actions of leaders and companies that do well by consistently doing good. I hoped to get to the bottom of what needs to happen for more organizations to thrive by championing environmental and societal sustainability. We also wanted to know what drives the bad actors such as the greenwashers and window-dressers. So, we designed a survey and collected data from 10,000 respondents.

The results were in line with our conference poll and confirmed our hypothesis that:

- Regulations, incentives and cheaper capital are important but do not adequately address environmental or societal challenges. They often fail to prevent and even cause, bad behaviour, let alone motivate good behaviour.
- To drive positive environmental and social action and innovation, we need proactive genuine leadership intent to do well by doing good.

The details of the survey are in the appendix, but here is a summary and some key questions the data raises that we will address throughout the book:

The top 3 challenges of the 21st century

We asked respondents to list the most pressing issues of the century. 67 per cent included climate change in the top three, making it the most widely acknowledged challenge in our survey. 38 per cent included cyber vulnerability, making it the second most cited challenge. Crime and violence at 34 per cent, corruption at 32 per cent and socioeconomic inequality at 31 per cent were next, making 'social' issues the next set of top-of-mind challenges.

Should the business world take responsibility to address these challenges? If so, how?

Sincerity of the corporate world as a whole in addressing today's existential challenges

- Only 13 per cent believe that the corporate world is extremely sincere about going beyond rules and regulations to proactively create solutions.
- 31 per cent chose 'sincere', which was defined as playing by the rules, abiding by the law and avoiding harmful action.
- 41 per cent said the efforts were 'not sincere' (i.e., paying lip service, more form than substance) and

- 15 per cent chose 'not sincere at all' (i.e., blatant greenwashing and deceiving).

What do businesses need to do to earn more trust and reputational capital? And in today's highly transparent and connected world, what will be the consequences of not doing so?

Reasons for the rampant greenwashing and deceit as seen in the cases of Volkswagen and Boeing

75 per cent of our respondents pointed towards poor or toxic organizational culture (i.e., misguided values, excessive pressure to drive sales and profits and ineffective consequences for unethical behaviour) as the driver of bad behaviour.

What is the G (corporate governance) of ESG failing to address?

The effectiveness of rules and regulations in driving the innovation needed to create long-lasting positive impact

83 per cent agreed or strongly agreed that while important, by itself, regulation is inadequate in driving the extent of positive action needed to solve challenges like climate change, cyber vulnerability and socioeconomic inequality.

With so much focus on regulatory compliance within ESG these days, what are we missing?

The primary motivation of the leaders and companies most sincere in proactively addressing environmental and social challenges

Responses to this question were mixed, but 'genuine proactive leadership intent to do well by doing good' received the maximum votes at 30 per cent.

That genuine proactive leadership intent, rather than regulation or incentives, is the primary driver behind the actions of the E and S champions is also confirmed by our qualitative research, as shown in the stories in Part Two.

How can corporate boards encourage/ensure such leadership intent?

The leadership we need

86 per cent of our respondents agreed or strongly agreed that strong steward leadership is needed to meaningfully address today's existential challenges.

What is stewardship? What is steward leadership and how can it be practised?

* * *

Stewardship and steward leadership

Coming back to the track records of Faber-Castell, Tata and Doi Tung thus far, we can see that their leaders were driven by steward leadership intent. In this chapter and the next, I will describe this intent in detail. This chapter will dive deep into the personal aspect of steward leadership, whereas in Chapter 3, we will discuss organizational application. To fully understand steward leadership, let us begin by unpacking its main ingredient—*stewardship.*

Leaders like Lothar von Faber, Count Anton-Wolfgang, Jamsetji Tata and Princess Mother Srinagarindra see themselves as stewards of planet Earth and humanity. Instead of waiting to be incentivized, regulated, measured and rewarded or punished, they proactively lead themselves to do the most they can for the planet and society. Their worldview is something like this: I have the opportunity to make the world a better place through my work—this is the very reason I exist. They see their role in life as taking care of what exists and making it better. They want to define their legacy not in terms of how much they acquired during their lifetime but in terms of stewardship—how much good they created and left behind.

At Stewardship Asia Centre, we define stewardship as 'creating value by integrating the needs of stakeholders, society, future generations and the environment'.

In my previous books *Too Many Bosses, Too Few Leaders* and *Open Source Leadership*, I made the distinction between bosses and leaders. I argued that bosses merely use authority to get others to do what they want. Leaders, on the other hand, strive to create a better future and never give up, no matter how hard it gets. They do not give up because their motivation to strive is driven by a deep sense of values and purpose. Their strong conviction in their own values and purpose gives them a unique type of energy—*leadership energy*[32]—which keeps them going despite the toughest of resistance and hardship. I used examples like Nelson Mandela, Gandhi and Martin Luther King Jr. from the socio-political sphere and the likes of Howard Schultz (former CEO of Starbucks) and Soichiro Honda (founder of the Honda Motor Company) from the business world to illustrate leadership energy. My argument was simple:

1. Leadership is about creating a better future, not about title or authority.
2. Any attempt at creating change will be met with resistance.
3. The key difference between leaders and non-leaders is the former's resilience in the face of resistance.
4. To keep going amidst resistance, you will need long-lasting leadership energy. This is the energy that kept Mandela from giving up even through twenty-seven years of prison.
5. Only a 100 per cent honest belief in a personal set of values and a purpose based on those values will evoke such leadership energy.

So, over the years, I have urged my readers, viewers and students to keep looking until they can fully understand their true values and purpose in life. While I have provided detailed guidance on how to uncover one's values and purpose—and therefore one's leadership energy—until recently, I left the choice of values and purpose to each individual to figure out for themselves. My emphasis was on the consistent application of values, whatever they may be. The idea here was that if you believe in any set of values that you never compromise, no matter how difficult a situation you might find yourself in and if you pursue a purpose based on those values, you will experience long-lasting leadership energy. I did talk about the need for emotional integrity[33], which is the courage to look in the mirror and be honest with oneself about what one truly desires in life, but I have thus far refrained from prescribing any specific values or any type of purpose as a leader.

Steward leaders

However, in light of the existential challenges we face today, our understanding of leadership must evolve. Based on research, I now strongly believe that if we want to save our planet and humanity, we need to mature into s*teward leaders*—leaders that proactively pursue stewardship as defined above. Not only must today's leaders take care of what is entrusted to them, they must grow it and make it better. In business, this means benefitting not just shareholders, but along with them, a wide variety of stakeholders, society, future generations and the environment. Therefore, the leaders of today must choose steward leadership, which is 'the genuine desire and persistence to create a collective better future'.

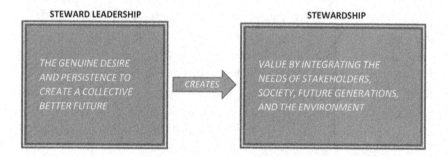

The evolution of the steward leadership concept

As the term suggests, steward leadership is the combination of two words: Stewardship and leadership.

But before we combine the two words, we will need to upgrade them in light of current concerns.

The Merriam-Webster dictionary defines stewardship as:

1. the office, duties and obligations of a steward
2. the conducting, supervising or managing of something, especially, the careful and responsible management of something entrusted to one's care

So, traditionally, stewardship has been seen as 'taking care of' or 'serving'. Given today's existential challenges and the urgent need to address them, we at Stewardship Asia Centre offer an upgraded definition:

Stewardship is creating value by integrating the needs of stakeholders, society, future generations and the environment.

Similarly, leadership has traditionally been seen as the action of leading a group of people or an organization or having a position of authority. Again, in today's context, I felt the need to upgrade this definition. Rather than being seen as the action of directing and telling others what to do, i.e., seeing leadership in terms of a leader's relationship with her followers or in terms of titles and positions—CEO, Prime Minister or President—in recent years, I have defined leadership differently.

'Leadership is the art of harnessing human energy towards the creation of a better future.'

However, as explained earlier, to address today's environmental and social challenges, leaders need to see themselves as stewards of planet Earth and society and maximize their leadership energy by developing honest clarity of values and purpose. So, at first glance, it seems that all we need to do is to add the word steward before leadership to arrive at steward leadership.

> 'Steward leadership is the act of harnessing human energy towards the creation of a better future.'
>
> But this would not answer the question: A better future for whom? To ensure that the better future is not too narrowly focused on oneself and/or one's shareholders, we need to borrow from our definition of stewardship, which says that value must be created in a way that addresses the needs of multiple stakeholders, the environment and society at large. In other words, stewardship requires the better future to be a collective one. Additionally, the desire to create a collective better future must be 100 per cent genuine and driven by intrinsic rather than extrinsic motivators. Introducing these elements into our definition, we can now arrive at a refreshed one:
>
> 'Steward leadership is the genuine desire and persistence to create a collective better future.'

A $10.1 trillion annual opportunity

Steward leadership is neither anti-shareholder nor anti-profit. On the contrary, it boils down to accepting the 21st-century leadership challenge, which is to drive superior shareholder returns by addressing the very challenges that threaten us today. If the World Economic Forum is to be believed, climate change alone represents $10.1 trillion a year in new business opportunities and can generate millions of new jobs by 2030[34]. So, the idea here is to make profit while addressing the biggest pain points of today's society—climate change, income inequality, cyber vulnerability and social unrest to name a few. This will require extremely high creativity, innovation and resilience, which governance alone will not activate. We will need honest steward leadership. Somehow, we need to motivate more business bosses to choose steward leadership so that enough innovation can take place to save us and our planet. Innovation and resilience can neither be legislated nor driven by extrinsic motivators alone.

So, as proposed at the conclusion of the previous chapter, the scope of the ESG framework must be upgraded to include leadership.

But not leadership in the traditional hierarchical sense. We need steward leadership—the genuine desire and persistence to create a collective better future. It is about seeing oneself as a steward of planet Earth and humanity and taking ownership to address environmental and social challenges.

Personal steward leadership

Let's be clear, stewardship is hard. Creating economic value for shareholders the normal way is hard enough, but creating value by integrating the needs of stakeholders, society, future generations and the environment is much harder. There will be a million obstacles and difficulties along the way. To stay resilient, leaders who choose to pursue stewardship will need a very deep reservoir of leadership energy. This is where steward leadership comes in. Only by maximizing their personal leadership energy can they create value the stewardship way. In recent times, no one exemplifies such *steward* leadership energy in business more than Paul Polman, the former CEO of Unilever. Before we unpack what it takes to become a steward leader, let's take a detour and look at Polman's attempt at steward leadership.

Paul Polman at Unilever

On January 1, 2009, Paul Polman became the Chief Executive Officer (CEO) and Executive Director of Unilever. At the time, Unilever was the 60th-largest company in the world by market capitalization and was valued at more than $100 billion. By 2009, however, its stock had been on the decline for a decade and management was distracted by frequent restructuring. At the same time, the 2008 financial crisis had shone a spotlight on the role of responsible business at the global stage. Unilever drastically needed a transformation.

Polman knew the world was rapidly changing, with issues such as poverty, climate change and increasing food prices beginning to impact Unilever's future business prospects. He foresaw consumers becoming more vocal about companies not living up to their roles in society, particularly with the growth of social media and other digital platforms.

On his first day on the job, Polman announced that Unilever would no longer be providing quarterly earnings guidance to Wall Street. He even told hedge funds that they were not welcome as investors looking to profit in the short term. Wall Street was predictably displeased with the statement and Unilever's share price plummeted 8 per cent on the day and a further 12 per cent over the next several months. The media weighed in, declaring, 'Unilever could use some guidance.'[35] Yet, Polman didn't flinch. 'I figured they couldn't fire me if I did it on my first day,' he said cheekily and kickstarted a wholesale transformation of the company.

To ensure the success of his vision, Polman replaced or reassigned 75 per cent of top management to ensure that his team was aligned with the new strategy. Polman also set out to alter Unilever's leadership culture to imbibe key leaders with a growth mindset that extended beyond financial returns. 'You cannot save your way to prosperity,' he elaborated, as high performing leaders were crucial in delivering the company's socially responsible goals. With this in mind, he launched the Unilever Sustainable Living Plan (USLP) in 2010 to double its growth, halve its environmental impact and triple its social impact.

Underpinned by multiple commitments and time-bound targets, the USLP signified a first-of-its-kind plan, in terms of its breadth, size, scope and ambition[36]. USLP has been responsible for Unilever's growth in their purpose-led brands like Dove, Lipton, Seventh Generation and Pukka tea. According to a 2019 article on Unilever's website, these 'sustainable living brands' grew 69 per cent faster than the rest of their business[37]. Even more, these brands have enabled them to achieve cost savings of over €1 billion since 2008 by improving water and energy efficiency in their factories and by using less material and minimizing waste[38].

Nevertheless, while the USLP provided a framework for Unilever's long-term vision, particularly for its external operations and output, there remained the concern of pushing forth a growth mindset throughout the organization and especially among its leaders. As such, in 2010, the Unilever Leadership Development Programme was launched to invest in authentic leadership development, assess company talent and enable Unilever to further develop leaders across its operating geographies. The programme forced managers to examine how their lives, work and leadership purpose could seamlessly intersect in a meaningful way to align with the company's goals and foster stronger relationships and connections internally and externally.

In addition, prior to Polman's arrival, many senior managers were being rated as over-performing while the company as a whole was underperforming. In response, Unilever introduced its '3 plus 1' output measures, whereby individual managers set three business objectives plus one personal development goal in their performance plans to focus attention on critical, long-term goals. Bonuses were then based on achieving these output measures. By developing such a standard, Unilever prioritized success measures that were much higher than before to emphasize Unilever's long-term focus for their managers. Ultimately, this cultivated a growth strategy that would reward accountability for the longterm and expose underperformers who were heavily focused on promoting their own careers rather than Unilever's vision[39].

Overall, while Polman persisted with his vision to transform Unilever, the internal systems and structure he put in place were heavily influenced by the purpose he believed was necessary to create value for everyone, not just the shareholders. However, it cannot be ignored that by pursuing such a vision, Unilever delivered a total shareholder return of 290 per cent over Polman's tenure[40]. Even after Polman's departure from Unilever in 2019, Unilever continues to lead the world in sustainability and performance[41].

We will discuss the Polman story in two parts. In this chapter, I will address aspects related to him being a steward leader personally and in Chapter 3, I will dive into the organizational aspects of steward leadership. Before you read any further, take a pause to ponder over a few questions:

1. What type of values did Polman believe in and practise?
2. What sort of purpose was he pursuing as Unilever's CEO?
3. What gave him the strength and conviction to stay the course during the first two very difficult years?

From our extensive research ever since the inception of Stewardship Asia Centre, we know that leaders like Polman strongly believe in four specific stewardship values:

1. Interdependence
2. Long-term view
3. Ownership mentality
4. Creative resilience

Even though they may not be labelled exactly as above, these four values lie at the heart of steward leadership. To become a steward leader is to have an uncompromising conviction of these values within one's personal belief system. They must become so deeply rooted in one's brain and heart that one acts according to the values without thinking. We will come back to this 'automatic values-based response' a bit later. Let's look at each of the values in more detail first:

Interdependence: A strong belief in the idea of interdependence forms the foundation of steward leadership. Steward leaders see the world as an integrated and interconnected web in which the success of each constituent is coupled with that of other constituents. Rejecting the notion of a zero-sum game, they develop the win-win habit and view their own success in terms of growing along with others rather than against them. Paul Polman understood early on as CEO of Unilever that the company could not be successful without taking the needs of different stakeholders into account. Poverty, climate change and increasing food prices were beginning to impact Unilever's future business prospects and he fully expected consumers to reward companies who do what they can for society's pain points. His belief in interdependence led to the formation of the Unilever Sustainable Living Plan.

Similarly, based on his firm belief in the value of interdependence, Faber-Castell's Lothar von Faber provided employee benefits like health insurance and housing to employees a full forty years before they became the law in Germany.

Starbucks, under former CEO Howard Schultz, became the first company in the United States to provide full healthcare benefits even to

part-time workers because of Schultz' firm belief in interdependence.
More about Starbucks when we discuss creative resilience.

Long-term view: Steward leaders are long-term thinkers. They are
willing to forgo short-term gains to achieve enduring returns. They
also build organizations that make the world a better place for current
and future generations. As confirmed by our survey, environmental
sustainability is one of the most pressing issues facing our planet
today. Depending on their stance on sustainability, business leaders'
actions can positively or negatively impact future generations. Danish
companies Orsted and Chr. Hansen Holdings and Neste Oyj of
Finland take up the top three spots in the list of large companies
doing the most for sustainable business practices[42]. Clearly, the
steward leaders at these companies have decided to be mindful of
the needs of future generations and do what they can to minimize
environmental harm.

Count Anton, whom we mentioned earlier as the last family member
to serve as CEO of Faber-Castell, invested in a sustainable forestry
project in Brazil in the mid-1980s. The benefits of the project would
accrue only after twenty years when the 300,000 *Pinus caribaea* trees
planted and tended to every year would be ready for harvesting. Not
only would the trees provide a steady supply of wood for producing
pencils, but they would also neutralize the company's carbon footprint
by absorbing 900,000 tonnes of carbon dioxide.

In the case of Polman, he knew that transforming Unilever into a
purpose-led organization would require long-term thinking. Stopping the
practice of providing quarterly earnings guidance was the first signalling
of his long-term view. While there were early setbacks, his long-term
vision kept him going. It is interesting to note here that 75 per cent of his
top team either did not have a long-term view or did not believe in the
new strategy. As things started going downhill before getting better, they
jumped ship. To their credit, Unilever's board, on the other hand, took
a long-term view and kept the strategy on track despite the early snags.

Ownership mentality: Steward leaders imagine an inclusive better
future and take it upon themselves to create it. Driven by the mantra

of 'If it's to be, it's up to me', they take responsibility and make things happen. In business, this means thinking and acting like an owner, even if one is just a manager or an employee. Polman was successful as a steward leader first and foremost because he took ownership and chose to do business the stewardship way.

I witnessed another great example of ownership mentality during the 2008 global financial crisis while I worked at Morgan Stanley. During the crisis, John Mack, who had risen through the ranks, was the CEO of the firm. After Lehman Brothers and Merrill Lynch had both perished in September of that year, regulators put considerable pressure on Mack to sell the firm at a throw-away price to save the markets from collapse. This would probably stabilize the markets, but most Morgan Stanley employees would lose their jobs and much of their savings, which were in company stock options. Being personally wealthy in his early 60s and having had a great career, Mack could have capitulated and retired into a life of luxury at that stressful and difficult time.

However, his strong sense of ownership did not allow him to do so. He decided that it was his responsibility to save Morgan Stanley and the jobs of 40,000 employees. So, he took the biggest risk of his life by going against the regulators to do just that and eventually succeeded. He was able to make what was probably the most difficult decision of his life with great conviction because of his psychological ownership.

Perhaps there is no better illustration of ownership mentality than the Doi Tung Development Project story I mentioned briefly earlier and will elaborate in Part Two. Not only did Khun Chai take ownership to make the Princess Mother's dream of making the project self-sustainable come true, but he also instilled ownership mentality in the farmers by turning them into entrepreneurs.

Recently, I met Frank E. Mars, the Chairman of the Board and a strategic advisor to Mars, Incorporated. Part Two has a case study on Mars' history of environmental and social sustainability. While I hosted Frank for a fireside chat at the Singapore Management University, he made an interesting point about ownership mentality. He differentiated between accountability and responsibility. 'Accountability is given to you, responsibility is what you feel,' he explained. Steward leaders clearly feel for the planet and society and take ownership to do something positive for both.

Creative resilience: An undying belief in interdependence is the foundation of steward leadership. Long-term view and ownership mentality are enablers that make it happen. But it is creative resilience that is the fuel that keeps it going. Steward leaders understand and acknowledge the enormity of challenges associated with creating economic value by integrating the needs of stakeholders and society at large. They realize that they will need both creativity—the ability to find innovative models to fuel growth—and resilience—the tenacity and persistence to not give up in the face of failures. The latter comes from their genuine desire to create a collective better future. Their own visualization of the collective better future they wish to create is so powerful that it keeps them in the game despite multiple failures and obstacles. As Mandela is credited to have famously said, 'I never lose. Either I win or I learn.'[43]

To unleash the much-needed creativity and innovation, steward leaders both challenge themselves to constantly come up with new ideas and build conditions in which innovation can thrive. Polman did just that. First, he personally conceived a new strategy. Then, he rolled out the authentic leadership development programme, assessed his leaders' strengths and development opportunities and created a performance-based compensation plan to ensure continuous innovation.

Starbucks' Schultz was rejected over 230 times in 1987 before he could raise $3.8 million to buy the then tiny Seattle-based coffee bean store chain[44]. What kept him going after so many rejections? His dream of creating 'a company my father never had a chance to work for', where everyone would be treated with respect and dignity and where even part-time workers would have full healthcare benefits. Much later, after Starbucks became a multinational corporation, it hit a rough patch financially. Bankers and consultants told Schultz to trim employee benefits, but he would hear none of it. He doubled down on finding innovative ways to re-kindle growth without sacrificing employee benefits. And he succeeded.

Becoming a steward leader

Step 1: Integrate the four stewardship values with your personal values

So, the first step towards becoming a steward leader is to firmly embed these four values within one's personal belief system. Behaviour based on these values must become one's automatic response system. This is not easy because the default human wiring is designed to 'take' rather than 'give'. To become a steward leader is to accept the idea: 'The more you give, the more you get'. Counter intuitive as it may sound, this is what steward leaders believe. They derive a very special kind of joy in giving. They are not selfless. Rather they believe that to maximize their own gain, they must work hard to make others successful. They believe in playing win-win-win where shareholders, employees and society at large all win together.

In today's dog-eat-dog world, it might be difficult to believe in the virtues of giving, so this win-win-win mentality needs to be developed deliberately. My friend Nipun Mehta, who runs a non-profit technology firm called Servicespace in Berkeley, California, says it best, 'It is only when you understand the joy of giving, do you realize what it means to receive. You give externally but you receive internally.'

He tells a story about a couple of interns that worked at his non-profit over a summer. One of the requirements of the job as an intern was to do one random act of kindness a day continuously for ninety days. The interns were expected to do something kind for someone else each day and report it. 'Why did you have them do it compulsorily every day?' I asked Nipun. 'I wanted them to feel the joy of giving and I wanted them to develop giving as their default operating system,' he replied. By doing a random act of kindness every day and by talking about how they felt doing it, their brain would rewire permanently and make them givers for life, he explained.

Even if one has honestly arrived at a set of values one deeply believes in, the behaviours do not become the default because of the lack of deliberate practice from a very young age. If we want values-based behaviour to become our default operating mode, not only do we need to very honestly examine what we really want (our values), but we also need to deliberately practise behaving according to those values until such behaviour becomes muscle memory. Parents need to create conditions—much like Nipun did for his interns—wherein, at a very young age, a child begins to think about his or her values and starts practising them regularly until they become hardwired in them. They must create regular opportunities for deliberate practice and setup reward and consequence systems accordingly. In the next chapter, we will discuss what organizations need to do to develop their collective muscle memory for stewardship values.

Brain science has now established the fact that the brain can indeed re-wire itself through brain rehearsals and deliberate practice, an ability called neuroplasticity. Unfortunately, most of us do not think deeply about our values and purpose. Worse still, we do not engage in deliberate practice to change our default settings. Neglecting this very important part of self-development not only exposes one to the danger of unethical action, but it also prevents people from discovering their true leadership energy and therefore from creating a powerful legacy. The original default setting is to maximize one's net worth and social status. By deliberately re-wiring the brain as explained here, one moves from maximizing *net* worth to maximizing *life* worth. And the best part is, in doing so, net worth often takes care of itself. You either end up making a lot of money because you have discovered your passion and turned it into your work or you are so happy giving and serving that you do not need much money.

So, while the first step to becoming a steward leader is to integrate the four stewardship values within one's belief system, I would like to offer some words of caution. Steward leadership demands honest belief in the four values. It is true that you can rewire your brain to behave in any way you want with deliberate practice but underpinning the deliberate practice must be 100 per cent *emotional integrity*, not just emotional intelligence.

Emotional Intelligence	Emotional Integrity
• Recognize, understand and manage one's own emotions. • Recognize, understand and manage the emotions of others[45].	• The ability to honestly admit to oneself what one really wants out of life without worrying about how society might perceive it[46].

As mentioned earlier, steward leadership is hard work. Only a 100 per cent honest belief in stewardship values will create the resilience needed to navigate the ups and downs of the journey. If the belief in values is anything short of 100 per cent, you will run out of leadership energy. And in today's era of near-total transparency, it is almost impossible to fake it.

Step 2: Define personal stewardship purpose—the collective better future YOU aspire to create

With firm conviction in their values, steward leaders now articulate their purpose. As with their values, their purpose is greater than themselves and seeks to create a collective better future for a wide variety of stakeholders, if not for society at large. The core difference between steward leaders and regular business leaders is the focus of their purpose. Most business leaders believe that their sole duty is to maximize shareholder returns. Steward leaders aim bigger—they too want to create value, but not at the expense of other stakeholders, society, future generations or the environment. Starbucks' Schultz, whom I mentioned earlier, had exactly this in mind. He certainly wanted to create wealth for himself and his family, but he also wanted employees and other stakeholders to succeed with him. In other words, he gave himself the purpose of creating a collective better future.

Decades ago, Mandela did the same. His version of the collective better future he wanted to create for South Africa envisioned people of all races, including whites, thriving together. His strong belief in interdependence gave rise to his inclusive purpose. Instead of punishing the whites for what they did to the black population during the apartheid regime, he forgave them and visualized a 'rainbow nation'. A true steward leader indeed.

Step 3: Ensure everything you do is aligned to and governed by your Steward Leadership Compass

Developing values and purpose clarity are foundational steps. Step 3 happens day in and day out. Now, the steward leader uses his or her values and purpose as a personal compass to make every decision. Real steward leaders walk the talk and never compromise their values even if it hurts their personal interest in the short term. When the majority population wanted revenge, Mandela forgave. He even went against the wishes of the very people who voted him to power and against his own family, in forgiving white people. His belief in his values and purpose was so strong that he was unafraid of losing even the people closest to him—his wife and daughter.

In essence, steward leadership involves articulating and activating one's personal Steward Leadership Compass.

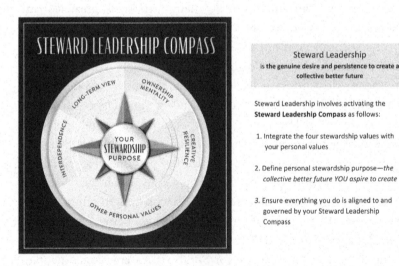

Figure 5: Personal Steward Leadership Compass. Source: Stewardship Asia Centre.

As mentioned above, Step 3 is where the rubber hits the road.

The following table summarizes the leadership maturity continuum from boss to leader to steward leader:

Leadership Maturity Continuum		
Boss	**Leader**	**Steward Leader**
Leadership is a position of authority.	Leadership is the desire and persistence to create a better future.	Leadership is the genuine desire and persistence to create a *collective* better future.
Doing something to others—directing, coaching, guiding, encouraging—to achieve desired results.	Doing something to oneself ('be the change you want to see in the world') to inspire others with own example.	
The focus is largely on one's own success, using a win-lose mentality.	The focus is on creating win-win success for oneself and a small set of stakeholders.	The focus is on creating *win-win-win success*, where individuals, the organization and its shareholders and society at large all thrive together.
Power coming from one's position and hard work are used to maximize influence.	Strong conviction in a set of personal values and purpose are used to maximize inspiration.	Stewardship values—interdependence, long-term view, ownership mentality and creative resilience—along with stewardship purpose—a purpose greater than oneself or one's shareholders—are used to maximize collective welfare.

Happiness, success and self-worth are measured in terms of power and wealth.	Happiness, success and self-worth are measured in terms of living and pursuing personal values and purpose.	Happiness, success and self-worth are measured in terms of living stewardship values and pursuing a stewardship purpose.
Leadership Energy —the resilience to keep going—is low because it is driven by power stemming from one's position.	Leadership Energy is high because it is driven by personal values and purpose.	Leadership Energy is high because it is driven by collective values and a purpose larger than oneself. This also makes the leader fearless.
Fundamental Question		
How to lead my team to generate the best possible results for the organization so that I can advance in my career?	How can I create a better future for myself, my family, my organization or my country?	How can I help solve the most pressing problems of today and through my work, create a better future for humanity?

Source: This table was first published in one of my articles on Forbes.com[17].

Regardless of title or position, anyone who considers themselves a leader in today's context must honestly search for answers to the fundamental question in the bottom right cell of the table: How can I help solve the most pressing problems of today and through my work, create a better future for humanity?

You may be doing well financially, but besides the wealth you have earned, what legacy will you leave behind for your children? What stories will your children tell about you with great pride? Will you leave the world slightly better than you found it? In other words, are you a steward leader? To find out, score yourself as honestly as possible on the statements below and reflect on your answers. If you are not already, this will get you thinking about shaping your own steward leadership journey.

Rate yourself on a 1–5 scale where 1 is strongly disagree, 2 is disagree, 3 is neither agree nor disagree, 4 is agree and 5 is strongly agree.	
1. I view the world as in integrated web in which the success and well-being of constituents is interdependent.	
2. Keeping both current and future generations in mind, I take a long-term view on value creation.	
3. I am self-motivated enough to take ownership and address problems even if they are not a part of my job or do not impact me personally.	
4. I routinely listen, learn and reflect with a view to innovate and add greater value.	
5. I have incorporated the four stewardship values in my personal set of deeply held values.	
6. I stand by my values even when it is inconvenient and challenging.	
7. I have established a clear purpose in life based on my values.	
8. My purpose aims to create a better future for a wide range of stakeholders, not just myself.	

Source: This table was first published in one of my articles on Forbes.com[18].

There are no good or bad scores. The key is to reflect, be comfortable with where you are or do something that will get you there. Whatever you do, be totally honest with yourself.

Chapter 3

Enterprise-wide Steward Leadership

Before we get into the organizational practice of steward leadership, let us revisit a fundamental question. Should commercial organizations be expected to do business the stewardship way?

Remember, stewardship in business is creating value by integrating the needs of stakeholders, society, future generations and the environment. Integrating the needs of so many constituents may come at the cost of shareholder gains. Should businesses be expected to sacrifice some profit for social good?

The Friedman Doctrine

As mentioned briefly in Chapter 1, noted 20th-century economist and Nobel laureate Milton Friedman, in his seminal 1970 *New York Times* op-ed, strongly opposed the idea of sacrificing some profit for social good. He concluded his famous op-ed saying:

'There is one and only one social responsibility of business—to use its resources and engage in activities designed to increase its profits so long as it stays within the rules of the game, which is to say, engages in open and free competition without deception or fraud.'

He made powerful arguments to support his conclusion. I have selected and adapted these few paragraphs from Friedman's op-ed to illustrate his thinking[49].

1. Holding businesses socially responsible for eliminating discrimination, avoiding pollution and providing employment is akin to socialism and goes against the grain of free markets.

In a free enterprise, private-property system, a corporate executive is an employee of the owners of the business. He has direct responsibility to his employers. That responsibility is to conduct the business in accordance with their desires, which generally will be to make as much money as possible while conforming to the basic rules of the society, both those embodied in law and those embodied in ethical custom[50].

2. Doing social good must mean that he is to act in some way that is not in the interest of his employers. For example, he is to refrain from increasing the price of the product in order to contribute to the social objective of preventing inflation, even though a price increase would be in the best interests of the corporation. Or that he is to make expenditures on reducing pollution beyond the amount that is in the best interests of the corporation or that is required by law in order to contribute to the social objective of improving the environment. Or that at the expense of corporate profits, he is to hire 'hard core' unemployed instead of better qualified available workmen to contribute to the social objective of reducing poverty[51].

3. In each of these cases, the corporate executive would be spending someone else's money for a general social interest. Insofar as his actions, in accord with his 'social responsibility', reduce returns to stockholders, he is spending their money. Insofar as his actions raise the price to customers, he is spending the customers' money. Insofar as his actions lower the wages of some employees, he is spending their money. If he does this, he is in effect imposing taxes on the one hand and deciding how the tax proceeds shall be spent on the other[52].

4. The whole justification for permitting the corporate executive to be selected by the stockholders is that the executive is an agent serving the interests of his principal. This justification disappears when the corporate executive imposes taxes and spends the proceeds for 'social' purposes. He becomes in effect a public employee, a civil servant, even though he remains in name an employee of a private enterprise. On grounds of political principle, it is intolerable that such civil servants—insofar as

their actions in the name of social responsibility are real and not just window-dressing—should be selected. If they are to be civil servants, then they must be selected through a political process. If they are to impose taxes and make expenditures to foster 'social' objectives, then political machinery must be set up to guide the assessment of taxes and to determine through a political process the objectives to be served[53].

For much of the fifty years following the publication of this op-ed, capitalism has operated based on shareholder primacy. The idea was simple—businesses exist to make profits and pay taxes on the profits. It is the government's role to deploy the taxes for social good. By running ethical and lawful businesses, business owners create employment and fund social good through taxes. Holding businesses responsible for much more would violate the spirit of a free-market mechanism like capitalism.

Until 2019, the United States Business Roundtable, an association of CEOs of leading American corporations, agreed with Friedman's views and upheld shareholder primacy in corporate governance. However, in that year, 181 CEOs signed a new statement on the Purpose of a Corporation, which commits to meeting the needs of all stakeholders—customers, employees, suppliers, communities and shareholders. Here is the full text of the statement, as reported on the Roundtable's website:

Statement on the Purpose of a Corporation[54]

Americans deserve an economy that allows each person to succeed through hard work and creativity and to lead a life of meaning and dignity. We believe the free-market system is the best means of generating good jobs, a strong and sustainable economy, innovation, a healthy environment and economic opportunity for all.

Businesses play a vital role in the economy by creating jobs, fostering innovation and providing essential goods and services. Businesses make and sell consumer products; manufacture equipment and vehicles; support the national defense; grow and produce food; provide health care; generate and deliver energy; and offer financial, communications and other services that underpin economic growth.

While each of our individual companies serves its own corporate purpose, we share a fundamental commitment to all of our stakeholders. We commit to:

- Delivering value to our customers. We will further the tradition of American companies leading the way in meeting or exceeding customer expectations.

- Investing in our employees. This starts with compensating them fairly and providing important benefits. It also includes supporting them through training and education that help develop new skills for a rapidly changing world. We foster diversity and inclusion, dignity and respect.

- Dealing fairly and ethically with our suppliers. We are dedicated to serving as good partners to the other companies, large and small, that help us meet our missions.

- Supporting the communities in which we work. We respect the people in our communities and protect the environment by embracing sustainable practices across our businesses.

- Generating long-term value for shareholders, who provide the capital that allows companies to invest, grow and innovate. We are committed to transparency and effective engagement with shareholders.

Each of our stakeholders is essential. We commit to deliver value to all of them, for the future success of our companies, our communities and our country.

Given these contrasting views, how should we answer our question: Should commercial organizations be expected to do business the stewardship way?

At first glance, both arguments seem valid. The proponents of stakeholder capitalism who oppose Milton Friedman say:

It is all well and good to speak of government's having the responsibility to impose taxes and determine expenditures for 'social' purposes as controlling pollution or training the hard-core unemployed, but that the problems are too urgent to wait on the slow course of political processes, that the exercise of social responsibility by businessmen is a quicker and surer way to solve pressing current problems.[55]

On the other hand, Friedman's arguments seem equally compelling, particularly when one considers that he professes the pure pursuit of profit so long as it stays within the rules of the game, which is to say, engages in open and free competition without deception or fraud.

So, what made the US Business Roundtable change its long-held stance about shareholder primacy in 2019? The following points are worth considering:

- In 2010, there were 2.1 billion users of the internet. By the end of 2023, there will be 5.3 billion[56]. Connectivity has given people much empowerment and reach, but its misuse has also made us vulnerable.
- In 2010, the global population was 6.9 billion. At the time of this writing in early 2023, it has already crossed the 8 billion mark[57]. While this means bigger markets for businesses, it also places much greater burden on planet Earth in terms of resources, socio-political harmony and climate.
- Today, we live in a world where exciting growth opportunities co-exist with existential challenges to humanity. If we ignore the challenges, not only will we forgo the promise of the opportunities, but also destroy the planet and humanity.
- The 2008 financial crisis, the increased frequency of severe and destructive weather events and the Covid-19 pandemic are ample proof that no individual, organization or nation can thrive in isolation. All sectors of the global economy need to do their part.
- Ample research now suggests that today's digitally empowered customers and consumers—younger generations in particular—are demanding good societal and planetary stewardship from business leaders. Any individual or organization that fails to rise to the challenge risks becoming irrelevant.

The last point is perhaps the biggest driving force behind the change made by the Roundtable. Now, it is not just a question of corporate social responsibility. 'Doing well by doing good' is a business imperative. Research has shown that when consumers have a choice, they prefer products and services of companies they deem ethical and responsible.

As I see it, there is no conflict between Friedman's doctrine and the changed stance of the Business Roundtable. Both Friedman and the Roundtable firmly believe in free markets. This means the actions and decisions of commercial organizations must be guided primarily by market forces and stipulated laws of the land. Friedman too acknowledged that if some social good is in the interest of the corporation, it is perfectly okay:

> Of course, in practice the doctrine of social responsibility is frequently a cloak for actions that are justified on other grounds rather than a reason for those actions.
>
> To illustrate, it may well be in the long-run interest of a corporation that is a major employer in a small community to devote resources to providing amenities to that community or to improving its government. That may make it easier to attract desirable employees, it may reduce the wage bill or lessen losses from pilferage and sabotage or have other worthwhile effects. Or it may be that, given the laws about the deductibility of corporate charitable contributions, the stockholders can contribute more to charities they favor by having the corporation make the gift than by doing it themselves, since they can in that way contribute an amount that would otherwise have been paid as corporate taxes.
>
> In each of these and many similar cases, there is a strong temptation to rationalize these actions as an exercise of 'social responsibility'. In the present climate of opinion, with its widespread aversion to 'capitalism', 'profits', the 'soulless corporation' and so on, this is one way for a corporation to generate goodwill as a by-product of expenditures that are entirely justified in its own self-interest.[58]

I would like to make two final points to put this debate to rest.

1. Thanks to near universal connectivity, everyone in today's market—individuals, companies, governments—is almost naked. All our actions are now in full public view. If digitization continues at its current pace, it is probably safe to assume that whatever is left of privacy will continue to be eroded. While the death of privacy is a huge concern, one silver lining may be that it will become increasingly difficult for bad actors to hide their bad behaviour. Consumers and customers want businesses to be more responsible towards the planet and society and will vote with their feet and preferences if businesses do not comply.

    There is also increasing evidence to suggest that in the long term, positive and genuine E/S action is more likely than not to lead to higher and more consistent shareholder returns[59]. The key words here are *long term* and *genuine ESG actions*. So, doing business with a stewardship mindset and aspiring to become a steward leader would be akin to capitalism. Any business not paying attention to E and S challenges will be acting against the long-term interest of shareholders.

2. Whether you believe in the efficacy of the myriad of research reports showing a positive correlation between E/S action and financial returns or not, the other question is this: What legacy do you want to leave as a business leader? Do you want to at least try to have a positive impact on today's existential challenges while driving financial returns? Or do you want to completely ignore today's pain points and continue to print money for shareholders just because you can? In recent decades, several 'geniuses' in technology and finance have used their superior cognitive abilities to make money in an unethical way. Cambridge Analytica and FTX are just some of the examples. If one is really proud of their superior intellect and smarts, why not use the gifts to show the world how to address today's challenges and make superior financial returns at the same time? As stated earlier, according to the World Economic Forum, the challenges provide trillions of dollars' worth of new business opportunities. Why not capitalize on those, make money and save the world at the same time?

I hope the above arguments shed some light on the need for stewardship and steward leadership. Thanks to the spotlight on ESG, most companies are beginning to do something about it. The question now is, where does your organization want to be on the E/S Action Spectrum we introduced in Chapter 1?

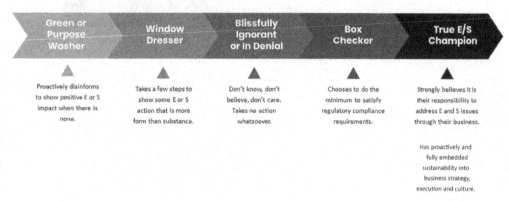

Figure 6: The E/S Action Spectrum. Source: Rajeev Peshawaria, Stewardship Asia Centre.

If you want to be on the far right-hand side, then ESL rather than ESG will be the way to go, because true E/S champions do not just stop at good governance. They create steward leadership DNA within their organizations so that everyone and everything can be guided and governed by stewardship values and purpose.

This move to ESL has implications for corporate boards as well. Besides compliance and risk management, boards must pay attention to ensure that a culture of steward leadership takes root within their organizations. Corporate governance is not just about preserving value. It also has another duty, which is to help enhance value. To fulfil that duty, boards must approach their work with a steward leadership mindset— *to create a collective better future*—and ensure that the organization's culture is based on the four stewardship values of interdependence, long-term view, ownership mentality and creative resilience. As we noted in Chapter 1, most boards tend not to spend adequate time on things like organizational culture and strategic innovation. Yes, the board must govern, but the G should be a subset of L—Steward Leadership.

So, let us change the picture and call the right-most champions steward leaders from now on and examine how steward leadership is practised at the organizational level. While doing so, we will also identify some pitfalls and suggest solutions.

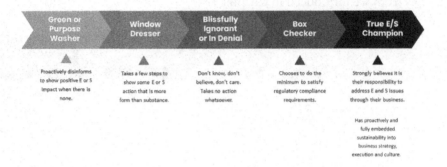

Figure 7: The E/S Action Spectrum. Source: Rajeev Peshawaria, Stewardship Asia Centre.

In Part Three, we will introduce the Steward Leadership Quotient—a tool that can help boards understand corporate culture and work with management to strengthen it.

Enterprise-wide steward leadership

The playbook for personal and organizational steward leadership is essentially the same. Creating an organization based on steward leadership tenets begins with clearly articulating and activating the organization's core Steward Leadership Compass. The three steps involved are the same:

1. Integrate the four stewardship values within the organization's existing values. This full set of values will now define the organization's culture.
2. Develop the organization's stewardship purpose—the collective better future you want the organization to create for a wide range of stakeholders and society at large.
3. Together, the stewardship values and purpose form the organization's core compass. Now, develop and maintain internal systems, structures and culture to ensure that

everything the organization does is aligned to and guided by the core compass.

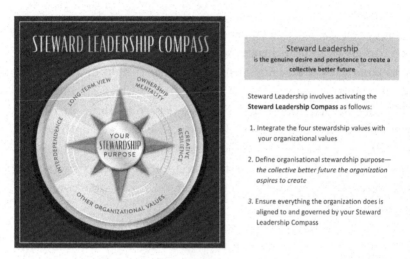

Figure 8: Organizational Steward Leadership Compass. Source: Stewardship Asia Centre.

As with personal steward leadership, Steps 1 and 2 are foundational and Step 3 is where the rubber hits the road. The consistency with which stewardship values and purpose guide the actions of the entire organization will determine the strength of its steward leadership culture.

Here are some common mistakes associated with the three steps and how to avoid them:

1. Values are articulated but not practised

In some organizations, values make great hallway posters and colourful slides in company presentations, but no one really practises them.

Real steward leaders do not just articulate values, they role model them personally and create conditions within the organization that enable the application of values in both strategy and execution. They understand that values-based decision-making is more powerful than rule-based decision-making. The now-famous story from Netflix illustrates this point very well.

Like most companies, Netflix had a detailed set of rules for travel related expenses. While reinventing their culture, they did away with it and replaced the lengthy policy with one sentence: 'Act in Netflix's best interest'.

Gone was the detailed guidance on how much to spend on airline tickets, meals or other expenses while on a business trip. Now it was left to employees' own judgement to do what is right in accordance with the company's values. Patty McCord, former Chief Talent Officer (CTO) of Netflix, found that Netflix's departure from an official travel and expense policy resulted in most employees complying with the adultlike, responsible behaviour expected of them. By setting out expectations of what 'Act in Netflix's best interest' means—to spend the company's money frugally, as if it were their own—the company's costs went down[60].

The point about values-based decision-making is this—if you have articulated values that are supposedly right for the company, then empower people to live them. The Netflix example above is one of many I have observed throughout more than thirty years of my corporate career, where freedom within a framework of values and purpose leads to more responsible behaviour by a vast majority of employees. Personally, too, I have led with values and freedom rather than rules throughout my working life. Except for rare instances, almost all my employees across the globe proved the point that trust begets trust. When given freedom within the framework of values, most employees behave responsibly. As a manager, this idea was liberating for me in many ways. By allowing employees to make values-based decisions, we almost always ended up exceeding performance expectations. Now I did not have the burden of telling people what to do. They used the organization's shared values to solve problems in ways that were often even better than what I would have done if I were the decision maker.

As a values-based steward leader, you have to give up control. This creates insecurity for a lot of managers. So, a pre-requisite for steward leadership is self-confidence. Only those managers who feel secure in their own skin can practise steward leadership. By choosing values-based guidelines over detailed rules and policies, Reed Hastings, CEO of Netflix, invited all employees to act as owners and leaders, while signalling his own comfort with letting go of controls.

Unfortunately, such leadership strength is rare. Most corporate bosses and therefore their companies, rely on rules rather than values to 'control' behaviour. The larger the company gets, the more rules and policies are instituted. When this happens, employees do not take ownership, do not use judgment and blindly follow the rules. The consequences of such a culture can be disastrous, as United Airlines learned the hard way. A few years ago, when United employees were handling an overbooked flight, they requested passengers to voluntarily give up a seat for a reward of $400. When no one volunteered, they applied the rule of randomly picking a passenger and asking him to leave. When he refused, he was violently dragged off the plane[61]. Instead of using company values to find a better solution, the employees blindly followed the rule. Perhaps they felt more compelled to apply the rule and less empowered to use judgement based on company values?

2. Values are written using catchy words or phrases rather than verbs

Another common mistake is to articulate values using buzzwords or phrases rather than simple sentences that clearly tell people what to do. Making a memorable acronym of the values is another obsession in the corporate world. To make the acronym fun and memorable, some companies end up diluting the message behind each value.

Rather than single words or catchphrases, we recommend articulating values using verbs. Instead of articulating the value of collaboration with a single word like 'teamwork', a sentence telling employees exactly what is expected of them would be better, like, *proactively help others to succeed*. The clearer the values are in terms of actions, the better.

3. 'Purpose-driven' is more form than substance

If you have been hearing the word 'purpose' in corporate lexicon more often recently, you are not alone. Terms like 'purpose-driven organization' and 'from profit to purpose' are everywhere. Every other company wants to transform itself into a purpose-driven company these days as it has become the management trend of the 2020s. Quick to respond, many consulting firms and business schools around the world have set up purpose practices and executive education curricula headed by self-styled purpose pundits who charge mega bucks for their advice. Books and articles on purpose are flying off the shelves like hot cakes. Google the phrase 'purpose-driven' and you will immediately know how powerful this trend is.

Isn't it great news that companies want to be purpose-driven? The customer, consumer and society at large will benefit, will it not? Yes and NO. I write the NO in uppercase because more organizations are getting it wrong than right. And the purpose pundits are not helping. I have nothing against the trend because it is much needed in today's context, but if you really want your organization to be purpose-driven, let's get a few things straight:

i. **Purpose is not new.** For CEOs trying to transform their companies into purpose-driven organizations, I have a basic question: Why now? Did your organization not have a purpose all along? One CEO I asked was quick to respond with, 'No, until now we only worked to maximize profit, now we must maximize purpose.' While this CEO spoke with good intentions to make a positive difference in society, like many others, he misunderstands the meaning of the word 'purpose'. According to Britannica, purpose is 'the reason why something is done or used; the aim or intention of something'[62]. By this definition, his company always had a purpose—to maximize profit. What the CEO was really trying to say is that he wants his company to consider the needs of society while establishing their business strategy. In other words, he wants the company to pursue a *stewardship purpose*, one that goes beyond just shareholder returns to create a *collective* better future. So, in our enthusiasm to jump on the bandwagon, let's not forget the purpose behind the drive for purpose.

ii. **Purpose is not necessarily positive.** I recently listened to a purpose pundit from a business school speak about the benefits of purpose in organizations. Purpose is motivational, purpose is inspirational, purpose is the glue that enables a higher level of collaboration . . . He went on and on about how an organization that articulates purpose attracts better talent and serves society better. Again, it made me question: Since when did purpose become a positive word in itself? If the dictionary definition is to be believed, purpose can be positive or negative. As I listened to the list of advantages of having a clearly defined purpose, I could not help but think about the mafia. They have very clear purpose which meets all the criteria this pundit was talking about—motivational, inspirational, common glue etc.

For purpose to be positive, it must be a stewardship purpose as described in point 1 above. It must be based on stewardship values described in Chapter 2—something that ought to get but is not getting enough attention in the current purpose mania. More on this in point v below.

iii. **Purpose statements alone are not enough.** Many organizations spend millions crafting and socializing new purpose statements and think their job is done. Simply having a lofty statement like 'To give people the power to build community and bring the world closer together' does not make the company a stewardship purpose driven organization. If you had not already guessed, the above is Facebook's purpose or mission statement. Similarly, Boeing flaunts this statement: 'To connect, protect, explore and inspire the world through aerospace innovation.' If indeed these companies really believed in their purpose, would they have sold our data or compromised our safety respectively?

iv. **Profit is not the enemy of purpose.** Another CEO I listened to recently said, 'We are undergoing two transformations, one from profit to purpose and the other from value to values.' Lofty words indeed. Here are my questions: Are you saying you will not look to make or maximize profits anymore? And what do you even mean by 'from value to values'? What does a commercial organization exist for, if not to provide value to society with its goods and services in exchange for profit? Let's be clear, stewardship purpose need not be at the cost of profit. If anything, the reverse is proving to be true. In today's totally transparent age where ordinary people have extraordinary access to information, customers and consumers are demanding stewardship behaviour from companies and will shun products, if they have an alternative available, of those that do not comply.

v.   **Purpose and values, not just purpose.** Finally, before an organization can realize its high-purpose dreams, it must honestly ask itself which values it holds most important and ensure two things:

a.   The purpose it articulates is based on stewardship values like interdependence, long-term view, ownership mentality and creative resilience. Stewardship values are those that are rooted in the belief that success and well-being are interdependent and cannot be maximized in isolation. In corporate parlance, this means believing that for the company to maximize shareholder returns in the long run, it must pursue strategies that create societal benefit.

b.   The values are lived and applied in everything the organization does, not just when it is convenient.

Another purpose pundit recently said that while values and behaviours form the culture of the organization, its purpose is the reason it exists. He drew a pyramid in which strategy and execution plans formed the base, values and behaviours formed the middle and purpose capped the top. By showing purpose at the top, he suggested that purpose was most important—the 'why' of a company's existence. I strongly disagree, because (a) purpose without the right values may not be the higher purpose that many CEOs today are hoping for and (b) whether the spirit of higher purpose is followed or not depends on the extent to which the right values are applied while making tough decisions. So, if you want to create a high-purpose organization, first clearly articulate the values that will drive behaviour, then make sure the values are lived and always applied. In this sense, purpose and values must have equal standing.

While I welcome and applaud all the efforts, CEOs should aspire towards transforming their companies into Stewardship Purpose Organizations (SPOs), not just Purpose-driven Organizations. The following figure summarizes the essence of an SPO:

Stewardship Purpose Organization

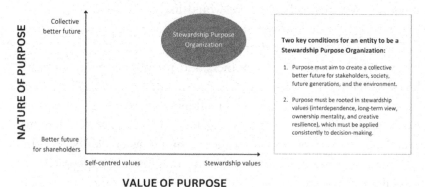

Figure 9: Stewardship Purpose Organization (SPO).
Source: Rajeev Peshawaria, Stewardship Asia Centre.

4. Strategy, internal systems and structures and culture encourage behaviours opposite to stated values and purpose

As mentioned earlier, many organizations are jumping on to the purpose bandwagon and publishing values and purpose statements, but the reality of action is just the opposite. A classic case in point is Enron.

Enron collapsed in 2001 following several investor lawsuits and an investigation by the US Securities and Exchange Commission (SEC). Many top-level executives, including Andy Fastow, whom we mentioned earlier, were indicted and served prison sentences. However, once hailed as the most admired and innovative company in the world, Enron's website boasted the following vision and values statements in its heyday[63]:

Vision

Enron's vision is to become the world's leading energy company—creating innovative and efficient energy solutions for growing economies and a better environment worldwide.

Values

Respect: We treat others as we would like to be treated ourselves. We do not tolerate abusive or disrespectful treatment. Ruthlessness, callousness and arrogance don't belong here.

Integrity: We work with customers and prospects openly, honestly and sincerely. When we say we will do something, we will do it; when we say we cannot or will not do something, then we won't do it.

Communication: We have an obligation to communicate. Here, we take the time to talk with one another . . . and to listen. We believe that information is meant *to move* and that information moves people.

Excellence: We are satisfied with nothing less than the very best in everything we do. We will continue to raise the bar for everyone. The great fun here will be for all of us to discover just how good we can really be.

As is now clear from the famous bankruptcy proceedings and several case studies, Enron's strategy, execution and culture were diametrically opposite to their vision and values.

In *Too Many Bosses, Too Few Leaders*, I presented an organizational leadership framework called Brains-Bones-Nerves (BBN) to shape company strategy (Brains), processes and structure (Bones) and culture (Nerves). Back in 2010 when I wrote the book, I highlighted that if employees agreed or strongly agreed with the following fifteen statements, it would be a good indication that the company's brains, bones and nerves were healthy.

Brains	Bones	Nerves
We have a compelling vision for future success.	We have top quality talent with the right skills and experience in all key jobs.	We have a well-defined cultural philosophy (who we are and what we stand for) and it is well understood by everyone.
We have a clearly differentiated strategy to achieve our vision.	Our supporting systems and structures (e.g., performance management, promotion processes) encourage desired performance.	Our compensation and rewards practices encourage desired behaviours in line with the cultural philosophy.
Vision and strategy are so clear that they guide resource allocation and decision making.	Roles, responsibilities and decision rights are defined as clearly as possible.	Through their actions, our leaders set the right example for others.
We have clearly recognizable core capabilities that give us our competitive edge.	Our people and resources are deployed in a way that best supports the execution of our strategy.	We focus both on short-term success and long-term capability building.
Everyone in the organization can clearly and consistently articulate our value proposition to clients.	Formal organization structure enables building and strengthening our core differentiating capabilities.	Our culture is one of listening, learning and constant renewal.

Source: *Too Many Bosses, Too Few Leaders*. Simon & Schuster, 2011. Peshawaria, Rajeev.

On a scale of 1 to 5 where 1 is strongly disagree, 2 is disagree, 3 is neither agree nor disagree, 4 is agree and 5 is strongly agree, any score below 4 would give management the opportunity to examine the situation and course correct as needed. Had Enron run a BBN survey for its employees, several red flags would have come to light long before it was too late to address them. If readers are interested in how to use BBN, a whole section of *Too Many Bosses, Too Few Leaders* is dedicated to it. So, I will not repeat it here. The reason I mention it here is to highlight the fact that to achieve stewardship purpose, stewardship values must be embedded in all three—brains, bones and nerves.

Figure 10: Organizational Steward Leadership Compass. Source: Stewardship Asia Centre.

Brains: If the organization wishes to pursue a stewardship purpose of creating a collective better future for stakeholders and society at large, then its strategy and business plans must include specifics on how to do so. Simply making lofty declarations such as zero-carbon pledges and printing glossy disclosure reports will not suffice. To meaningfully address E and S challenges, the senior management must proactively create innovative strategies to do so. As already stated earlier, this needs L (proactive steward leadership), not just G (governance). Innovation is not a matter of legislation, policy or compliance. Compared to 2011, when I wrote *Too Many Bosses, Too Few Leaders*, today's environment requires management to go well beyond creating a compelling vision and differentiated strategy. Today, companies must create a compelling vision and differentiated strategy to achieve their *stewardship* purpose. Faber-Castell, Tata and Doi Tung's Mae Fah Luang Foundation all deliberately created strategies to bring their stewardship purpose to life. Believing strongly that their success depended on the success of others (interdependence), they took it upon themselves (ownership mentality) to create a collective better future by finding innovative solutions to social and environmental challenges (creative resilience) even if it took time to do so (long-term view).

Peter Drucker, noted management consultant and author of thirty-nine books, once said, 'Every single social and global issue of our day is a business opportunity in disguise.' Steward leadership is all about addressing today's social and environmental challenges profitably. The value of creative resilience makes this happen. Founder of MycoStories and former managing partner at Ogilvy, Marc Violo, cites several examples in his article titled '25 Companies Carrying Out Corporate Social Innovation'[64]:

- **Vodafone** obtained a grant from the British government's Department for International Development to cover initial research and development for a new service aiming to give people in less developed countries access to financial services. The venture, M-Pesa, was kept separate from other Vodafone businesses, spent two years on in-market experiments. Once M-Pesa had demonstrated its commercial viability, local units of an established business financed its scale-up. Today, M-Pesa is managed by Vodafone's national subsidiaries and is one of the company's most important offerings. It accounted for 18 per cent of the revenue of Safaricom, Vodafone's Kenyan subsidiary. The experience encouraged Vodafone to link up with philanthropies and government agencies to experiment in other areas, such as agricultural information services and applications to remotely monitor and manage home energy consumption.

- **Danone**'s Nutriplanet group, drawing on nutritional, socioeconomic and cultural data has analysed the habits and health issues of populations in fifty-two countries to inform product development. After studying the diets of Brazil's youth, for example, Danone reformulated a bestselling cheese by reducing sugar and adding vitamins. In Bangladesh, children eat 600,000 servings a week of Danone's Shokti-Doi, a targeted nutrient-rich yogurt. R&D also extends into packaging. In Senegal, Danone developed a carton composed of local grain and a little milk that can be stored at room temperature.

Bones: Similarly, when it comes to designing internal processes, policies and systems, care must be taken to ensure that the talk about E and S is converted into action. We saw in Chapter 1, as well as in the case of Enron, how performance measurement and compensation systems can drive undesired behaviours. Management will need to be deliberate about ensuring that internal processes do not clash with stewardship intentions. Paul Polman succeeded for ten years at Unilever because he understood the importance of doing this. You will recall from Chapter 2 that after launching the Compass and the Unilever Sustainable Living Plan, he redesigned the company's performance management system to include the '3 plus 1' output measures. Bonuses would now be based on achieving these output measures. By developing such a standard, Unilever prioritized success measures that were much higher than before to emphasize Unilever's longterm focus for their managers. Ultimately, this cultivated a growth strategy that would reward accountability in the longterm and expose underperformers who were heavily focused on promoting their own careers rather than Unilever's vision.

Violo's article cites the example of Puma and its majority shareholder Kering using creative resilience in shaping the bones (people, internal processes and structure) of the organizations:

- **Puma** was one of the first companies to establish an Environment P&L in 2011. This new framework is meant to help them identify and manage the cost to nature of doing business, while simultaneously sharpening focus in pursuit of new and sustainable business opportunities. Their majority shareholder Kering further developed the methodology and expanded the EP&L to the entire Kering Group. Since then, they published the methodology as an open-source tool in 2016 and have launched an EP&L mobile app.

Nerves: Perhaps the biggest lesson we can learn from Enron, Theranos, Boeing and Volkswagen is the importance of culture. In all these cases, corporate culture had gone bad. Values were merely posters on the wall. Periodic attention to check if the values are alive and kicking is easy to do and can provide useful opportunities to course correct before it is too late. As I have mentioned before, driving growth and shareholder value while addressing today's existential challenges is hard. To ensure success, consistent application of the four stewardship values is a must. Senior management must role-model the values and encourage everyone else to follow suit. At Enron, the talk about values was just that—*talk*. What management really expected employees to do was to drive growth at any cost and by any means.

Violo cites the following examples of companies trying to create a culture of *ownership mentality* and *creative resilience* to do good:

- **Ferrovial**, a Spanish multinational that operates urban and services infrastructure, has sought to engage employees worldwide through an innovation contest. The programme, titled 'zuritanken', invites staff to offer solutions to challenges in the company's strategic business areas. The winning idea at the inaugural innovation contest was a walkway that harnesses kinetic energy generated by footsteps and converts it into electricity. The product, Floor Power, is now installed at Heathrow Airport, which Ferrovial manages.
- **Burt's Bees** has its own equivalent, the Greater Good initiative. The successful programme empowers employees through trainings in actionable environmental stewardship,

social outreach, natural wellness and leadership. The programme supports a company-wide goal to achieve 100 per cent employee engagement in sustainability.

- **Barclays Social Innovation Facility** is an internal accelerator for the multinational banking company to develop commercial finance solutions to social and environmental challenges. Launched with a £25 million financial commitment in 2012, the Barclays Accelerator provides a physical site and co-working environment for innovative employees and companies. Employees within Barclays develop their ideas in a three-day intrapreneur lab, then receive three months of internal mentoring before pitching their innovations to senior executives. Projects launched include a credit card aimed at millennials that 'rounds up' the charge at bank expense and donates the added funds to social purposes, loans with reduced credit charges for consumers who otherwise would not qualify for such rates and a suite of impact investing products.

- **Clif Bar** has embedded sustainability in its employees' benefits package, including incentives for actions such as making eco-friendly home improvements and purchasing a fuel-efficient car. Employees are rewarded for such positive behaviour and recognized at year-end.

- **Accenture Development Partnerships (ADP)** has undertaken more than 600 projects in 55 countries where its professionals, at 50 per cent salary reduction, partner for up to six months with NGOs to bring business solutions to humanitarian problems. For example, ADP worked with NGO consortium NetHope to launch and staff the first global IT help desk for international NGOs.

Another important aspect of creating a culture of steward leadership is to not shy away from tough decisions. When it becomes clear that some employees do not believe in and exhibit behaviour in accordance with the four stewardship values, they must be let go sooner rather than later. At Netflix, the employment condition was clear— you will have the freedom to do what you think is right in accordance with company values, but if you misuse the freedom or do not actively exhibit values-based behaviour, you will be let go. With freedom comes responsibility.

So, rather than simply creating beautiful posters, steward leadership requires senior management to proactively shape and maintain the company's brains, bones and nerves in a way that the four stewardship values are lived every day and its stewardship purpose is pursued relentlessly. While harder to do so, real steward leaders choose to do business with a stewardship mindset. Because they are driven by a strong sense of their own stewardship values and purpose, they do not cave in easily even when times are tough. In fact, it is their steward leadership track record that helps their organizations fare better than others during times of crisis.

* * *

By now, some might say that the entire concept of steward leadership is too idealistic. Recently I was discussing the need for steward leadership with a regulator. I made the same argument I have been making throughout Part One. Yes, we need regulations, but regulations will only set the minimum standards of responsible behaviour. We need ground-breaking innovation to solve for climate change and for that we need genuine steward leadership. After listening to me patiently, he said, 'Rajeev, I agree with everything you are saying. If we can convert everyone into genuine steward leaders, we won't need much regulation and I'll be out of a job. But how can we make sure everyone pursues genuine steward leadership? Is that possible? Most people are motivated by self-interest alone, so how can we expect everyone to adopt stewardship values and purpose?'

I thought the pushback was legitimate. He was absolutely right. There is no way we can convince everyone to buy into the concepts of steward leadership as laid out in this book. The average person will probably continue to act out of self-interest as opposed to the idea of interdependence.

But here is why I am still hopeful that we will succeed in saving planet Earth and humanity. We do not need all 100 per cent—8 billion people—to be convinced.

Wilfredo Pareto told us in 1906 that 20 per cent of causes or efforts create 80 per cent of effects or results. The Pareto Principle, aka the 80/20 Rule, is still alive and kicking in almost every walk of life. It is now well known that 20 per cent of the code creates 80 per cent of bugs, 20 per cent of customers are responsible for 80 per cent of sales, 20 per cent of employees produce 80 per cent of organizational results and so on. So, if 20 per cent of us choose steward leadership, it ought to be enough. While regulations should ensure that most of us, if not 100 per cent, minimize causing further harm, 20 per cent of us will use our creative resilience to unleash the breakthrough innovation needed to address today's challenges. History, based on the 80/20 rule, tells us that we have a good chance here.

Part Two

Steward Leadership in Action and Inaction

Introduction to Part Two

In Part One, I made the following points:

- The challenges we face today are existential. If not addressed by all sections of society, we will fail to secure the future of planet Earth and humanity.
- In business, we need proactive and inspired leadership, not just governance, to address the challenges. Consequently, ESG must upgrade itself to ESL, where 'L' stands for the higher form of leadership needed in today's context—Steward Leadership.
- Steward leadership is the genuine desire and persistence to create a collective better future. This collective better future integrates the needs of stakeholders, society, future generations and the environment while creating economic value.
- Steward leadership is practised by establishing and activating the Steward Leadership Compass at both personal and organizational levels. The Compass articulates clearly the collective better future an individual or organization wishes to create, based on four specific values: interdependence, long-term view, ownership mentality and creative resilience.

Part Two outlines nine stories. Five of them—Faber-Castell, Doi Tung, Tata, Mars and Farm Fresh—are about creating sustainable value with steward leadership over long periods of time. One of them—RGE—is about a company within a controversial industry taking steps to address environmental and social issues even in the most difficult of circumstances to the mutual benefit of all stakeholders. Two of them—Boeing and Volkswagen—show how great global companies momentarily strayed from the spirit of steward leadership as described in this book and faced disastrous consequences. Finally, the last story, Theranos, is of someone who started off with a good purpose in mind but went astray because they did not pursue it with stewardship values.

As you read each story, consider the following questions:

1. What elements of the Steward Leadership Compass stood out? Why?
2. What elements of the Steward Leadership Compass were weak or missing altogether?
3. What lessons can we learn from the story?

Chapter 4

Faber-Castell: More than 260 Years of Sustainability Enabled Profitable Growth

For the first time in 250 years, the next leader of the German family-owned business was not to be from the Faber-Castell family. Eighth-generation leader Count Anton Wolfgang von Faber-Castell passed away in January 2016 at the age of seventy-four after a serious illness. His three children decided that an external top manager should head the 6,500-employee company[65]. As the first CEO outside the family prepared to take charge in June 2017, the supervisory board of the company and the Faber-Castell family were confident that the legacy of the previous eight generations of family leadership will be intact. To understand why, we have to go back to the roots of Faber-Castell.

The founding

In 1761, just outside the city gates of Nuremberg, Germany, cabinetmaker Kaspar Faber set up his own pencil business, a common activity of the carpenter trade at that time. Throughout his lifetime, Kaspar Faber worked to grow his little workshop to a sizeable business that he was able to pass down to his son, Anton Wilhelm Faber.

During his tenure, Anton Wilhelm had expanded the small workshop into a flourishing business. He bought a land very close to the workshop, which remains the headquarters of Faber-Castell to this day. As tribute to his pioneering work, his initials were later incorporated into the company's name, A.W. Faber. For the next forty years, the pencil factory managed to pull through the wars and economic instability that plagued the Kingdom of Bavaria, but it was not until Anton Wilhelm's grandson, Lothar von Faber, took over that A.W. Faber entered the global stage.

Baron Lothar von Faber

Much of Faber-Castell's modern success has been attributed to its fourth-generation leader, Baron Lothar von Faber. His personal beliefs and attitudes in how he ran the business are immortalized in Faber-Castell's current core values or what it terms its 'Corporate Essentials': entrepreneurial and responsible, passionate and enduring, quality-driven and sustainable and open-minded and ambitious.

Armed with experiences in the major trading centres of Paris and London, twenty-two-year-old Lothar von Faber sought to modernize the family business with the goal 'to raise myself to the highest rank by making the best that can be made in the whole world'[66].

Lothar von Faber stayed true to this dedication to quality throughout his fifty-seven years at the helm of A.W. Faber. Since taking over the family business after his father's death in 1839, he constantly strived to produce quality pencils and was relentless in his efforts. 'At the time, I had powerful competition in Paris to contend with . . . Therefore, I had to think up the means of rising above that competition over the years. The best means is always the quality of a product . . .'[67]

Business innovations

During his time in Paris, Lothar had learned about the latest pencil production methods and acquired a taste for the French elegance. He came up with the idea of presenting pencils as a set, with pencils of different hardness in one encasing. He was particularly proud of this idea as 'no other producer has ever sold several grades in one encasing before'[68].

He understood that the quality of pencils should be reflected in its packaging as well. The set of ten pencils of different hardness was presented in a wooden box embellished in gold with the A.W. Faber name. 'I gave the finest pencils, the Polygrades, the prettiest outer attire so as to match their inner value. I had the pencils polished in black and decorated in gold.' Indeed, consumers had never seen pencils— plain, ordinary stationery—in such attractive packaging. The unrivalled Polygrades were launched in 1837 and remained part of A.W. Faber's top product line for decades before they were replaced by the green Castell pencil range in 1905[69].

Lothar's innovation shone through in the company's business model as well. Lothar went against convention at that time and found ways to cut out the middlemen. He wanted to be free of intermediaries and so travelled across Europe and sold his pencils himself. By directly interacting with his customers, he was able to uncover new needs and find ways to improve his products[70]. It could perhaps be due to these interactions that Lothar introduced the hexagonal pencils. Unlike the cylindrical pencils that dominated the market at that time, hexagonal pencils did not roll off tables. Lothar not only modified the shape of the pencil, but also set the standards for length, thickness and hardness, which were adopted by most other pencil manufacturers[71].

Lothar also secured control over raw materials. In 1856, he acquired the exclusive mineral rights to a graphite mine in Siberia after discovering that its graphite was of exceptional quality. Thinking way ahead of his time, Lothar had faith that his decisions would benefit the company in the long run.

The cost of transporting the graphite from far off Siberia to the factory just outside Nuremberg, Germany, was immense. From the mine, the graphite had to be transported to the nearest port by a reindeer across a vast distance without any trace of a road. After traversing the seas and finally docking in Germany, the graphite still had to be transported to the factory in Stein, which lies far from the coast of Germany.

The cost was high, to say the least, but Lothar knew exactly what he was up against. The English graphite that contributed to the early success of pencil sales in England and France was by now practically non-existent. With exclusive rights to the Siberian graphite, Lothar held all the trump cards. These 'Siberian pencils' went on to become bestsellers.

Besides modernizing the pencil, Lothar also improved the efficiency of his factory through technical improvements. Waterpower was harnessed, the sawing and planning of the wood were mechanized and later, the use of the steam engine provided even more power for the factory[72]. Lothar's efforts laid the foundation for quality production in Nuremberg, with other manufacturers popping up in the 19th century, including familiar names like Staedtler, Schwan and Lyra. By the end of the century, there were some twenty-five pencil factories in Nuremberg, producing up to 250 million pencils a year with a value of 8.5 million marks, about $26 million today[73]. Germany now led the world in pencil production, with most factories concentrated in and around Nuremberg.

Lothar was also the first pencil manufacturer to travel around Germany and abroad with his products. Confident in the quality of his pencils, he demanded prices that only English pencils could command at the time. Lothar's belief in quality as the key to success was proven and by the 1850s, A.W. Faber's pencils became sought after abroad and later, back home in Germany.

A businessman with a social conscience

While quality and innovation were his hallmarks on the way to market leadership, perhaps his bigger legacy was to combine business success with social good.

As Lothar scaled up production, he employed more factory workers. Lothar was acutely aware of the poor conditions that factory workers were facing at the time. During this period of early industrialization in Germany, Nuremberg was experiencing a population boom after it became part of the Kingdom of Bavaria in 1806. With new industries settling in the city, lots of smoke and dangerous dust were emitted. Many people died of infectious diseases like typhoid fever and tuberculosis. Bronchitis and deadly pneumonia were commonplace too. In the 1850s, the mortality rate of Nuremberg was 29.4 per thousand[74]. In comparison, Germany's mortality rate at the height of the coronavirus pandemic in 2020 was 12 per thousand[75].

So, in 1839, the same year he took over the company, he modernized production shops to include windows, 'making them light and airy, to take the health of the workers into account'[76].

Five years later, he set up one of the first company health insurance schemes in Germany, almost forty years before Germany's statutory health system was introduced in 1883[77]. Soon after, Lothar set up a savings bank and pension fund for his employees. He also had housing built for them and provided financial support for schools and a day nursery for employees' children. Without doubt, Lothar's social schemes generated returns for him. The benefits generated huge employee loyalty and dedication, which benefitted the business. But it takes a different kind of leader to *do well by doing good*. At the end of the day, it was his strong business acumen coupled with social conscience that created the win-win scenario where employees and owners both thrived together.

Lothar's social schemes were considered so exemplary that they reached the ears of the French emperor Napoleon III, who sent a delegate of experts to Stein in 1867 and appointed Lothar a chevalier of the Légion d'Honneur, the highest French decoration in military and civil society[78].

Before that, Lothar's contributions were already recognized locally. In 1862, Lothar was made a life peer for his services to the business world and in social matters. In 1881, he was raised to the hereditary peerage, therefore changing his name from Lothar Faber to Lothar von Faber.

When he handed over his business interests to his only son Wilhelm von Faber in 1877, he told him that his aim should be 'to make himself ever more useful, to develop himself ever more effectively and to shape his life ever more aesthetically'. He should do everything that is 'right, good and beautiful', while safeguarding as the highest good the 'individual liberty' of each and every worker, employee and representative of the company'[79].

The last descendant

Born in 1941 in Bamberg, Germany, Count Anton was expected to take over the family business when he grew up. However, Anton did not inherit his family's love for pencils. Instead, he went on to study law at the University of Zurich in Switzerland and continued his venture into the legal sector, taking on a year-long internship with a lawyer.

After graduation, the eighth-generation heir was determined to establish his career on Wall Street. In 1971, he joined Credit Suisse White Weld, one of the world's leading international finance companies. Anton's career took off. Within a span of five years, he moved to manage the London branch of Credit Suisse First Boston.

However, his father's demise in 1978 curtailed his short-lived career as an investment banker. Having been appointed to the management of the company three years prior, Count Anton-Wolfgang von Faber-Castell[80] was now the sole managing partner of Faber-Castell.

By the time he took over, the organization had reacquired several of its subsidiaries around the world. And thanks to a strategic decision made by Anton's father, the family owned the world's largest wood-cased pencil factory in Brazil.

Although Anton took on the mantel unwillingly, he discovered that he enjoyed the business. He was good at it too. Having grown up surrounded by pencils and all things Faber-Castell, it was no surprise that the reluctant leader knew the history and the products of the family business like the back of his hand—knowledge that would serve him well throughout his time at Faber-Castell. Armed with his business acumen and experience on Wall Street, Anton began executing his strategy for Faber-Castell. Over the next four decades, he would establish the German firm not only as a global premium brand, but one known for its unwavering commitment to the environment and society.

The foundation: Brand reputation

At the heart of Count Anton's strategy was the brand. He recognized its importance in the company's sustained success, right from when Lothar von Faber created the first branded pencils and fought hard against imitations.

'Lothar von Faber left his mark on the generations that followed, including me personally,' said the Count. 'His uncompromising efforts to build up the brand reputation, his social commitment, his creativity and his consistency he set about conquering new markets.'[81]

Throughout his thirty-eight years at Faber-Castell, Anton remained steadfast in his commitment to these four principles. Anything else was a distraction.

Building a brand takes time and it requires a long-term orientation. Count Anton recognized that it is easier for a family-owned business to adopt such a mentality. 'We family entrepreneurs naturally find it easier to think in terms of generations and to see through projects whose fruits will not be reaped for perhaps decades and only after setbacks. In a listed company, this attitude would have got me fired at least three times by now, especially in the days when shareholder value was the be-all and end-all and the goal of short-term profit eclipsed any long-term considerations.'[82]

But his patience and capacity for long-term thinking do not merely stem from the fact that Faber-Castell is a family-owned business. 'I don't think anything at all for short-term gains,' he said. Rather, Anton identified with the principles of the 'honourable merchant', a concept that has its roots in the Early Middle Ages[83]. An honourable businessman regards values and virtues such as integrity, honesty and decency as the basis of his actions[84]. 'For me, corporate ethics means "behaving decently" not only around people who are especially dependent on the company (for example, workers who need to retain their jobs), but also around partners such as clients and suppliers. This decency, which is based on values such as social responsibility, trust, honesty and fair mutual dealings, can be compatible with a healthy striving toward sustainable profitability, as only profitable companies can assume their social responsibilities on a continuing basis.'[85]

Commitment to quality

Like Lothar von Faber, Anton believed that quality is the key to success and people had to know that Faber-Castell produces quality goods. Anton had been known to hurl wooden pencils from the tower of his castle to the stone courtyard below. He had initially planned to prove the durability of the pencils by throwing bundles of them from the top of the Eiffel Tower. He was convinced that not a single pencil would break.

There was no way the Paris authorities would sanction this crazy stunt. Imagine the relief his public relations advisers felt when they heard the news!

'So I climbed up the highest window in the tower of our castle—it's 30 metres high—and threw the bundles from there,' said Anton[86].

His antics did not stop there. In 2012, Anton downed a shot of bright orange ink used in Faber-Castell's children's felt tip pens in front of a hoard of journalists. His then head of Research and Development Dr Gerhard Lugert chose a blood-red shot of ink to accompany the count. They definitely testified to the safety of the ink.

The count's seemingly flamboyant attitude was far from a thoughtless stunt from a marketing enthusiast. Anton had been nothing but consistent in his dedication to building the Faber-Castell brand and he was willing to go to great lengths to do it.

Anton felt a deep, personal responsibility towards the brand. He viewed himself as the brand ambassador and took this role seriously. Since 1978, he had repeatedly had his photo taken in front of the family castle to convey its brand positioning visually. He was always immaculately dressed in a neatly pressed suit and tie, with a pocket square tucked in his left breast pocket.

Anton was not blindly keeping a tradition going. To Anton, 'The point is not to cling to tradition for its own sake, but to preserve it, in keeping with the times, as a successful system of values.'[87]

Social commitment

And Anton had done just that, with the same heart and vigour as Lothar von Faber. Lothar's social schemes had left an indelible mark on his descendants. Lothar's great-grandson—Anton's father—continued the Baron's charitable work and spoke emphatically of the 'law' of his forefathers that a company must grow with social responsibility.

Given Faber-Castell's new global position and the extensive reach it has developed, Anton expanded the company's social commitment accordingly. In an unprecedented move, Faber-Castell and the IG Metall trade union ratified an agreement that they had worked out jointly in March 2000. This social charter is the first of its kind in the industry.

By signing the social charter, Faber-Castell had voluntarily committed itself to applying the guidelines of the International Labour Organization in all its factories and subsidiaries around the world. The charter includes, among other things, a ban on child labour, a guarantee of safe and hygienic working conditions and equal opportunities and treatment, regardless of race, religion, sex or nationality.

To Anton, signing the social charter was 'both an obligation and something I take for granted to face up to the challenges of globalisation'[88]. That Anton saw the social charter as an obligation points to an understanding of the scale that Faber-Castell has and the impact that it can make on its thousands of employees.

But this was more than pure 'business sense', as Anton had often put it. Personally, he also hated layoffs. Just as his father, he regarded them as a 'personal defeat'[89].

Anton was guided by a commitment to earning 'decent' money, in both the ethical and financial sense. After signing the initial social charter, he did not kick off his shoes and pat himself on the back for a job well done.

The year after, he set up the Graf von Faber-Castell Children's Fund Foundation, a charitable trust for children to sponsor the work of various humanitarian children's aid projects, particularly in developing countries. The foundation supports kindergartens, schools, children's hospitals, orphanages and other groups devoted to the care of children. The Children's Fund Foundation is most active in Brazil, Peru, India and Africa.

Responsibility to the planet

As a company that produces an astounding 2.3 billion wood-cased pencils each year[90], it is not hard to imagine the extent of damage it might cause to our environment. Not to mention the fact that using up such finite resources does not bode well for a company whose survival depends on them.

'For me as a businessman it is extremely important not to make profit at the cost of future generations,' explained Anton[91].

Anton did not confine his vision to the future generations of the Faber-Castell family but extended it to the future generations of our planet. In a move strikingly similar to Lothar von Faber's acquisition of exclusive mineral rights to the graphite mine in Siberia, Anton started a sustainable forestry project in Prata, south-eastern Brazil, in the mid-1980s. Except this time, the aim was not just to secure raw materials.

Faber-Castell planted and tended to ten thousand hectares of pine forests—almost the size of 14,000 football fields[92]. Every year, around 300,000 young trees of the *Pinus caribaea* species are planted and raised thousands of miles from the endangered Amazon rainforests. After about twenty years, these trees would be large enough to be harvested as environmentally compatible raw material for black lead and coloured pencils[93].

But beyond ensuring the continued supply of wood for Faber-Castell's production lines, the forests also neutralize the company's carbon footprint worldwide, absorbing 900,000 tonnes of carbon dioxide[94]. This extensive forestry project not only secures stocks of sustainable wood but also protects the environment through photosynthesis, which converts carbon dioxide into biomass.

While Faber-Castell could very well have just used all ten thousand hectares of pine trees for pencil production, they left almost a third of the forest untouched. This sacred area is dedicated to preserving the native environment and, as of 2022, has become home to more than 722 species, fifty of which face extinction elsewhere[95].

Again, this entire project reflects Anton's ethos: making decent money. Setting up the forests in Prata was a strategic choice. Thanks to Anton's father, who bought back their factory in Sao Carlos in 1967, Faber-Castell owned the world's largest graphite and coloured pencil factory. This factory, which employs about 2,800 employees[96], uses the wood from these forests, saving transportation and other logistical costs. So financially, Anton had it down.

But no one could have guaranteed the success of the project back when it started in the 1980s. It takes twenty years for the pine trees to mature; reaping the fruits of success, if any, demanded patience and the long-term thinking that Anton said would have gotten him fired three times over on Wall Street.

Still, he was dedicated to making this project a success—not just because it made business sense. Built into this project are plenty of checks and balances that show how Faber-Castell's sustainability efforts are not performative. The forests are managed in accordance with modern principles of sustainability. It meets the requirements of the Forest Stewardship Council, a panel of experts made up of international scientists and environment associations. A certification from the FSC widely counts as a seal of quality. The company sawmills and its production sites for wood-cased pencils are all FSC-certified[97].

Surviving crises

Anton's unwavering values allowed him to see the company through three major crises: the collapse of the slide rule business in the late 1970s, the sudden drop in sales of manual technical drawing instruments in the late 1980s and the burst of the dot-com bubble in the 1990s.

Throughout these tough times, Anton remained focused on his and the brand's core principles, sticking to what it does best—pencils. By constantly improving on its core competency, Faber-Castell has managed to thrive for centuries. While Anton acknowledges that this laser focus is 'dull', it was a simple recipe for success. During his time at Faber-Castell, Anton proved that this focus does not come at the cost of innovation.

The collapse of the slide rule business in the 1970s was a huge blow to Faber-Castell. With the rise of the electronic pocket calculator, slide rules were made redundant and demand fell dramatically. At the time, however, Faber-Castell's factory in Geroldsgrün in north Bavaria was one of the world's largest producers of slide rules and accounted for almost a third of Faber-Castell's revenue.

Faber-Castell Cosmetics

Instead of hopping on the bandwagon to produce pocket calculators, Anton chose to stick with what Faber-Castell did best. He established

Faber-Castell Cosmetics in 1978, initially producing wood-cased cosmetics pencils for brands in the cosmetics industry. Faber-Castell already had the manufacturing capabilities in place, along with over two centuries of experience making quality pencils. Yet, by venturing into a new industry, it had reached a brand-new customer base. The founding of Faber-Castell Cosmetics truly encapsulated Anton's belief that 'tradition means keeping the glow, not the ashes, alive'[98].

Although the product line was slightly different, the values that sustained Faber-Castell through the centuries were still seen within Faber-Castell Cosmetics. The company develops innovative, high-quality cosmetics products focusing on natural ingredients for clean and vegan textures as well as sustainable packaging such as FSC-certified wood or post-consumer recycled plastic caps[99].

Today, Faber-Castell Cosmetics makes up about 15 per cent of the group's turnover[100].

The Perfect Pencil

Even after coming up with such an innovative idea to diversify the company's product line, Anton did not become complacent. Although Faber-Castell had already made its name in the higher end of the fashion industry, Anton wanted to further elevate the brand.

In 1993, Anton broke into the premium stationery market by launching Graf von Faber-Castell, with 'Graf' meaning 'count' in German. Graf von Faber-Castell produced exclusive writing instruments, the most notable of which is the Perfect Pencil[101].

The Perfect Pencil was inspired by the sterling silver pencil holder that Lothar von Faber had created in 1885. First launched together with the Graf von Faber-Castell brand in 1993, the Perfect Pencil came with an eraser and extender[102]. The sleek, shiny extender that encased Faber-Castell's high quality wooden pencil certainly elevated the ordinary pencil. Today, the Perfect Pencil sets you back $258, at the very least.

Faber-Castell had found its recipe for success: directed innovation. By harnessing its expertise in pencil production and focusing on what it does best, Faber-Castell had tapped into new markets and revolutionized its industry.

Globalization in a modern era

Early on, Anton recognized the potential of the Asian markets and founded subsidiaries there, including India, China and Indonesia. One of the very first production sites Anton established in Asia was Faber-Castell Malaysia. Starting with only eight staff in 1978, Faber-Castell Malaysia produced natural rubber and PVC erasers. With Faber-Castell's system of values so entrenched in the organization, employees all the way across the world had no problem executing it. Keeping to Faber-Castell's motto of 'doing ordinary things extraordinarily well', the Malaysian production site became one of the world's largest eraser producers. Throughout the years, it continued to innovate and spearheaded improvements. Faber-Castell Malaysia also started producing environmentally friendly and child-safe erasers with PVC-free materials from 2006[103]. The same values-based entrepreneurial spirit subsequently made production sites in ten countries and sales companies in twenty-two countries extremely successful.

Throughout the thirty-eight years that Anton led Faber-Castell, he had created a strong culture based on long-held values and purpose. When the family ultimately decided to bring in the first outsider as CEO, they knew that the family's legacy would be safe.

Reflection questions

1. What led to the survival of Faber-Castell for almost three centuries?
2. What elements of the Steward Leadership Compass stood out? Why?
3. What elements of the Steward Leadership Compass were weak or missing altogether?
4. What lessons can we learn from the story?

Chapter 5

Doi Tung Development Project:
Self-sustaining Community Stewardship

Established in 1988 in the Golden Triangle where the borders of Thailand, Laos and Myanmar meet, the Doi Tung Development Project (DTDP) saw the transformation of an opium poppy cultivation area into a reforested area. Doi Tung is a mountain in the Chiang Rai province of northern Thailand, which, until about 1990, was bustling with unlawful drug production, prostitution and human trafficking controlled by independent militia.

Most villagers came to Doi Tung without official permits, rendering them stateless[104]. As nationless individuals, they were unable to access public benefits and infrastructure, including healthcare. The nearest hospital was not only hours away in the city, but villagers ran the risk of being caught by government officials if they travelled because they did not have the proper documents.

Schools were also far away from the villages, leaving most locals uneducated and consequently working low-paying jobs, leaving them vulnerable to exploitation. Drug lords or armed militia in the area would often coerce them into doing illicit activities, such as working in opium poppy fields. Even then, farmers would only be given a fraction of the profit. With no access to healthcare and with opium within arms' reach, the locals started replacing medicine with it, leading to widespread usage.

Figure 11: Armed militia patrolling the villages. Picture used with permission from Mae Fah Luang Foundation.

The villagers did not have many alternatives. Growing other crops on a large commercial scale was simply not viable. Without tools and infrastructure for irrigation, rainwater was the sole source of water for farming. The dramatic swings between high and low crop yields led to unstable income streams and locals lived in constant anxiety, wondering if the next harvest would be their last.

Poor cultivation methods also contributed to dismal harvests and crop production. Although Doi Tung was full of watershed areas, poor farming techniques, such as recurrent shifting cultivation on plots of land or slash-and-burn, resulted in soil sterility and erosion. Almost 55 per cent of the watershed forests in Doi Tung were devastated[105]. What was once a lush forest was now akin to an arid desert.

With agriculture unviable, some women resorted to prostitution to feed their families. Some women were even victims of sex trafficking, kidnapped from their homes and thrown into illegal sex work, making them susceptible to sexually transmitted infections like HIV and AIDS. When they returned home, the women unwittingly spread the disease to locals, resulting in the rise of HIV or AIDS within Doi Tung.

Figure 12: Doi Tung, stripped of vegetation. Picture used with permission from Mae Fah Luang Foundation.

The crippling reliance on opium as well as the dismal quality of life in Doi Tung was an inescapable cycle of crime and poverty. Life in a desolate land left villagers disillusioned. With hung heads and slumped shoulders, most walked as if they were weighed down by hefty shackles and chains.

Mae Fah Luang Foundation

But all of this began to change with the arrival of Her Royal Highness Princess Srinagarindra—the Princess Mother. The Mae Fah Luang Foundation would transform underdeveloped areas under her leadership. 'Mae Fah Luang', meaning Royal Mother from the Sky, was a title given to the Princess Mother by the ethnic groups. To reach the inaccessible grooves of the mountains, the Princess Mother visited the villages by helicopter. Backlit by the sun, her chopper seemed to appear almost surreally from the blue of the horizon, as if the Princess Mother herself was descending from the sky.

The Princess Mother's devotion to 'developing communities, society, environment and cultures' cascaded to everyone in the Foundation. The Mae Fah Luang Foundation's goal was to 'create happiness, sustainability and stability' for all, regardless of background. To achieve that, the Princess Mother strongly believed that the Foundation's approach should be to 'help people to help themselves', as long-term sustainable development can only be achieved when the community itself is involved and leading the charge.

Supporting the Princess Mother was her Private Secretary and the Secretary-General of the Foundation, Mom Rajawongse Disnadda Diskul, also known as Khun Chai. He knew that the Princess Mother would not be returning to her old home in Switzerland upon turning ninety, as she wanted to stay in Thailand to help her countrymen. Khun Chai started looking for underdeveloped remote areas where the Princess Mother could do developmental work and make meaningful impact.

In a conversation with a government officer from the Royal Forestry Department, Khun Chai was offered 2,000 rai (320 hectares) of land in Doi Tung, which Khun Chai thought would be a great area for development. He travelled with the government officer up the mountain and found that the vast area of Doi Tung, full of opium poppy cultivation and social illnesses, was aligned with the Princess Mother's initiative of reforestation and livelihood development.

On January 15, 1987, as the Princess Mother stepped out of her helicopter and onto the reddish barren lands of Doi Tung, she declared, 'I will build my house here, but if there is no DTDP, then I will not live here. I have wished to plant forests for over ten years now.'

Doi Tung Development Project

When Khun Chai asked why she wanted to redevelop Doi Tung, the Princess Mother remarked, 'No one wants to be bad, but they do not have the opportunity to do good.' Those who were busy trying to make ends meet did not have the time and energy to educate themselves about sustainable and ethical practices. Those without state protection and education had to rely on unethical and dangerous livelihoods to survive. Cementing her resolve to bettering Doi Tung for its people and the environment, the DTDP was initiated by the Princess Mother and driven by the Foundation in 1988.

An uphill battle

In its infancy, the immediate goals of DTDP were reforestation and creating dignified and stable jobs for the locals. However, government funding for reserved forests was non-existent and the team lacked capital for its reforestation efforts. At the forefront of the project's development was Khun Chai. A driven and ambitious man, Khun Chai set his sights on making the DTDP a world-class development model. To gather the necessary funds, he came up with a creative solution. The Princess Mother was turning ninety soon and she was the darling of Thailand. What could be a better opportunity than her birthday to leverage and request donations in the form of gifts for the Princess Mother? Khun Chai went to all seventy-three provinces in Thailand and requested monetary gifts to sponsor the Princess Mother's new project for her ninetieth birthday celebration. He got some funding to reforest 9,900 rai (1,584 ha) of Doi Tung's watershed forests from people all over Thailand, including government officials, ministers, security forces and provincial governors[106]. The 9,900 rai of watershed forests was a portion of the 50,000-rai land that Khun Chai had mapped out for reforestation.

A significant portion of the land slated for reforestation was agricultural lots used by the villagers. Khun Chai had intended to borrow their land for about thirty months to replant trees in the area. However, this meant that the local farmers would lose their livelihoods as they would be unable to cultivate opium or practise shifting cultivation. Realizing this, the Princess Mother reminded Khun Chai and his team to limit the disruptive effects of the DTDP while providing the locals with new job opportunities. Thus, Khun Chai developed Navuti in 1989, a company that would manage and conserve 'economic forests' by hiring locals and providing them with various jobs. These economic forests would contain cash crops that would not only provide locals with profit but also help with the area's reforestation.

As an enterprise, Navuti could apply for a low-interest loan for developmental work from Japan International Cooperation Agency (JICA) and even receive investments from other private businesses.

Khun Chai went from company to company, proclaiming, 'You're doing business in Thailand. What good have you done to our country? You've taken a lot from us. It's time to pay back.' Khun Chai felt it deep within his heart that everyone had to give back to society. Moved by his determination, six companies agreed to invest in Navuti. A start-up capital of ฿30 million ($900,000) was thus consolidated.

Having gained the momentum it needed, the DTDP expanded its scope to include the creation of economic forests, food processing, agriculture, preserving the ethnic method of making handicrafts and tourism.

Growth of economic forests

The Foundation ran a three-part reforestation effort:

1. Economic forests managed by Navuti, which generated income for the people through the agriculture of market-driven cash crops
2. Watershed forests, which would become a source of water for the locals
3. Sustenance forests, which people could tap on for food

To achieve their immediate goal of providing villages with alternative stable and dignified forms of income, Navuti paid close attention to economic forests. Different cash crops were examined and, in the end, Arabica coffee and macadamia were shortlisted to be grown in Doi Tung. Arabica coffee flourishes at similar altitudes to opium, which had clearly thrived in Doi Tung. Arabica coffee also flourishes under shade and can be grown under taller trees. Given that the locals' income would depend on the quality of Arabica coffee, which is in turn reliant on the cover provided by surrounding greenery, the community was incentivized to care for both the Arabica coffee cash crop and nearby trees.

The other cash crop identified by Navuti was macadamia nuts. Macadamia was also found to grow well in the mountainous environment of Doi Tung and was a high-selling product with high market demand, marking it incredibly lucrative[107].

Figure 13: Coffee cherries and macadamia nuts found in the economic forests of Doi Tung.
Pictures taken from doitung.com. Used with permission from Mae Fah Luang Foundation.

Despite Khun Chai's best intentions, most villagers were doubtful about the plans that Navuti had for the economic forests. Though the land was illegally obtained and utilized by the locals, they felt like their farmland and main source of income were stolen by Navuti for the economic forests. The villagers had little to no confidence that the Foundation would be successful. The other government agencies that tried implementing developmental projects had failed.

To gain their trust, Khun Chai communicated with key members of the community frequently and as openly as possible throughout the implementation of the DTDP. He also worked to produce tangible outcomes that the villagers could witness and benefit from. Through numerous discussions with the community, Khun Chai was able to convince the villagers to work with his team to make the DTDP successful. The benefits of growing coffee and macadamia were indisputable—the demand for Arabica coffee and macadamia nuts was high and both cash crops were lucrative.

Seeing to his promise that the DTDP would be able to uplift the community, Khun Chai recruited hundreds of villagers to work for him under the Navuti company and provided them with stable income flows from legal means. The average income of $106 per person per year, most of which came from the production and sale of opium, rose to $409 per person per year in the first few years of the project[108]. Job security as well as better pay led to greater trust in the Foundation and villagers started getting involved in various developmental activities of the DTDP.

Yet, unbeknownst to them, more challenges were coming their way. Despite the villagers receiving training in making high quality coffee, productivity of the coffee and macadamia plantations was lower than anticipated. Although Arabica coffee yields were predicted to be about 1 kg of coffee cherries per year, only half that amount was produced and the quality of some harvested coffee cherries did not meet market standards.

After some investigation, the team realized that the poor harvest was because the farmers and farmhands lacked the willpower to work hard and did not strictly adhere to proper farming procedures. As they were paid a daily wage, the farmers gave little regard for the quality of coffee beans, picking coffee cherries to harvest even if they were unripe so that they could clock out earlier from their jobs[109].

Due to lower yields and quality of cash crops, revenue generated from coffee cultivation was very poor. This disheartening situation was further exacerbated by the Asian financial crisis in 1997. With the drastic depreciation of the Thai baht, the JICA loan taken by Navuti doubled from about 27 million to nearly ฿55 million[110]. With a gargantuan debt to pay and abysmal prospects, DTDP seemed to be in an irrecoverable situation. The Board of Directors of Navuti held an intense discussion on next steps and almost decided to shut the DTDP down.

However, Khun Chai remained steadfast in his desire and persistence to improve the social well-being of the people in Doi Tung and requested the Board to reconsider its judgement. He knew that too many villagers were now dependent on the DTDP for their livelihood. If DTDP were to be abandoned, they would be thrown back into their previous lives of illicit dealings and job insecurity.

Determined to turn things around, Khun Chai sought to raise the productivity of the coffee and macadamia plantations. To equip the farmers with practical knowledge, he sought foreign experts on coffee and macadamia.

Khun Chai brought Navuti's general manager and supervisors to the farm of Andy Roy, situated in Kona, Hawaii, where the second-best Arabica coffee in Hawaii is produced, to train on-the-job for a month. When they returned to Doi Tung, they shared their learnings and became in-house practical experts for the farmers.

For macadamia, Khun Chai turned to Australia, a major producer in the global market. He invited Ron Barnett, who ran his own macadamia farm, to be an advisor in Doi Tung. Barnett visited the economic forests of Doi Tung and gave practical tips to the staff and workers on proper farming and harvesting techniques for macadamia nuts. Navuti's general manager was also sent to work on Barnett's farm, gaining much needed experience and knowledge in macadamia nuts from germination to harvest. Both experts provided insightful advice to Navuti's management team, who were able to pass on the practical knowledge to the farmers, improving productivity of the crops in the later years.

After further deliberation, Khun Chai realized workers were also not incentivized to grow and harvest high-yielding and high-quality crops due to the lack of ownership and willpower. They were given the same wage regardless of the productivity and quality of the harvest.

Recognizing this, Khun Chai proposed a radical change to the labour system of coffee and macadamia cultivation in Navuti. Instead of hiring farmers, he recommended that coffee trees be rented to workers willing and able to nurture them. This created small enterprise opportunities for individual farmers who would grow and sell Arabica coffee on their own, instilling a sense of ownership within them. So that the villagers would have a sense of responsibility and pride while farming on land that is not legally theirs, they were asked to pay a symbolic fee of ฿1 ($0.04) per tree per year in the coffee plantations. The Foundation paid half of the farmers' rental fees to Navuti to alleviate their financial burden.

Navuti only purchased high-quality ripe coffee cherries from farmers, guaranteeing payment for workers while ensuring the finest quality of their coffee beans. As a result, locals took greater care of their coffee trees, resulting in higher yields and better-quality coffee cherries within a year. This led to a win-win outcome for both the Foundation and the farmers, as there were increases in both income for the locals and revenue for Navuti. Coffee cultivation quickly rose to become one of the community's most profitable income streams. In 1988, coffee provided an average income of $547.4 per annum per household. By 2012, villagers earned an average of $15,751.80 per annum per household[111].

Separately, this change in ownership aided in the reforestation efforts of DTDP as the community could appreciate the viability of caring for economic forests. For the economic forests to continue producing high-quality coffee beans and macadamia nuts, locals had to preserve and conserve the environment from which the cash crops were growing. A symbiotic relationship formed, with the Princess Mother's vision of 'a mutual and sustainable coexistence between man and forest' for Doi Tung realized. In 2018, 58 per cent of the forest area was reforested[112]. According to the Mae Fah Luang Foundation, 86.8 per cent of Doi Tung's forest has been regrown as of 2023.

Figure 14: Doi Tung today. Credit: SAC researcher Jane Ang.

With the coffee and macadamia plants bearing fruit, Khun Chai and his team had to put their heads together once again. What was the best way to add value to the crops for maximum profit? Charting the value chain for each cash crop, the team thought of different ways coffee and macadamia could be processed to make different, high value products. For example, a coffee roastery was set up in Doi Tung to produce roasted coffee beans which could be sold at a higher price than processed green beans from coffee cherries. In fact, packaged Doi Tung branded roasted coffee was sold for five times more than green beans in 2000.

The Foundation also sold coffee under the Doi Tung brand in Cafés DoiTung, generating another income stream for the community. Cafés DoiTung can be found not only in Doi Tung but also in other parts of Thailand. Coffee drinks were sold at almost 300 times the price of green beans, at $177 per kg. Designing and owning the entire value chain of its cash crops was an innovative method to maximize profit, generating a total income of more than $4 million per annum for the community[113].

With the major challenges behind them, Navuti was able to repay their JICA loan[114]. Since 2001, the DTDP has been financially self-sufficient and profits are invested back into development activities[115]. Today, the Doi Tung name is ubiquitous. Doi Tung coffee and macadamia products are widespread and profitable though they are just a part of the five business streams of the DTDP. Through food processing, handicrafts, cafés, tourism and agriculture, the DTDP continues steadily in its purpose of uplifting the community and improving their livelihoods while reforesting the natural environment.

Food processing, cafés and agriculture

Doi Tung coffee has allowed communities to coexist with forests in a mutually beneficial and sustainable manner. Doi Tung coffee grown in the economic forests is of high quality and is endorsed and utilized by companies such as Thai Airways and Muji[116]. Doi Tung coffee was also accorded the Geographical Indication (GI) certification in 2006 for its quality coffee beans and received quality assurance by the Specialty Coffee Association of America.

Like Arabica coffee, macadamia nuts are processed into a range of value-added products to generate maximum profit from one cash crop. Products such as roasted macadamia, macadamia cookies, macadamia spread and macadamia honey can be sold for a much higher price than pure macadamia nuts. With the expert help of Ron

Barnett and the pioneering work of farmers to grow macadamia in Doi Tung, the sale of macadamia nuts has become a viable and profitable business stream.

Reusing waste to enhance business streams

Additionally, to reduce waste generated from production and post-harvest processes, the DTDP developed innovative ways to repurpose by-products and waste through its zero-waste model. Macadamia husks are composted or laid on soil to maintain soil moisture levels. Macadamia shells are used as biofuel to produce energy at the Doi Tung handicraft production centres and macadamia processing factory. Ash from burnt macadamia shells and coffee grounds is used to make grey and brown dyes respectively for handicrafts made by women from ethnic groups, which is another business stream of the DTDP. The rest of the waste products from macadamia and coffee are incorporated into creating and designing decorative mulberry paper produced at the paper production centre in Doi Tung, resulting in beautiful and unique paper patterns.

Preserving traditions in ethnic art

As part of the Princess Mother's desire to preserve the ethnic handicrafts and traditions and facilitate the integration of the ethnic communities into Thai society[117], a handicrafts production centre was set up with four facilities: weaving, paper production, dyeing and ceramic production.

Handicraft production under the DTDP allows for local ethnic knowledge and craftsmanship, such as embroidery, sewing and weaving, to be preserved and passed on in a sustainable and viable manner. Ethnic women can profit from their use of traditional methods to make handicrafts, earning a livelihood and gaining financial support. The larger community also feels a sense of self-respect as their form of ethnic art is in demand and appreciated by the general Thai populace.

Figure 15: Traditional weaving method by the ethnic women of Doi Tung.
Picture taken from doitung.com. Used with permission from Mae Fah Luang Foundation.

To ensure that the handicrafts are well-received in the market, the Foundation hires modern, world-class designers to hone the skills of the local artisans and adapt traditional craftsmanship to contemporary trends. These experts have designed for famous luxury brands like Prada and Isabel Marant and are well-positioned to give advice and training on how to repurpose and re-innovate traditional crafts for the modern palate. However, the local women do not stray from their ethnic roots, still employing the traditional techniques passed on from one generation to the next, maintaining the core ethnic identity and culture of their community[118].

Mainstream commercial outlets have also identified the beauty and exquisiteness of Doi Tung branded handmade crafts. Companies like IKEA work with Doi Tung to produce limited edition collections like the LOKALT and Allvarlig while employing locals and providing them with jobs[119,120]. Local artisans are taught how to work with clay to create dishes, bowls and vases with designs that are an intersection between traditional craftsmanship and modern design.

The total income of workers in the DTDP's handicraft business was $2.77 million by 2022, with jobs created for over 300 locals[121]. Additionally, craftswomen were earning more than workers in a local handicraft company unrelated to DTDP[122]. Undoubtedly, the DTDP has created new avenues for ethnic communities to earn a livelihood while preserving their traditions and culture.

Educational tourism

With its success as a sustainable living development model, the DTDP has been designated as a 'living university', disseminating information about its sustainable approach and welcoming more than 1 million tourists every year[123]. Organizations and leaders from around the world converge at Doi Tung to learn more about sustainability, community development and how to implement it.

While at the mountain of Doi Tung, visitors are also exposed to the values of zero waste and sustainability, both of which are crucial to the DTDP. Residents, DTDP staff and tourists are given training and workshops on the proper methods of reusing and recycling waste at the Waste Management Centre by the locals.

At the Thai–Myanmar border, tourists can also have a bird's eye view of the lush forest and bear witness to the success of the DTDP's reforestation efforts. It is also the base of Thai soldiers who patrol the mountain to protect the residents of Doi Tung and to prevent any forms of drug smuggling or trafficking across the border. Overlooking the valley is a café that a group of soldiers has set up on their own to sell coffee. The entrepreneurial spirit burns bright within the community.

Figure 16: The SAC team stops by Café Phamuang, run by soldiers at the Thai–Myanmar border, for a cup of coffee. Picture credit: SAC researcher Jane Ang.

An enterprise for a better world

Since 2001, the DTDP has been self-sufficient in its financial gains and profits are invested back in development activities[124]. For its residents, their average household income of less than $2,580 per year in 2006 increased to about $13,879 per year, over a third greater than the average household income in the province[125]. To facilitate this, the Foundation created the Social Development Department to work closely with the community and the DTDP reinvested profits into community development[126].

Despite DTDP's phenomenal success, the Foundation members stated that Khun Chai never credited the success of Doi Tung to just himself and the Princess Mother. He believed that the DTDP would have done just as well so long as there was effective management and strong leadership. The underlying message of empowering the residents of Doi Tung to be the changemakers of their own community was always present, as the Foundation worked tirelessly to forge leaders within the community[127]. In 2017, the DTDP passed ownership of social operations and the torch of leadership to the locals. The people of Doi Tung showed resilience and protected the nature they lived within wholeheartedly. They were given a wide variety of occupations to choose from in their communities, while some became entrepreneurs establishing their own brands of coffee, cut flowers and handicrafts. Currently, the DTDP only manages the Doi Tung business enterprise and curates new environmental initiatives and opportunities for youth development.

When Khun Chai reflected on his work in the DTDP, he mused that he was only thinking of giving back to the Thai people. He had only wished to 'reforest the land and help the poorest of the poor'. The DTDP was the culmination of his firm belief that the sort of investment made by a business where it gives back to society is one that will '(last) forever'[128].

The Mae Fah Luang Foundation continues its purpose of empowering disenfranchised communities, implementing the DTDP model of sustainable living development in fragile local communities and in other countries like Myanmar, Afghanistan and Indonesia.

At present, the Mae Fah Luang Foundation continues to share its experiences and best practices in sustainability with a widespread audience, drives its mission of sustainable livelihood development with a focus on Myanmar and elevates its expertise in nurturing forests through a carbon credit verification programme known as 'Carbon Credit from Community Forests for Sustainability'. The Foundation empowers and builds the capacity of local communities to verify carbon credit from their forest and register carbon credit with government entities while forging strong partnerships with private organizations determined to reduce and offset its carbon emissions, creating a win-win situation for everyone involved.

Reflection questions

1. Why was the DTDP project so successful?
2. What did Khun Chai do particularly well as a leader?
3. What elements of the Steward Leadership Compass stood out? Why?
4. What elements of the Steward Leadership Compass were weak or missing altogether?
5. What lessons can we learn from the story?

Chapter 6

The Tata Group: A 155-Year Legacy

The country's first international airline. Its first steel mill. Its first affordable car. The Tata Group has been instrumental in bringing India's name to the global stage. Established in 1868 in Mumbai, India, the country's largest conglomerate is not only known for its pioneering spirit, but also its prestige and reliability. The range of products and services it provides is extensive, with ten business verticals ranging from technology and automotive to tourism and telecom. In the financial year 2021–22, the combined revenue of all Tata companies was $128 billion and they collectively employed more than 935,000 people[129]. As of March 31, 2022, there were twenty-nine publicly listed Tata enterprises with a combined market capitalization of $311 billion[130].

Despite the sheer size of the conglomerate, the Tata Group has remained one of India's most respected business houses throughout its 155-year history. How has it sustained the breadth of its growth across industries and continents while maintaining its reputation?

Rooted in its core

One would think the size of the conglomerate was a result of the Tata Group's focus on factors like market dominance or financial gain. Yet, from the beginning, its founder Jamsetji Nusserwanji Tata did not think a business should focus on market dominance or profit maximization. He believed:

In a free enterprise, the community is not just another stakeholder in business, but is in fact the very purpose of its existence.[131]

A cotton mill that Jamsetji established in 1874 became a laboratory where he experimented with technology and labour welfare in a way never seen in India. Polluted water was a common cause of illness, so he installed a water filtration plant and arranged for sanitary huts[132]. He then opened a grain depot and a dispensary, before introducing a provident fund and pension schemes for his employees[133].

Industrializing India

The measures introduced at this cotton mill were just a precursor to more extensive employee welfare initiatives that the Tatas would introduce alongside their efforts to industrialize India. Although the Industrial Revolution had taken Britain by storm, it had missed India. Jamsetji recognized that India's path out of poverty depended on widespread industrialization and the integration of modern science and technology into the nation's economy[134]. He was determined to build India's first steel and iron plant.

In 1902, five years before the plant was built, Jamsetji wrote to his son Dorabji:

> Be sure to lay wide streets planted with shady trees, every other of a quick-growing variety. Be sure that there is plenty of space for lawns and gardens. Reserve large areas for football, hockey and parks. Earmark areas for Hindu temples, Mohammedan mosques and Christian churches.[135]

Jamsetji had planned an entire township for those who work at the plant. Although Jamsetji would not live to see the plant and township built, his son Sir Dorabji Tata and his cousin R.D. Tata successfully opened it in the remote village of Sakchi in 1912, laying the foundations for what would become Tata Steel. Dorabji and R.D. Tata were not just executors of Jamsetji's dreams—they embodied his spirit and values. Four years before the plant was even built, the Tatas had set up a hospital in Sakchi to make medical care more accessible to the people of the region. When the plant was built, they implemented an eight-hour working day for labourers, long before shorter working hours became the norm. They introduced free medical aid in 1914, the maternity benefit scheme in 1928 and the retirement gratuity scheme in 1937[136]. A few years later, accident compensation was introduced through a scheme called 'Suraksha'[137]. None of these initiatives were indicated in Jamsetji's letter to his son back in 1902, nor were they even close to being codified in the law, but Sir Dorabji Tata and R.D. Tata embraced the values that Jamsetji embodied. Jamsetji's dreams of an industrialized India did not stop with Tata Steel. He also wanted to provide clean, pollution-free power to Mumbai, a city that was choking on the fumes of textile mills. He dreamed of setting up the first hydroelectric power plants in the Western Ghats, a mountain range that runs parallel to India's western coast. The power plants would be accompanied by a hydroelectric dam that would harness the power of flowing water to create electricity[138].

As he did with the township, Sir Dorabji Tata took on the responsibility of bringing this project to fruition. This time, he did it with his younger brother, Ratanji Tata. Jamsetji did not live to see the dam built. The brothers continued to build on the preliminary work done during their father's lifetime and built hydropower units near Mumbai and the first grid connection around Lower Parel. Over the next three years, three more hydroelectric entities were incorporated and were collectively referred to as the Tata Electric Companies. The two original units in Mumbai were amalgamated into the Tata Power Company in 2000[139].

Today, Tata Power is India's largest integrated power company, with about 35 per cent of its power sourced from clean energy. Of its overall output of 14,076 megawatts of power, 9,000 megawatts are thermal and the remaining 5,000 megawatts are from renewable sources: 900 megawatts of wind power, 2,900 megawatts of solar power and 1,200 megawatts of hydropower[140].

Tata Power has provided Mumbai with a reliable power supply for more than 100 years, a privilege no other part of the country enjoys[141]. Tata Power continues to work with the government to provide power to other Indian states and is currently fulfilling 3 per cent of the country's energy needs.

India's resurgence

Besides industrialization, Jamsetji believed that the integration of modern science and technology into India's economy was paramount to bringing the country out of poverty. But Jamsetji was not one to just hand out money or donate to charity. He wanted to build a system that would enable India to nurture its finest minds. He started by establishing the JN Tata Endowment in 1892. This supported Indian students, regardless of caste or creed, in pursuing their higher studies in England.

Jamsetji personally selected two women doctors—Freany K Cama and Krishnabai Kelavkar—as the first recipients of the JN Tata Endowment[142]. Jamsetji was aware of India's high infant mortality rates. Infants were dying not because there was not modern medicine available, but because of the scarcity of female doctors and Indian women's strong reluctance to go to male doctors[143]. India's future generations were essentially being wiped out before they could grow into productive citizens. By choosing Freany and Krishnabai, Jamsetji hoped to encourage more women to follow in their footsteps and ultimately lower India's infant mortality rate.

The JN Tata Endowment eventually became the Tata Scholarships. By 1924, just thirty years after the funding was set up, two out of every five Indians entering the civil service were Tata scholars[144]. Beneficiaries of the scholarships have included former Indian president K.R. Narayanan, physicist Raja Ramanna, astrophysicist Jayant Narlikar and violinist Mehli Mehta[145].

Systems of success

Jamsetji did not stop at setting up the endowment. His hopes for India's progress led to him pledging ₹3 million from his personal fortune towards setting up an institution that would nurture Indians in the sciences. He donated half of his personal wealth—fourteen buildings and four landed properties in Bombay (as Mumbai was then called)—

to create this institution[146]. He gathered support from the Viceroy-designate and, later on, at the request of the Secretary of State for India, the Royal Society of London asked Nobel laureate Sir William Ramsay for help. Sir William found Bangalore the most suitable place for the institution and it was there where the Indian Institute of Science was established[147].

The construction of the IISc eventually became a tripartite venture, when the government and the Maharaja of Mysore offered 372 acres of land—at no cost—and promised other necessary facilities[148]. Through a collaboration among the government, the maharaja and the Tata Group, the first stone of the IISc was laid in 1911.

Although Jamsetji did not live to see any of the great visions for his beloved nation come to life, his contributions were no less significant. By placing the community at the heart of his business, Jamsetji had also shaped the conglomerate's business strategy—offering a wide portfolio of services and tapping into emerging markets. Despite the size that the Tata Group grew to, Jamsetji never lost sight of the goal he started out with—to make the community the heart of his business.

Tata Trusts

Jamsetji's giving spirit deeply inspired his sons, leading them to lay the foundations for Tata Trusts. Beyond bringing his father's dreams to life, Jamsetji's elder son Sir Dorabji Tata also left his own legacy. Less than a year after his wife's death, Dorab put all his wealth into a trust focused on the advancement of learning and research and relieving distress. In honour of his wife's memory, he also set up the Lady Tata Memorial Trust, which he endowed with a corpus for leukaemia research[149]. He also formed the smaller Lady Meherbai D Tata Trust for the training of women in hygiene, health and social welfare[150].

While Dorab was bringing their father's plans to fruition, his younger brother Ratanji Tata devoted himself to philanthropy. Ratanji supported a range of benefactions, from lesser-known public welfare initiatives to high-profile ones, like his support to the Servants of India Society and Mahatma Gandhi's anti-apartheid movement in South

Africa[151]. Upon his death in 1919, the Sir Ratan Tata Trust was set up in accordance with his will. It had a corpus of ₹8 million[152].

Ratanji did not just leave behind a sum of money. He instructed the trustees on the causes they could devote the funds to, such as education and learning. He also specified that the institutions receiving the funds had to subject their accounts to periodic audits by the trustees and the ventures using the funds had to have their schemes carefully prepared by competent personnel[153].

To this day, the Sir Dorabji Tata Trust and Sir Ratan Tata Trust remain the two main foundations of the Tata Group. Since then, five more trusts have been established. Together, these seven trusts make up Tata Trusts, holding about two-thirds of Tata Sons, the principal holding company of the Tata Group, allowing them to ensure that the group operates in a socially responsible manner.

Diversification

The next major chapter in the Tata Group's history was J.R.D. Tata's five-decade-long leadership. J.R.D. Tata took on the mantel as Tata Group's chairman in 1938. During his fifty years at the helm of the Tata Group, the name 'J.R.D. Tata' became synonymous with the conglomerate. The diversification of Tata's business verticals came to characterize J.R.D's leadership. When he took over the group in 1938, there were fourteen enterprises under Tata. By the time he left in 1988, there were ninety-five. He grew Tata's assets by more than 50 times, from $100 million to over $5 billion[154].

The ninety-five enterprises could not have been more different. Tata Chemicals, Titan Watches, Tata Consultancy Services and Tata Tea were just a few enterprises in J.R.D. Tata's portfolio[155]. Some of these enterprises were even formed across different countries and cultures. When asked what binds them other than the 'Tata' name, here is how he answered: 'If someone were to ask me, what holds the Tata Companies together more than anything else, I would say it is our shared ideals and values which we inherited from Jamsetji Tata.'[156]

Throughout his career, J.R.D. had demonstrated that same heart for his employees and India. One of J.R.D.'s key contributions was the establishment of Tata Aviation Service. After a joy ride in a plane in northern France at fifteen, J.R.D. had his heart set on becoming a pilot and he took that dream to India. He became India's first commercial pilot in 1929[157]. That same year, it came to pass that a British air service was being planned to carry mail on a London–Karachi–Calcutta route. The rest of India was left out and the Tata Group drew up a proposal for an airmail service to connect those excluded[158]. After three years of not receiving support or approval, the Tata Group finally decided to provide the service at no cost to the government or taxpayer[159]. In 1932, Tata Air Mail was formed and its inaugural route connected Karachi, Ahmedabad, Bombay (now Mumbai), Bellary and Madras (Chennai was called Madras then). Just two years later, it was already making a profit and, in the following year, it expanded to new routes.

An aviation fanatic, J.R.D. himself flew the plane on the airline's maiden flight from Karachi to Bombay (Mumbai). In 1938, J.R.D. renamed the company Tata Airlines[160]. But just a little over ten years later, Nehru's government nationalized all Indian airlines as part of a broader policy to nationalize key industries. This resulted in two corporations—one for domestic flights and the other for international flights[161]. Tata Air Services was then renamed Air-India International. J.R.D. was later invited to lead Air-India and Indian Airlines, the domestic carrier. He became the chairman of Air-India and sat on the Board of Directors of Indian Airlines, serving in both positions until 1978[162].

During his time at Air-India, J.R.D. sought to make the airline the best globally because it brought India's flag to the world. After the airline's inaugural international flight, he said, 'It was for me a great and stirring event . . . seeing the Indian flag displayed on both sides of the Malabar Princess (the name of the aircraft) as she stood proudly on the apron at the airports of Cairo, Geneva and London filled me with joy and emotion.'[163] He was so committed to his vision that after every flight he took, J.R.D. Tata would send notes to the management, summarizing his observations and included encouragements or criticisms. In a note he wrote after flying from Europe to India, he said, 'The tea served on board from Geneva is, without exaggeration, indistinguishable in colour from coffee . . . I do not know whether the black colour of the tea is due to the quality (of tea leaves) used or due to excessive brewing. I suggest that the Station Manager at Geneva be asked to look into the matter.'[164] His attention to detail did not go to waste. In 1968, Air India topped the list of airlines in the world[165].

National interest

Like his predecessors, J.R.D. Tata was not only concerned with the bottom line. When it came to major decisions, his first question was not 'What does Tata need?' but 'What does India need?'[166] Throughout his time heading Tata, J.R.D. had championed many national causes including family planning and population control[167]. For his contribution to population control, he received the UN Population Award in September 1992[168]. Like Jamsetji, J.R.D. was also passionate about literacy and education, particularly among women and children, which he believed would raise the standard of living for the country.

J.R.D. also helped to establish many key institutions, including the Tata Institute of Fundamental Research and the National Centre for the Performing Arts. He also played a key role in setting up the National Institute of Advanced Studies in Bangalore (now Bengaluru). As a custodian of the Ratan Tata Trust, J.R.D. also had a decisive role in planning India's first cancer hospital: the Tata Memorial Hospital for Cancer Research and Treatment, now known as the Tata Memorial Hospital[169].

At forty, J.R.D. further built on the trusts his ancestors had established and he set up the JRD Tata Trust by donating many of his shares of Tata Sons Limited and other companies. A cause that he and his wife Thelma held close to their hearts was the plight of disadvantaged women in India. To support this cause, he established the JRD and Thelma J Tata Trust specifically to serve this group of women[170].

India was always at the forefront of J.R.D.'s mind. During the last years of World War II, J.R.D. was primarily concerned with building up the country's industrial capacity. He gathered other industrialists and technocrats to work on a plan for India's industrialization and this culminated in the two-part publication of 'A Plan of Economic

Development for India' in 1944. This plan came to be known as the 'Bombay Plan'[171]. The Bombay Plan was not intended as a scheme of economic development for post-independence India, nor was it a blueprint for action. Instead, it only provided a basis of discussion for the economic planning in India and the general direction it should proceed in[172]. Although not formally accepted by the new government of independent India, the Bombay Plan represented the views of India's big businesses and showed their commitment to uplifting the nation and not just their individual corporations.

Ratan Naval Tata

While J.R.D. Tata diversified the Tata business verticals, Ratan Tata sought to globalize the Tata businesses, in line with India's period of economic liberalization. Ratan Tata took over from J.R.D. Tata as chairman of Tata Sons in March 1991.

After the rapid expansion of the Tata group under J.R.D.'s leadership, Ratan Tata took over a decentralized, unevenly controlled company. He first amended the Tata Sons' articles of association to consolidate operations. As part of this strategy, he asked Tata Group firms to pay brand fees of 0.25 per cent of their revenues to Tata Sons to use the brand name[173]. This would increase Tata Sons' stake in the various companies, which were alarmingly low in the 1990s[174]. He also implemented a retirement age of seventy and had subsidiaries report directly to the group office.

Beyond organizational restructuring, Ratan Tata also ensured that the values that guided the Tata Group from its genesis were explicitly made known and practised throughout the organization. In 1998, the Tata Code of Conduct was released[175]. Although the Tata Group had always remained firmly grounded in its values and principles, they were never codified. With the release of the Tata Code of Conduct, employees were explicitly guided on the company's values, ethics and business principles. To implement the Code, the company created the position of 'ethics counsellor' at the senior management level in every department. The Code provides guidance on employee behaviours, dealings with customers, local communities, suppliers, government and the environment[176]. The consistent enforcement of the Code instilled in employees a sense of pride by being associated with a company with such strong values. This respect for the company also fostered a stronger sense of commitment and, in turn, encouraged better performance and created a better company image[177].

With a proper code of conduct in place, Ratan Tata went on to expand the group's operations overseas. In 2000, the Tata Group acquired London-based Tetley Tea for $431.3 million and, in 2004, it purchased the truck-manufacturing operations of South Korea's Daewoo Motors for $102 million[178]. In 2007, Tata Steel completed the biggest corporate takeover by an Indian company when it acquired the Anglo-Dutch steel manufacturer Corus Group for $11.3 billion[179]. The next year, Tata Motors acquired Jaguar and Land Rover from Ford in an all-cash transaction for $2.3 billion[180].

The Tata Nano

Like his predecessors, Ratan Tata had the community's welfare in his heart. He often saw Indian families on scooters, usually with a child sandwiched between his mother and father and they rode on slippery roads. Drawing on his background in architecture, Ratan Tata began doodling, trying to figure out how he could make scooters safer. The two wheels eventually became four, the frame had no windows, no doors and was just a 'basic dune buggy'[181]. But he decided that it should be a car. And so, the quest began to create an affordable car for the Indian families who could not afford the likes of the Maruti 800 and Alto.

After four years of hard work, the Tata Nano was launched in 2008 for about ₹100,000 or around $2000[182]. But as with every business, not everything turns out as successfully as planned. Despite the good intentions behind the product, consumers were reluctant to be associated with a 'cheap' car—the Nano was heavily marketed as such[183]. Although the stigma attached to the Tata Nano led to dwindling sales and its eventual withdrawal, the initiative was another demonstration of Tata's commitment to society.

A heart for the people

Besides innovation in the automobile industry, Ratan Tata was dedicated to providing equal opportunity to students from India. He endowed a scholarship fund of $28 million at Cornell University, where he had earned his degree in architecture in 1959, to provide aid to undergraduates from India[184]. In 2010, the Tata Companies, the Sir Dorabji Tata Trust and the Tata Education and Development Trust donated $50 million to the Harvard Business School to build a new facility for the school's executive education programmes[185].

The Tatas have never viewed profit maximization as the sole goal of the organization and Ratan Tata was no exception: 'Business, as I have seen it, places one great demand on you; it needs you to impose a framework of ethics, values, fairness and objectivity on yourself at all times. It is not easy to do this; you cannot impose it on yourself forcibly because it has to become an integral part of you.'[186]

As the Tatas have shown through the decades, their ability to strike the delicate balance between values and profit has led to pioneering innovations that uplift their communities.

Tata today and tomorrow

Under the leadership of N. Chandrasekaran, Tata Sons' current executive chairman since 2017, the Tata Group has spent five years cleaning up its balance sheets, paying off debt, exiting and merging unprofitable businesses, among other strategies[187]. It is now moving on to the next stage, with a renewed dedication to a sustainable future not just for Tata, but for the world.

The Group has pledged to achieve carbon net zero before 2045[188]. This is five years earlier than the 2050 deadline that 196 countries agreed upon when they signed the Paris Agreement in 2015[189]. 'We are focusing on a three-phased architecture approach for electric vehicles (EVs) and plan to launch 10 EVs in 5 years,' said Shailesh Chandra, MD, Tata Motors Passenger Vehicles and Tata Passenger Electric Mobility[190]. EVs are just one prong of Tata Motors' arsenal of strategies.

Tata Power is also one of the forerunners leading the charge towards the Tata Group's aim of becoming net zero by 2045. With

35 per cent of its energy already sourced from renewable sources and a 19 per cent reduction in greenhouse gas emissions so far, Tata Power seems well on the way to its 2045 target[191].

With its business strategy renewed and its entities cleaned up, the Tata Group has its eyes set on further international expansion. Chandrasekaran announced at the Uttar Pradesh Global Investors Summit—the flagship investment summit of the Government of Uttar Pradesh—in February 2023 that Tata is 'going to build an integrated multimodal air cargo (hub) through Air India SATS with our partner Zurich Airport in the new Jewar airport.'[192] The Tata Group also has new investments of $90 billion lined up, including Tata Power and Tata Steel investing more than $10 billion in renewable energy[193] and Tata Motors and Jaguar Land Rover investing $25 billion to improve its industrial footprint and to become an electric-first automaker[194]. Jaguar Land Rover also promised another new electric Jaguar by 2025[195].

With the house of Tata expected to record its highest annual growth in history at about 20 per cent in 2022–23, it continues to prove that a business conglomerate driven by stewardship values does not have to sacrifice profits for the sake of the greater good[196].

Reflection questions

1. How did multiple generations of the Tata family, involved in many diverse businesses, remain successful for 155 years?
2. What elements of the Steward Leadership Compass stood out? Why?
3. What elements of the Steward Leadership Compass were weak or missing altogether?
4. What lessons can we learn from the story?

Chapter 7

Mars, Incorporated: The Role of Corporate Values in Anchoring Purpose

'Accountability is given to you, responsibility is what you feel,' said Frank E. Mars, Chair of the Board and strategic advisor, Mars, Incorporated, at a fireside chat I hosted with him at the Singapore Management University in early 2023. In distinguishing between accountability and responsibility, Frank's comment clearly reflects how purpose at Mars has taken on a rare level of importance at the company. Mars has inculcated within its corporate culture the notion that the company and by extension its employees (also known as Associates), are responsible for its footprint and impact on its stakeholders, society and the environment.

Mars' approach to purpose is in stark contrast to that taken by many other corporates, where purpose may be superficially tagged on to existing business operations rather than embedded within them. Conversely, purpose at Mars has been defined by Mars, for Mars and is undergirded by the company's core business values, also known as the Five Principles. In the case of Mars, a 100 per cent family-owned company, these business values have been developed and stewarded by the Mars family across generations. The story of the business dynasty illustrates how a corporate culture rooted in a clear value system enables businesses to adopt purpose in more meaningful and transformational ways.

Mars has its origins in candy and confectionery products and over the years has diversified to be a global leader in various other markets, including pet care products, main meal food and staples, snacks and more recently, veterinary services. Now in its fourth generation of family leadership, Mars remains completely privately held, is America's third largest private corporation and is widely recognized as a purpose-driven company[197]. The company recently stepped into the spotlight with major commitments to environmental and social sustainability, notably through its $1 billion commitment in 2017 to its Sustainable in a Generation plan. Reflecting on this, Grant Reid, then-CEO of Mars, explained, 'Mars has been in business for four generations and intends to be for the next four generations.'[198]

The company's mission statement, 'The world we want tomorrow starts with how we do business today', effectively summarizes its purpose-centric approach to business and echoes the values and principles that have guided the company for decades[199]. These values have been diligently passed down from one generation of the Mars family to another, are entrenched in the company's culture and have enabled it to find success for nearly 110 years.

The origins of Mars, Incorporated

The business has its origins in the butter cream candies products sold by Frank C. Mars and his wife Ethel V. Mars in 1911 in Tacoma, Washington. As a young boy in Minnesota, Frank contracted polio, which prevented him from walking to school and attending lessons. His mother thus schooled him at home in their kitchen, where she also taught him the art of hand-dipping chocolate. This sparked Frank's passion for chocolate and candy-making. In 1920, he moved to Minnesota and launched 'Patricia Chocolates', which was named after his daughter. In 1922, he launched the Mar-O-Bar, a sticky combination of chocolate, caramel and nuts[200].

Frank's sales skyrocketed upon his creation of the Milky Way bar in 1923, which was inspired by a trip to a five-and-dime store with his eldest child Forrest Sr. Forrest had asked his father, 'Why don't you put a chocolate-malted drink in candy bar?'[201] The rest was history. As he maintained a strong emphasis on quality, taste and value, Frank's business soared with close to no marketing. Mars, Incorporated was established in Minnesota in 1926 and, in 1929, the company was relocated to a full-production plant in Chicago. The business would continue to develop new confectionery products and see success even through the challenging years of the Great Depression[202].

Frank brought Forrest Sr. into the business in 1929 and Snickers was launched in 1930, although the pair disagreed on how it should be run. In 1932, Forrest Sr. moved to the UK with $50,000 from his father and the foreign rights to the Milky Way bar, determined to forge his own path and work towards his dream of a perfect business[203].

Forrest Sr. proceeded to set up shop in a one-room factory in Slough, a small industrial town just outside London, where he learned the ropes of the chocolate business during the Great Depression. This time would prove to be instructive for Forrest Sr. as it moulded and honed the values he would later adopt and inculcate into his own business practices. He observed the practices of a few family-owned confectionery firms, such as Cadbury's and Rowntree's, which were known for running their businesses ethically and taking good care of their workers. These companies thrived despite the economic downturn, leading Forrest Sr. to believe that accounting for social and ethical considerations was simply the smart approach to business[204]. While in the UK, Forrest Sr. developed the Mars Bar, a new version of the Milky Way bar, which quickly became a bestseller. Over the years, Forrest Sr. continued to find success in Europe, establishing a confectionery and a canned petfood company[205].

After Frank C. Mars passed away in 1934, Forrest Sr. returned to the US. Over the next two decades, he purchased his father's company piece by piece. When he eventually gained ownership of the company in 1964, he merged it with his own, Food Manufacturers. A perfectionist at heart, Forrest Sr. had always envisioned building Mars to become an empire in more ways than one. Upon taking the helm of the company, he aimed for Mars products to be staples in pantries across the world and expanded into a range of industries. Concurrently, he had pictured building Mars around a value system and set of business practices that he had himself honed over the years of running his own company. As such, he was determined to immediately put the company's affairs in order the way he saw fit[206].

Forrest Sr. had a vision of a successful business model that embodied his core values and swiftly implemented a radically egalitarian system, rejecting bureaucracy and status. In this vein, he introduced several then-unorthodox business practices, many of which remain to this day. For instance, all employees have since been called 'Associates'[207]. Forrest Sr. also encouraged Associates to adopt his business philosophy and rewarded such dedication by compensating them significantly more than other similar companies at the time[208].

Forrest Sr. knew that a successful legacy hinged on longevity and his own succession struggle had been a harsh reminder of the importance of long-term planning. He mused, 'Many companies began as Mars did, but as they grew larger, they sold stocks or incurred restrictive debt. We believe growth can be achieved another way.'[209] As such, Forrest Sr. developed a clear succession plan well ahead of time to keep the business entirely family-owned and prepared his children for an organized and clean succession when the time was right. In 1969, Forrest Sr. retired and his two sons, Forrest Jr. and John, took on more senior roles as Group VPs in the company. Forrest Jr. led confectionary and John took control of Petcare and Vending. In 1975, Forrest Jr. and John became joint Office of the President (what a CEO at Mars is called). Annual revenue at the time stood at a clear $1 billion and the company was debt-free.

Building a family business dynasty

As Forrest Sr. moulded his business around his values, he adopted the same approach with his family. With explicit intentions of handing over the Mars empire to his children, Forrest ensured they not only understood these values but adopted them as their own. Victoria Mars, Forrest's granddaughter, shared, 'As a child, I grew up with these principles as part of how we lived as a family. They weren't hanging on a wall, posted on the kitchen fridge. But they guided our family and me on how we interacted with people.'[210]

Through their upbringing, Forrest's children, Forrest Jr., John and Jacqueline, were well poised to take the business forward and build on the foundation their father had put in place. After Forrest Jr. and John had completed their university studies, they joined Mars and were tasked with expanding the business in the Netherlands and the UK respectively. Forrest Jr. and John went on to have roles in France, Canada and Australia. These new roles proved to be trials that would allow the brothers to come to an intimate understanding of the Mars core values in practice and to gain a sense of ownership and ambition around expanding the business to new markets[211]. Jacqueline joined the business later in 1982 to lead the project to codify the Five Principles. She later went on to become Group VP for Food.

Forrest Sr.'s children effectively leveraged the backbone he had established and built the family business dynasty that is today. A commitment to maintaining family ownership and emphasizing long-term thinking has endured, thus ensuring the family has control over the business' practices and core value system[212]. Forrest Jr. and John were devoted to the Mars empire and took forward their father's value system and business practices while making it their own. They emphasized product quality and excellence and continued the practice of paying Associates above-average wages while demanding above-average loyalty. Over the years, Forrest's children worked tirelessly to break into new markets across the world and successfully brought the company to China, Russia, the Middle East, Africa and Latin America[213]. Today, annual sales at Mars stands at well over $45 billion, far outstripping the revenue growth of other global consumer goods companies in the same period[214].

Codifying corporate values: The Five Principles

Having taken over the helm of Mars for a few years, Forrest Sr.'s children saw the importance of codifying the values that had driven the company forward over the years. Thus, in 1978, they gathered the senior business leaders to deliberate on the core values that had brought the company to where it was and that would shape the company's future in time to come. The Five Principles of Mars, namely, Quality, Responsibility, Mutuality, Efficiency and Freedom, were thus published in 1983. Today, the Principles ground the Mars company culture, with the company and its Associates firmly believing that it is the Principles that differentiate Mars from its competitors. When Mars receives any media attention, the Five Principles, now almost synonymous with the company itself, are typically mentioned as well[215].

The Principles of Freedom and Mutuality are particularly unique, especially important to the Mars family and less likely to be found in other corporations' value systems[216]. The Freedom Principle refers to the need to remain family-owned and profitable to remain free from being answerable to other shareholders and ties in with the Mars family's dedication to long-term planning. In turn, the Mutuality Principle likely stems from a letter written by Forrest Sr. in 1947, in which he states that the business' objective is to create a mutuality of benefits for all stakeholders[217].

Mars believes that a mutual benefit is a shared benefit and that shared benefits are those that will endure in the long run. At the heart of Mars' business practices is a focus on thinking about others' interests and building win-win relationships that create long-lasting benefits for the business, Associates, business partners and society at large. The embedding of the Freedom and Mutuality Principles in the Mars corporate culture helped to set a solid foundation and naturally orientate the business and its Associates towards doing business with purpose and with society's broader interests in mind.

Integral to the corporate culture, a twenty-four-page brochure on the Principles can be found on the desks and tables in every Mars factory and each new hire at Mars receives a copy signed with the names of family members (now including generations three, four and five). The Five Principles have since served as a guiding framework that informs business decisions, unites Associates across geographies and generations and influences relationships between Mars and all its stakeholders. Taken to be non-negotiable, the Principles also serve as a way for the Mars family to anchor the business in the values they believe in and to guide decision-making accordingly. Victoria Mars explained, 'You can get managers that can come along who might say we need to change aspects of the Principles, but the family will say, "You don't understand; these are

our principles, our values. You don't have the right to change them."
We own these principles and values. The business doesn't own them;
we own them.'[218]

Efforts to maintain the Five Principles as Mars' foundation continue
till this day to ensure that all business units and Associates conduct
their work in accordance with the Principles. Former Chair and Board
Director Pamela Mars-Wright recalled a staff survey years ago with
disappointing results, 'What was evident was that we weren't living the
Five Principles. We weren't the company we thought . . . So we decided
to go back to the Five Principles and to really focus on them.'[219] A
greater conscious effort was thus made to consistently incorporate the
Principles in day-to-day work; for instance, the Principles are now used
as a framework for running meetings, with decisions being made and
outcomes being evaluated against them. When Mars ran the survey
again in 2013, the results were significantly improved compared to the
survey prior[220].

Today, the Five Principles effectively serve as a guiding philosophy
for Mars in its commitment to being future-facing and purpose-
driven. As Victoria Mars explained, 'The Five Principles are all about
the "how" versus the "what" at Mars and they serve as a solid base
upon which we build everything. Mixed with a sense of entrepreneurial
adventure that has permeated the business since the beginning, they
create a workplace where our associates can be proud and business can
thrive.'[221]

Considering purpose versus performance: The economics of mutuality

The influence of the principles in shaping the company's culture
meant that Mars was ahead of the curve in considering the question of
how the company would define its purpose in relation to its financial
performance. The Mutuality Principle and Mars' corresponding focus
on mutual benefits for all stakeholders, has had an especially crucial
role in determining Mars' approach to purpose and sustainability.

In 2006, John Mars, son of Forrest Sr., while in conversation
with then-CEO Paul Michaels and then-CFO Oliver Goudet, posed

an interesting question, 'What should be the right level of profit for Mars?'[222] While many shareholders would define the optimum level of profit as the maximum level possible, John Mars was concerned that Mars' profit level was too high and at the expense of its value chain partners and other stakeholders. He feared that by way of the company extracting more than it had a right to from its value chain, a domino effect would be created where each stakeholder puts undue pressure on another, ultimately creating imbalance and shortfall that would likely cost Mars in the long term[223].

Knowing there was no straightforward answer to this question, Mars' leadership team handed the question over to Catalyst, the internal think-tank Forrest Sr. had established to challenge traditional business thinking and explore new business management models based on mutuality. The Catalyst team established the Economics of Mutuality (EoM) programme, where they explored what constitutes value beyond financial capital and developed a set of non-traditional metrics to account for the value of non-financial capital pertaining to both people (human and social capital) and the planet (natural capital)[224]. This provided a jumping off point for the Catalyst team to analyse the performance trajectories of over 3,500 companies over a forty-year period.

Catalyst found that a long-term and holistic approach is ideal when determining an optimal level of profit, as a broader approach towards value creation across stakeholders would drive stronger performance for the company in the long run. Catalyst thus proposed that Mars should focus not only on financial performance metrics, but also the impact of the business, be it value created or destroyed, on the three pillars of performance, people and planet in any ecosystem where Mars operates[225].

Through the programme, both Catalyst and Mars have jointly explored various pilot programmes in its business ecosystems in Africa, where performance and purpose are both aligned and social capital is deeply accounted for. As stated by a Mars External Peer Review Panel in July 2013, this question posed by John Mars and Catalyst's findings marked the start of Mars' explicit focus on 'the path to becoming a long-run investor in a holistic business future as opposed to a short-sighted, profit-only driven entity.'[226]

Adopting a purpose-driven approach: The Mars way

With the Five Principles as the heart of Mars' corporate culture, the Mars family had been committed for some time to the power of business as a force for good. In line with John Mars' question around the 'right' level of profit, Mars, Incorporated began to undertake the process of defining what purpose meant to the company, particularly as conversations burgeoned in the mid-2000s around corporate sustainability.

The question of sustainability and what it meant for Mars was raised in 2007, at which point the company did not have a sustainability plan outlined. Mars' business leaders put together an executive-level team to assess the relevance and risks of sustainability to Mars and to report back with their findings thereafter. The team knew that in order to undertake this process in earnest, it was vital that they took the concept of sustainability and made it Mars' own. Mars' Five Principles meant that a clear philosophy and value system had already been in-built into the company culture and adopting externally imposed approaches such as corporate social responsibility and sustainability reporting was less likely to have a deep and meaningful impact internally.

As such, the team focused on sustainability through the lens of Mars products and developed data-driven sustainability stories for each of the top brands under each business segment. These stories created crucial insights for the company and encouraged all Associates to consider the intricate relationship between Mars' products, business operations and sustainability considerations. Through this process, both the Mars family and Mars' business leaders saw the needs and merits of integrating sustainability as a core component of Mars' operational and corporate strategy moving forward[227].

With Mars having been principles-led for many years, placing purpose at the centre of Mars' work was a natural progression that built upon the values already fundamental to the company's culture.

The Mars family has actively worked to adapt the Five Principles as needed to ensure that they suit the company's present-day needs and context while still maintaining their essence. As purpose came to the fore within the company, the family adapted the Five Principles to reflect this renewed focus, thus placing a purpose-oriented approach at the core of the company's work.

'Purpose has a clear role to play in business. Performance without purpose is meaningless and purpose without performance isn't possible. We're a large company and with that scale comes both the responsibility and the opportunity to have a positive impact,' declared Grant Reid, CEO of Mars, Incorporated from 2014 to 2022[228]. Today, Mars' business leaders are strong advocates for purpose and the sustainability agenda and are unified in their conviction that performance and purpose go hand-in-hand.

Purpose in action: The Sustainable in a Generation Plan

Guided by the Five Principles, Mars takes a long-term and holistic approach when accounting for the company's impact and footprint on all its stakeholders, including society and the environment. Grant Reid shared, 'As a company, you want to be sustainable, both in the way that you operate but also in what you put back into the ecosystem in which you operate.'[229] These considerations are clearly reflected in the ways in which Mars has approached its purpose-driven activities, most of which fall under Mars' Sustainable in a Generation (SiG) Plan.

SiG was launched in 2017 with a $1 billion investment and clearly elucidates how Mars' leadership puts purpose at the centre across all its business segments. The SiG Plan maps out a series of tailored initiatives and ambitious targets derived from Mars' measurement of climate impacts and data analysis. This detailed measurement and analysis have enabled it to identify where its focus areas should be. For instance, the company identified that as much as 80 per cent of its emissions stemmed from 'agricultural and land use change'. This spurred the company to focus its sustainability efforts on supply chain

management and agriculture production and by extension, to set a goal
to attain net-zero value chain emissions by 2050.

Grant Reid shared, 'I don't underestimate the size and complexity
of our own commitment to get to net zero across the breadth of our
entire supply chain . . . The old ways of doing business will not deliver
the changes required and it's clear that a transformational redesign of
business supply chains will be critical.'[230]

(i)   **Enabling a sustainable supply chain: Cocoa for
      Generations programme**

      'One of our key aims is to source more sustainably
      produced raw materials, boosting farmers' incomes and
      create mutual benefits for the communities that supply
      them,' said Frank E. Mars[231]. Along this vein, the Cocoa for
      Generations programme aims to enable sustainable cocoa
      production by transitioning smallholder farmers to more
      sustainable approaches to cocoa farming and by holistically
      investing in these rural communities. Aiming to source 100
      per cent traceable and responsibly sourced cocoa by 2025,
      the company has launched two farmer-first programmes in
      Cote d'Ivoire and Indonesia to support 14,000 smallholder
      farmers by tackling persistent barriers to their ability to earn
      a sufficient income[232].

(ii) **Enabling a sustainable supply chain: Coral reef
      restoration efforts**

      Since 2007, Mars' Sustainable Solutions team has
      been working to develop socially, economically and
      environmentally sustainable solutions that positively impact
      the communities that supply Mars' raw materials. One of
      the projects the team has developed is the Mars Assisted
      Reef Restoration System (MARRS). MARRS is a low-cost
      scalable method of restoring the coral reef ecosystem near
      Makassar, Indonesia, where the company's cocoa operations
      are located. Today, this has been put in place off the coasts
      of various islands in Indonesia where Mars operates and
      has led to one of the world's largest restored coral reef

ecosystems, with over three hectares of coral reef being rebuilt. In the restoration process, the team also undertakes a participatory approach and ensures involvement of the local community. In doing so, the restoration activities drive behavioural change amongst the communities involved and enable sustainable 'reef-based' livelihoods[233]. This method is being rapidly scaled around the world where coral reefs are threatened.

(iii) **Strengthening communities: Ending pet homelessness**
Driven by their purpose 'A better world for pets', Mars Petcare has introduced a series of programmes to address pet homelessness concerns across the world. To ensure that initiatives are well-targeted in different countries and contexts, Mars Petcare has partnered with an advisory board of leading animal welfare experts to release the State of Pet Homelessness Index, mapping the scale and factors of pet homelessness by country. Mars Petcare has rolled out several programmes under their top pet care brands to combat pet homelessness, such as PEDIGREE Foundation's grant programmes for dog shelter and rescue organizations[234].

Institutionalizing purpose: The Mars Compass

The launch of the SiG and all the aforementioned pragmatic initiatives that Mars has spearheaded, has been a resounding signal that the company is committed to consciously undertaking business endeavours and decisions that are purpose-centric. While many of the SiG initiatives were already underway, the Mars family saw the need to go beyond the plan and institutionalize purpose within the company. It is key to ensuring long-lasting and transformational change in the way the business and its Associates approached all aspects of work. As such, to guide all business units in incorporating purpose-related dimensions and metrics into their respective strategies, the family introduced the Mars Compass in 2018. The Mars Compass is a set of shareholder objectives and it requires the board and management to think long-term and holistically about how the company creates value[235].

The Compass outlines a set of strategic objectives for the company's long-term strategy and emphasizes how performance and purpose go hand-in-hand. The objectives of Financial Performance and Quality Growth capture the financial or 'performance' dimensions, whereas the objectives of Positive Societal Impact and Trusted Partner capture the non-financial or 'purpose' dimensions of the strategy[236]. To foster the long-term thinking needed for transformational change, a three-year integrated value creation plan process was introduced to actively bring the Compass into the business planning for all segments. By implementing this process, Mars has enabled its teams to create business plans on a longer timeframe with a focus on sustainability priorities as opposed to a strictly one-year planning cycle that prioritizes short-term financial performance.

As Poul Weihrauch, current CEO of Mars, Incorporated shared, 'Anchored by our Purpose, the Mars Compass establishes expectations from the Family for how we should lead our business and provides a clear definition of success. It ensures we link purpose and performance and gives us the freedom to think in generations, not quarters.'[237]

Purpose-driven for generations

Looking ahead, Mars will be taking purpose forward via its SiG Plan and the Compass. While the eventual outcomes of the SiG Plan remain to be seen, the bold posturing of Mars' approach is testament to how it has embedded purpose at the heart of the business and has committed itself to undertaking deep and transformational change. By thinking in terms of generations, Mars inherently adopts a long-term and holistic view and is able to approach purpose as a process, grounded in the understanding that the future is shaped by how business is conducted today. Purpose-driven activities are thus poised to be meaningful, reflective and responsive to changing stakeholders' needs and contexts.

Adopting and embedding purpose in this manner has been made possible by Mars' Five Principles and its role in shaping a clear corporate culture at the company. The presence of a values-driven corporate culture that ties the company and all its business segments together has enabled purpose to be more easily adopted by business units and its Associates. This is further enhanced by the Mars family's and business leaders' efforts to consistently update the Five Principles and tie the company's focus on purpose back to them.

With a forward-looking approach deeply rooted in established corporate values, Mars and its Associates seem to be well-positioned to take ownership of its purpose and business impact and ultimately undertake purpose-centric activities to generate positive outcomes for all its stakeholders.

Reflection questions

1. Why does a privately held debt-free company like Mars pursue a strategy based on 'mutuality'?
2. What elements of the Steward Leadership Compass stood out? Why?
3. What elements of the Steward Leadership Compass were weak or missing altogether?
4. What lessons can we learn from the story?

Chapter 8

Farm Fresh: Dairy, Just as Nature Intended

It was the wee hours of dawn. Loi Tuan Ee, founder of the Malaysian dairy company Farm Fresh Berhad, was ready to start his day as a salesman at the supermarket to promote his dairy products.

In the early 2000s, Loi had to work closely on the ground to persuade market goers to purchase his goods as his business was still in its infancy. Malaysians found it hard to trust a homegrown dairy company, sticking to more renowned large multinational brands. Some of them even perceived local dairy to be 'dirty' or 'low quality', which Loi thought was a huge shame as he knew that his cattle and farmhands always produced delicious, high-quality milk.

Loi's foray into sales was not exactly smooth sailing. Selling his dairy products was always a nagging worry in his mind as he had only a meagre supply of milk produced every day. It did not really make much sense to start a dairy farm in a tropical country like Malaysia. The heat and high humidity do not provide optimal conditions for the temperate Holstein Jersey cows he brought from Australia to produce milk efficiently. When kept in warm climates, milk yield is significantly lower than average milk yield in temperate environments.

These challenges were a real headache for Loi, but his conviction to nurture a homegrown business for fresh dairy was unshakeable. When Loi went on his grocery runs, he noticed that most dairy products sold in the supermarket chillers advertised as 'fresh milk' was instead made from powdered or reconstituted milk. Some of it was even pumped with unnatural additives such as processed sugars and unhealthy preservatives, which he felt was incredibly unnecessary for human consumption. At a glance, Loi estimated that 95 per cent of the milk in the chillers was reconstituted or powdered milk[238]. Food, in his opinion, was becoming overly processed. Loi shuddered to think of the situation where children were exposed to unnatural preservatives and excessive sugars in their growing years.

With a market gap to fill and the desire to provide Malaysians with fresh and pure dairy, Loi left his high-paying job in the packaging industry in his forties, bought a small plot of land in Mawai Kota Tinggi, Johor and imported sixty Holstein Jersey cows from Australia. When he started, nature-loving Loi vowed that the company would never stray from its customer-centric values and adhere to its purpose of providing natural fresh milk to its customers while also loving the environment it operates in and uplifting the local community.

Loi's journey was not an easy one. Compared to other perishables in the market, fresh milk has an incredibly short shelf life. Coupled with the near non-existent dairy culture in Malaysia as well as the tropical heat and humidity, it was incredibly costly to run a local dairy business. There was little to no economies of scale to leverage and operational costs were steep. Loi had to figure out how to sell fresh milk to the Malaysian populace and deliver what little milk he had gotten from his cows to far flung areas of Malaysia while preserving its freshness. For a moment, he allowed himself to indulge in the possibility of extending the shelf life of his fresh milk through the addition of preservatives[239]. Maybe that could allow him to sustain his then rocky business?

Shaking his head to expel those thoughts, Loi berated himself for entertaining that notion. 'If I want to ensure the longevity of my business while building my customer base, I need to stay true to my belief that if a business puts their customers first, their customers will respond in kind,' he said to himself.

Building a Malaysian business for Malaysians

Strategizing ways in which he could emerge successful in the Malaysian dairy industry amidst huge competition from larger brands and multinational companies, Loi felt that there was value in branding Farm Fresh as a local company *for* Malaysian families—the aunties and uncles, as all middle-aged and senior citizens are fondly called in

Malaysia and Singapore. If positioned correctly, branding Farm Fresh as a homegrown business could accord him a competitive advantage against the established larger businesses dominating the market.

His conviction was reinforced during one of his countless supermarket visits when he was on the ground conducting sales pitches. Noticing a familiar face, he walked up to a middle-aged woman moving to grab a carton of fresh Farm Fresh milk off the shelves. He realized that she was a repeat customer. When he asked why she had returned to buy his milk, she laughed and said, 'My children really love it and I appreciate that it is made of natural ingredients!'

This was what Loi pinpointed as Farm Fresh's key to success. With the wide variety of dairy products in the market for consumers to choose from, it was imperative for Farm Fresh to build its customer-centric brand and differentiate itself. To create a brand that customers would adore and trust, Farm Fresh had to be a business that always placed its customers' welfare at heart. While operating and making crucial decisions for the business, Loi always paused to think, would this be beneficial to our customers? 'To build a brand where the customer loves you, your core values are to please the customer's well-being and interest first,' Loi reasoned. 'If you begin to sway, it is only a matter of time when the customers who supported you and your values will no longer hold any value.'[240]

At that time, Malaysia did not have a self-sufficient dairy industry as the market was dominated by large, multinational companies. These MNCs would sell powdered milk reconstituted from fresh milk produced by local farmers and only pay them a fraction of the profit. Although Khazanah Nasional Berhad, the sovereign wealth fund of Malaysia, invested in smallholder farmers and small-scale dairy production, commercial dairy farming remained unviable for locals. Most dairy companies would close during festive seasons, leaving farmers with no way to sell the milk they get from their cows daily.

Knowing this, Loi offered double the pay his competitors from larger companies were giving[241]. He purchased milk at higher than prevailing market prices, which led to RM38.1 million ($9.5 million) more income for dairy farmers in rural Malaysia since the implementation of the initiative in 2013. As of 2022, 72 per cent of employees across Farm Fresh's farms and processing facilities were recruited from local rural communities[242].

Additionally, Loi and his employees at Farm Fresh work every day—even during the holidays—to transport, process and sell fresh milk produced from local commercial dairy farmers. This minimizes waste while generating more profit for Farm Fresh, especially during festive seasons when most dairy companies are closed.

Understanding that the quality and quantity of its fresh milk supply is dependent on the success of its local dairy farmers, Farm Fresh also kickstarted the rural farmer network to provide dairy farmers with upskilling opportunities through training and mentorship to increase milk yield and quality. With local farms producing higher quality milk at larger quantities, Farm Fresh was able to process and sell more delicious dairy products for its consumers.

A gene-ious idea

In 2009, Loi had just imported sixty Holstein Jersey cows from Australia. The conception rate of Australian cattle was high, which was imperative to the growth of a dairy business at its infancy as it meant that the cattle population could grow at faster rates[243]. However, the executive-turned-dairy-farmer was still wet behind his ears and he grew to realize that Holstein cows were more accustomed to temperate climates. In hot and humid Malaysia, they demonstrated clear signs of discomfort and heat stress, producing lower milk yield than predicted.

Undeterred, Loi went back to the drawing board to brainstorm ways to increase milk production and efficiency at the farm. How could he make his dairy business viable in such unfavourable conditions of high heat and humidity? The odds were dramatically against him. After all, he could not possibly transform the tropical climate of Malaysia. His breakthrough occurred when he realized that there was something within his means to change—he could improve the resilience of his cattle through genetic engineering. In 2012, Loi hopped on a plane to Australia to acquire an Australian genetic company established by the Queensland government in the late 1960s. Employing the use of crossbreeding between the heat-tolerant Indian Sahiwal and Holstein-Friesian breeds to develop the Australian-Friesian-Sahiwal (AFS) breed, Farm Fresh now had more access to dairy cattle which was more ideal for the tropical climate. Today, Loi believes that this crossbreed builds an indispensable foundation for Farm Fresh's high fresh milk production. At the rapid speeds at which Farm Fresh is growing now, Loi deeply appreciates that he and his team had the foresight to invest in more heat-tolerant cows to keep up with ever-growing demand[244].

To further strengthen the AFS breed to improve milk yields in tropical climates, Farm Fresh also created an in-house team to intensify research on crossbreeding genetic technology. To foster a collaborative culture within the Malaysian dairy community and encourage knowledge exchange between peers, Farm Fresh pledged to share the results of the research with the Malaysian government under the National Dairy Industry Development (NDID) programme[245]. Through partnerships and raising the collective capabilities of the Malaysian dairy industry, Loi believes that the future that Farm Fresh envisioned, where Malaysians and other people around the world could consume fresh natural dairy, can be achieved.

Happy cows, happy milk

With an increased tolerance to heat, the AFS cows were producing better quality milk in greater quantities for Farm Fresh to sell. As a dairy farmer, Loi was acutely aware that his cows formed the backbone of his business' success. If Farm Fresh could become a reliable source of safe, delicious and nutritious dairy, consumers would be more incentivized to trust and purchase their products while investors would feel more assured in funding the business.

As Loi loves to quip, 'Happy cows, happy milk.' To produce the creamiest and highest quality milk, his cows had to be happy and well taken care of. This comes easy to Loi, who loves his cows so much that he affectionately refers to them as 'his ladies', a term which many others in his company also adopted. Sometimes, he proudly shows off pictures of his cows to his wife, compliments and praises spilling from his lips[246].

Ensuring that his 'ladies' are always well taken care of and content, Loi and his team in Farm Fresh take a holistic three-pronged approach. The 'ladies' are fed organic feed full of nutrition, have a dedicated team of veterinarians to conduct daily health checks and are provided with comfortable living conditions. The AFS and Holstein Jersey cows, being vulnerable to stress from the heat and humidity, live in barns with water sprinklers that spray water on them to cool them off. Currently, tunnel ventilation barns are being installed at all Farm Fresh farms, providing the 'ladies' more comfort and keeping them happy.

Farm Fresh was awarded the Certified Humane(R) accreditation in recognition of its comprehensive animal welfare policies and practices, making it the first dairy company in Asia to obtain the accreditation[247].

Spreading the Farm Fresh word

With the 'ladies' of Farm Fresh happy and producing high-quality, fresh and natural dairy, it took little time for the Farm Fresh name to be ubiquitous in the major cities of Malaysia. However, a significant number of people had come up to Loi, lamenting that they could not find Farm Fresh products in their local supermarkets or grocers. Unfortunately, Farm Fresh's dairy farms were located close to the bigger cities at the southern end of the Peninsular Malaysia. As fresh milk has a short shelf-life, Loi could only transport chilled fresh dairy to larger cities with a proportionately large market.

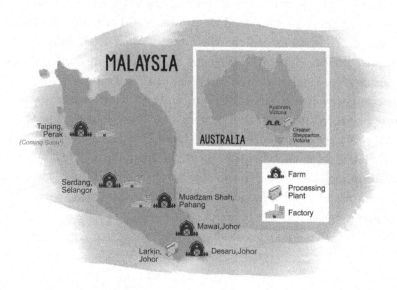

Figure 17: Farm Fresh facilities located across Malaysia and Australia.
Picture taken from https://www.farmfresh.com.my/. Used with permission from Farm Fresh Berhad.

It was perplexing that there was a huge untapped market outside of the cities that Loi had no capacity to engage. If he could sell his fresh dairy products to those located in the rural corners of Malaysia, he could grow the business even further and spread the Farm Fresh name to the rest of Malaysia. Ruffled by this missed opportunity, he spoke to his long-time friend and business partner, Azmi Zainal, the current Chief Operating Officer (COO) of Farm Fresh.

The two thought long and hard about how to scale up their distribution network. Was there a way to cost-effectively distribute quantities of fresh milk in bulk? What if they could minimize delivery costs by dispatching a large enough quantity of milk to rural parts of Malaysia where someone well-acquainted with the neighbourhood could sell and distribute them? Not only would Farm Fresh be able to sell more of their dairy products, but they could also empower people in the rural communities to become micro-entrepreneurs and have an additional source of income. If it worked, it would be a win-win solution, thought Azmi.

To test the waters, the Home Dealers' Network was pioneered in 2016. Since the dairy products that Farm Fresh offered were chilled and had a short shelf-life, the network was initially established in major towns in Johor and Kuala Lumpur. Loi knew that there needed to be a fundamental shift to their products if Farm Fresh wanted to expand. Thus, to extend the shelf life of their fresh dairy, Farm Fresh developed ambient UHT (Ultra Heat Treatment) milk. As its name suggests, it is fresh milk that has been heated to extreme high temperatures, sterilized and cooled to ambient temperatures so that it can be stored at room temperature and for a longer time. This kickstarted a momentous shift in the Home Dealers' Network. With UHT milk in its arsenal, Farm Fresh could distribute its UHT milk to rural communities situated in the remotest of areas as it was cheaper to distribute and had a longer shelf-life for micro-entrepreneurs to store and sell over a longer period.

Figure 18: Farm Fresh distribution network of home dealers located across Malaysia as of March 31, 2023.

Picture taken from https://www.farmfresh.com.my/. Used with permission from Farm Fresh Berhad.

Through the establishment of the Home Dealers' Network (Figure 2), many rural and suburban Malaysians were given the opportunity to become micro-entrepreneurs by being a Farm Fresh distributor. In six years, the network expanded from zero in 2016 to 900 home dealers in 2022[248]. By selling Farm Fresh products in their local community, these micro-entrepreneurs, who were mostly housewives or women, earned about RM700 to RM5,000 ($142 to $1,050) per household per month. The revenue generated from the Home Dealers' Network was 30 per cent of Farm Fresh's revenue in the financial year 2022, as of March 2022. Evidently, Farm Fresh had cultivated this symbiotic relationship with their micro-entrepreneurs, uplifting rural and suburban communities while generating more profit.

More than a homegrown local dairy darling

Farm Fresh has grown from a small local dairy farm in Mawai Kota Tinggi, Malaysia, to a large business with operations across the Asia-Pacific region. The brand that was once loved largely by local aunties and uncles is now adored by markets outside of Malaysia, such as Singapore, Australia and Brunei[249].

To meet the burgeoning demand, Farm Fresh has plans to scale up their Kyabram facility in Australia, which will be the hub for dairy exports of Farm Fresh products in the Asia-Pacific region. Farm Fresh also aims to expand into the Indonesia and Philippines markets, which are rapidly developing economies with large populations and thus have a larger potential for growth. Loi seeks to build the home dealership network in Indonesia and Philippines through replicating the successful Malaysian model, generating profit for the company while providing jobs for suburban and rural communities. Additionally, Farm Fresh is gearing up to expand into the consumer dairy market in Hong Kong, employing the same sales and distribution model that was utilized in Singapore[250].

The secret ingredient to tasty natural dairy . . . and success

When questioned about the reason for Farm Fresh's success in an interview with *The Peak* in 2017, Loi stated matter-of-factly, 'We've given what we promised to our customers and stuck to our traditional values and for the past five or six years, we've had uninterrupted growth of between 60 to 70 per cent each year.'[251] To ensure that the company values cascade down to every employee in Farm Fresh, from admin staff to farmhands, Loi believes that a strong culture is vital. Every chance he gets, he reinforces the notion that one of Farm Fresh's best values is putting their customers' interests and well-being first. In his opinion, 'The moment you don't keep to your brand promises, yes, you will make gains in the short run, but it will catch up to you over the long run.'[252]

To Loi, Farm Fresh's customer-centric values set the foundation for the local success and regional expansion of the business. It was precisely because Farm Fresh put their customers' welfare in mind that they responded in kind, becoming loyal consumers of the brand. Brimming with pride, Loi remarked in an interview with Singapore-based news outlet Channel NewsAsia, 'We were doing RM9 million ($2.25 million) in business for the whole year (in 2012) and then fast forward nine years later, we are doing RM9 million business a week.'[253] In 2022, Farm Fresh's net profit stood at RM78.6 million ($19.65 million), which was a 139 per cent increase from its net profit in 2021 of RM32.8 million ($8.2 million)[254].

Resilience in turbulent times

With recent black swan events such as geopolitical tensions and Covid-19, Farm Fresh, like any other company, had to combat rising costs. The previously private company's recent venture to go public with an Initial Public Offering (IPO) has garnered distressingly close attention from investors. Loi laments that shareholders tend to be more worried about short-term pressures than long-term gains. He stands by his words that no matter the challenges that come his way, so long as Farm Fresh sticks to its values, its consumers—the local aunties and uncles—will persist in their love and support for Farm Fresh. With a loyal customer base, Loi trusts that any business can continue to be resilient. By keeping to their brand promise, Farm Fresh has only raised their prices once within two years while its competitors rose prices three or four times. Ensuring that fresh milk remains affordable to all despite trying circumstances, he gains his customers' trust and support for the Farm Fresh brand.

Looking ahead, Loi comments, 'I would hope that over the years I will be able to convince these big fund managers to look into Farm Fresh as a long-term investment because our yardstick here is that we don't lose our customers, which builds brand resilience.'[255]

Reflection questions

1. What did Loi do particularly well as a leader through the initial growth phase of Farm Fresh?
2. What elements of the Steward Leadership Compass stood out? Why?
3. What elements of the Steward Leadership Compass were weak or missing altogether?
4. What lessons can we learn from the story?

Chapter 9

Riau Ecosystem Restoration (RER): Finding Purpose in Adversity: An Asian Story

'The fact that we're an Asian company with Indonesian origins, by de facto, you're already negative five, in the perception of sustainability,' shares Anderson Tanoto over lunch in an interview with *The Straits Times* in Singapore[256].

Tanoto, the thirty-four-year-old scion of the Tanoto family, has been the topic of conversation for Indonesia's booming forestry and agricultural industries as he endeavours to cultivate sustainability leadership from within Royal Golden Eagle (RGE). Headquartered in Singapore and founded in 1973 by Tanoto's father Sukanto Tanoto, RGE has risen into a resources heavyweight group of eight manufacturing companies with assets of $30 billion and a workforce of 60,000 in Singapore, Indonesia, China, Brazil and Canada. Combined, RGE's companies manage more than 1 million hectares of forests in Indonesia and Brazil. While its core competencies lie in growing and harvesting trees and energy resource development, RGE's companies have also produced sustainable natural fibres, edible oils, green packaging and natural gas. What sets RGE apart from its competitors, however, is that close to 50 per cent of its 1 million hectares is set aside as conservation areas.

Indonesia ranks eighth among the world's pulp and paper exporting nations, as of 2022[257]. It is unsurprising that Indonesia's concentrated efforts on natural resource extraction have triggered substantial repercussions for its rainforests, communities and businesses that operate across the archipelago. Indonesia's largest players, including RGE, have been shrouded for years with allegations of deforestation, land disputes with indigenous groups and drainage of carbon-rich peatland habitats that have outraged advocacy groups as recently as 2021[258]. A catalogue of multinational corporates from Unilever and Proctor & Gamble to PepsiCo, Mondelēz and Nestlé have also frequently come under scrutiny from advocacy groups to suspend sourcing from Indonesian firms.

Reading RGE's controversial headlines of its associations with environmental and societal degradation would quickly repel the most neutral consumer. Recent data is finding that consumers across all generations—from Baby Boomers to Gen Zs—are now willing to spend more for sustainable products[259]. In today's world, a company risks losing customers to competitors that are seen as more environmentally and socially responsible.

An important question therefore emerges from the throng of controversy impacting companies like RGE: Is there room for companies with such a rich and controversial history to change course and earn back trust?

With the guidance of a young, fresh and 'green' leader, RGE and its subsidiary group of companies, including APRIL, seem to have found the inspiration needed to springboard the conglomerate into a direction that is striving to make sustainability the core of its business.

Indonesia's landscape at first glance

Indonesia is renowned as a treasure chest of biodiversity. The vast archipelago hosts between 10 and 15 per cent of all known species of plants and mammals.

Located on Indonesia's Sumatra Island, the rainforest restoration project known as Riau Ecosystem Restoration (RER) is no less than a beacon of transformation and hope for industry-led conservation efforts.

RER was set up by APRIL in 2013 to restore and protect an area of biodiverse and peatland-rich rainforest that is twice the size of nearby Singapore. The RER project began with an initial 20,265 hectares of land on the Kampar Peninsula, which has expanded to over 150,693 hectares across Kampar Peninsula and Padang Island. RER comprises five sixty-year ecosystem restoration concession licenses granted by the Indonesian Ministry of Environment and Forestry[260].

The reserve is home to a vast array of rare and critically endangered animal species including pangolins, sun bears and the Sumatran Tiger, of which only about 400 to 600 are left in the wild. They are accompanied by thousands of other species that are continuing to be counted within the reserve each year, including 838 species of fauna and flora, five of Sumatra's six cat species and sixty-nine globally threatened species[261]. Preliminary estimates have even put the entire Kampala Peninsula's peatland carbon storage above 6.5 million tonnes, making it an area of growing interest to the burgeoning global carbon credit market and the Indonesian government, which has its sights set on a 2060 net-zero target[262].

Figure 19: Mosaic Plantation in Kerinci, May 2018.
Photo reproduced with permission from RGE.

A critical element of the RER project is the adoption and maintenance of an integrated production-protection ring landscape model. This model demonstrates how peat landscapes can be responsibly managed to provide forest products for society and protect biodiversity. The 'plantation ring' provides a renewable fibre resource to produce value-added products such as pulp, paper and viscose that generate economic returns and provide employment opportunities while creating a buffer zone that mitigates human encroachment, illegal logging and fires.

In August 2022, a small research team from the Stewardship Asia Centre (SAC) witnessed the unique landscape firsthand. Guided by RER's Head of Operations, Brad Sanders, through a helicopter ride, the first thing we observed as we entered the Kampar Peninsula was hectares of fibre plantations—the plantation ring—along the coastline of the peninsula, which acts as a buffer for RER concession areas. It protects and conserves the biological diversity found within the natural peat forests, which in return provides ecosystem services to downstream communities such as water storage and supply, carbon storage, fisheries and other non-timber forest products[263]. This production-protection model recognizes that development and sustainability are two sides of the same coin in Indonesia.

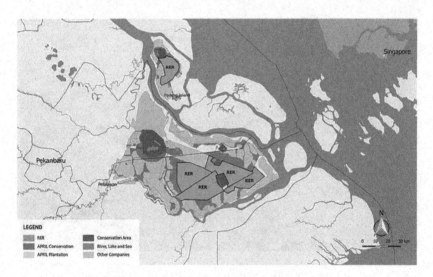

Figure 20: The Kampala Peninsula in eastern Sumatra. Reproduced with permission from RGE.

Speaking on the RER project's uniquely interdependent ecosystem, Sanders says, 'In very simple terms, the plantations need the forest as a source of water and the forest needs the plantations as a source of finance to pay for protecting and restoring it.' He further explains, 'From another business perspective, if a customer has a choice between our paper and someone else's and everything else is equal—price, quality, service—then what makes us different from the other guy? Hopefully this makes us different, because of this commitment, active management and the monitoring work that we're doing.'[264]

RGE's Anderson Tanoto shares this sentiment. 'Many people believe that it's business versus the environment and that if you harm the environment, it's actually more profitable. From a medium-to-long-term perspective, it is not and this is how we approach our business.'[265]

Laying the foundation of transformation: Riau Ecosystem Restoration (RER)

Another factor that has allowed the RER project to cultivate such an interdependent system has, in part, been Indonesia's forestry laws. Many of the forests across Indonesia are state-owned. Around half of these areas are leased to private companies in zones known as concessions, which are then largely used to turn the land into timber or palm plantations.

In 2004, however, mass environmental degradation within Indonesia's most vulnerable ecosystems caused concern as many conservation groups demanded action to reverse the trend in forest loss. In response, the government created a new classification known as Ecosystem Restoration Concessions (ERCs)[266]. These fostered public–private partnerships to 're-establish a biological balance'. Companies partnered with environmental groups to manage concessions for forest conservation and restoration, rather than for production of palm oil or timber. Companies who have been granted ERCs are able to generate income through other means such as ecotourism and carbon credits.

However, the main challenges some practitioners face in creating successful business models include high costs and the difficulties in realizing sufficient income from carbon markets, non-timber forest products and ecosystem services. Since 2004, when ERC licenses were first introduced, only sixteen licenses have been awarded to ten license holders. RER is one of the few examples of progress through such a scheme[267].

RER essentially uses a multi-stakeholder approach to conservation, working with local communities, NGOs and government agencies to develop sustainable land-use practices and protect important habitats for endangered species. In addition to collaborating with key partners such as environmental group Fauna & Flora International and local rural communities' NGO Bidara, it is still largely managed and funded by APRIL.

At the UNFCCC COP 21 in Paris in December 2015, APRIL pledged $100 million to initiate the project during the first ten years of the license period to support conservation and restoration of the RER area. Five years later, APRIL launched APRIL2030 in November 2020, its vision for meeting the challenges of the next decade[268]. As part of its Vision 2030 commitments, APRIL pledged to invest $1 in its conservation activities for every tonne of wood fibre harvested on its plantations each year. To this day, this funding commitment ensures a steady, regular budget for RER and other APRIL conservation initiatives and supports that currently stand at around $12 million to $14 million a year, which affords the staff a level of long-term planning and investment that is crucial to the sustainability of the project[269].

Overall, APRIL's decision to take on the concessions that comprise RER formed a key part of the enhanced environmental strategy it began pursuing a decade ago. Their 'one for one' commitment has even been supplemented by a pledge to halt expansion of plantation areas. With such ambitious targets, the company is now almost closing in on that target, with 480,000 hectares of managed plantations within its stable versus some 360,000 hectares of forest restoration areas and another 40,000 hectares it has identified as targets for further ERC concessions[270].

According to Craig Tribolet, APRIL's sustainability operations manager, 'The challenge now of course is there's not a lot of (natural forest) areas left in Indonesia. So, as we start to look for how to fill that remaining 80,000 hectares (of the target) it's become a much more difficult discussion: Where are we going to get it from?'[271]

He is therefore looking beyond the ERC model at potential plans that could see APRIL working with communities outside its concessions to protect and conserve smaller tracts of natural forests, perhaps totalling 10,000 to 15,000 hectares at a time. Looking for creative solutions to achieve their goals has pivoted APRIL to look beyond Riau towards the communities they can further contribute to the most.

From sustainable value creation to innovative research

Amongst the swath of conservation areas and plantations, the SAC research team was also one of the first corporate visitors to RER's eco-research camp site just on the edge of a nearby plantation site where APRIL has allocated a small area to build the camp. Located at the heart of Kampar Peninsula, the Eco-Research Camp is RER's operational base and houses the Tropical Peatland Science Hub for further study of this ecosystem. This pseudo luxury hybrid solar powered camp acts as a scientific hub for peatland, flora and fauna research and a place to stay for APRIL's corporate guests.

The eco-camp promises to bring scientists, academics and conservationists from across the region and around the globe to RER to facilitate the collection of crucial data. Its location provides strategic access to the restoration activities on the ground, which helps visitors to really understand the challenges of managing and restoring a landscape of that size[272].

Figure 21: Aerial view of the Eco-Research Camp on nearby plantation site wherein APRIL has allocated a small area to build the camp. Photo is taken in August 2022 by SAC Research Team.

As research is a key pillar of the RER project, located 18 km from Eco-Research Camp, visitors can also learn more about APRIL Group's science-based approach in measuring greenhouse gas (GHG) flux in a natural peat swamp ecosystem. We were able to visit and scale one of the four GHG flux towers operated by APRIL's scientists to gather robust data on the exchange of GHG across four different landscapes of peatland and forests. APRIL has funded these greenhouse gas monitoring towers to the tune of $1 million each, where scientists have been mapping seasonal changes in methane and carbon emissions from the forest.

Figure 22: SAC's research team had the opportunity to scale one of the 48-metre-tall GHG flux towers near the Eco-Research Camp, alongside Mr Bey Soo Khiang, Vice-Chairman of RGE and Chairman of APRIL and Ms Sharon Chong, Vice President, Group Sustainability and External Affairs. From Left to Right: Joanna Soh, Bey Soo Khiang, Annisah Smith, Sharon Chong and Rajeev Peshawaria. Source: Stewardship Asia Centre.

Access to the eco-camp additionally allows research opportunities in camera trap installations to pinpoint key species, bird monitoring, exploration of native tree nurseries, restoration planting and much more.

Transparency amidst a chequered past

APRIL is one of the world's largest manufacturers of wood pulp and fibre, the basis of myriad everyday products from office printing paper to viscose fabrics. Its products are utilized every day in households globally. The very fact that they have embarked on such lofty goals is to be lauded, especially for other countries seeking examples of companies in the developing world moving towards conserving and restoring previously degraded lands. However, a question remains. Given the economic pressures Indonesia is facing and its heavy reliance on its natural resources to drive its growth, is it possible for the country's plantation business sector to co-exist with transformational goals that marry nature restoration and profit?

Many environmental groups acknowledge some of the success achieved at RER and the progress APRIL has made towards addressing its environmental impacts over the past decade. Even so, some critics remain and contend that the company's path to becoming a truly environmentally sustainable enterprise remains an ambitious task due to the nature of being a pulp and paper business in Indonesia's complex political and economic environment.

However, this does not seem to discourage RGE's next-generation leader Anderson Tanoto. According to Tanoto, 'Putting yourself up for scrutiny is healthy. There's no replacement for transparency, monitoring, reporting and verification. In some sense, companies build their credibility by doing that. When you share success stories, but also failure stories—things that did not work in terms of sustainability, it gives a very humbling and very real story of the sustainability journey.'[273]

Transparency is therefore becoming a key commitment among RGE companies, with APRIL leading the way towards remedying a legacy of environmental and social scrutiny.

APRIL set up a Stakeholder Advisory Committee of independent forestry and social experts to oversee the implementation of its Sustainable Forestry Management Policy. To strengthen its commitments to forest conservation and respecting the rights of indigenous and local communities, the committee also selected independent verification auditor KPMG to assess APRIL's progress towards meeting its policy goals[274]. Audit reports are published on APRIL's website. As part of its role, the committee facilitates stakeholder dialogues to enable stakeholders to share their concerns and feedback on APRIL's operations so APRIL can address them accordingly. Where relevant, the committee and KPMG also investigate and review NGO claims and publicly report details of any required action.

APRIL also has in place a grievance mechanism that was developed following consultation with local and international NGOs. The mechanism provides external stakeholders, especially local communities, a transparent way to raise their concerns related to APRIL's operations and those of its suppliers. Another example of APRIL's transparency and accountability was its public efforts to regain Forest Stewardship Council (FSC) certification for its products. Although APRIL withdrew from the FSC in 2013 after several NGOs filed a complaint against the company for large-scale deforestation activities, APRIL has since been seeking reassociation with the FSC, aware of the credibility that certification carries[275].

To secure FSC association and potentially gain FSC labels on its products in future, companies considered to have driven deforestation in the past are required to take proactive actions to address their past harm. To begin that process of reassociation, a company must publicly acknowledge its past environmental and social impacts. After this, FSC develops a bespoke roadmap, setting out a multitude of criteria and remedial actions that the company must fulfil, including the restoration of deforested and degraded lands and reconciliation efforts with effected communities[276]. Additionally, through the new definitions of corporate group, FSC now recognizes the importance of assessing the harm caused by associated companies across the entire operations of their corporate groups, including shadow companies.

By FSC's assessment, 'Since 1994 over 530,000 hectares of forest cover change has taken place within lands managed by APRIL and its suppliers, including almost 436,000 hectares of "irreversible forest conversion" from dense forest to commercial plantations.'[277] It was a stark reminder of the environmental damage already done and in 2020, APRIL officially wrote to the FSC and acknowledged that very assessment.

'On behalf of the management and shareholders, APRIL Group expresses its acknowledgement of the impact of its operations since 1993, including the associated potential environmental and social harms, in Riau, Indonesia, where it operates,' the letter states[278]. 'APRIL Group is committed to fully and sincerely engage in the process of remediation and ending disassociation with FSC.' Given the potential reputational and legal risks attached to such a letter, it is no insignificant acknowledgement.

Looking towards the future

In his role as Managing Director at RGE, Tanoto is targeting that by '2030 the asset base of the group will increase by more than $30 billion to top $60 billion'[279]. To do so, APRIL is about to take a sizable risk towards achieving Tanoto's ambitious sustainability goals by investing $2.2 billion into a new paperboard facility located at its integrated production base in Riau. This new facility is one of the largest investments that APRIL has made since its founding in 1993 and is scheduled to begin operations in June 2023[280].

Tanoto hopes that such a massive investment will meet the rising global demand for recyclable packaging to replace those made from plastic. 'I believe the transition away from plastic waste packaging will happen sooner than later,' Tanoto exclaims. 'And the only way we can make it happen sooner than later is to make . . . our packaging scalable, big, good quality and low cost.'[281]

While one of the biggest challenges the company continues to face is perception, this is just one of the steps Tanoto is taking to revolutionize the work and legacy of the RGE group to move the firm towards achieving their sustainable development vision[282].

In the last ten years alone, APRIL has made huge strides towards advancing their business models. In addition to acknowledging some of the past environmental harm associated with its business, it is investing in the needs and transformation of the future, while spending millions of dollars a year on a challenging rainforest restoration project, which it argues is inherently a long-term investment for the island of Sumatra and their business. APRIL 2030 is its vision for meeting the challenges of the next decade[283] and the company has made good progress on its pledge since its launch in November 2020[284].

With APRIL bolstering its own sustainability commitments as it sets its sights on achieving a net-zero-emission, nature-positive future, accusations of greenwashing will undoubtedly continue. Some may even view the operational changes RGE and APRIL are experiencing to be a path towards redemption. Nonetheless, we could consider it to be a complete shift to purposeful action. It is important to recognize that the investments that RGE and APRIL are undertaking will not only benefit the company as a whole, but the research, partnerships and sustainable value in which they are investing today will inevitably have trickling impacts on the societies and the environments they operate in for years to come.

Many will inevitably object and exclaim, 'How can such recent acts absolve RGE of their past?' In truth, this is a difficult question to answer. However, considering the magnitude of their ongoing transformational change, APRIL could very well come to pioneer more than a unique, multi-million-dollar rainforest reserve. With consumer demand for sustainable products, coupled with a looming climate change crisis on the horizon, the RER project could progress into an Asian story worth paying attention to in the years to come.

Only time will tell if the company fully achieves its sustainability ambitions. Meanwhile, however, it is encouraging to see the next generation of leaders like Tanoto championing sustainable change in a region fraught with environmental degradation and development constraints, while pushing the boundaries of sustainability 'to show the world that Asian companies like us, a privately owned family organization, can still take a lot of policies on sustainability that are as good, if not better, than the MNCs'[285].

Reflection questions

1. Will Anderson Tanoto succeed in his endeavour to make sustainability the centrepiece of his business strategy? Why or why not?
2. What elements of the Steward Leadership Compass stood out? Why?
3. What elements of the Steward Leadership Compass were weak or missing altogether?
4. What lessons can we learn from the story?

Chapter 10

The Boeing 737 Max Twin Tragedies

This story is collated entirely from publicly available information about the crashes and their subsequent investigations.

Monday dawned on Tanjung Kawarang, West Java, Indonesia. Thirty-one-year-old captain Bhavye Suneja was set to fly Lion Air's latest addition to its fleet—the Boeing 737 Max 8. It was Boeing's latest update to the older 737 models, touted as the latter's more fuel-efficient sibling. Having amassed more than 6,000 flight hours[286], the Indian-born captain was no stranger to flying. This short, one-hour domestic flight was but a walk in the park. Even then, the ever-methodical captain had arrived early to complete preflight inspections[287].

But what he could not have possibly known was that a different crew had experienced a problem with the aircraft the evening before. It had flown from Jakarta to Bali, where a malfunctioning angle-of-attack sensor was replaced[288]. A plane's AoA sensors are in its nose, measuring how high it is pitched up or down. It plays a crucial role in warning pilots of a potential stall.

On the flight back to Jakarta, the pilots had struggled to control the plane and made a distress call. Only with the help of a third pilot who was hitching a ride had they managed to restore manual control[289]. But because the issue was not recorded properly, the aircraft was allowed to take off the next day[290].

At 6.18 a.m., Lion Air Flight 610 was cleared for take-off. Four seconds after take-off, the plane's sensors started recording two different airspeeds. The on-board sensors were also giving altitude readings more than 200 ft apart.

Not knowing which reading to rely on, First Officer Harvino asked the air traffic controller to confirm the altitude of the plane. It was 900 ft. On the plane, one display said 790 ft and the other said 1,040 ft.

Ten seconds later, the controller noted that the plane's altitude was decreasing from 1,700 ft to 1,600 ft. The plane's controls still showed different speeds. Suneja and Harvino agreed that the plane should climb to 5,000 feet.

Eight seconds later, an alarm warned that the plane was flying at a steep angle. The plane suddenly descended 600 ft. Oddly enough, one AoA sensor said the plane's nose was pointing 18° up while the other said it's pointing 3° down. The plane then warned of low speed. Just four seconds later, it warned of a possible stall. The plane was warning of both too much speed and not enough speed.

Eleven seconds later, an automatic system activated. It pushed the nose down for two seconds before Suneja interrupted it, pushing the nose up for six seconds. The system activated twenty times in the next five minutes, pushing the plane's nose down each time until Suneja interrupted it.

Suneja and Harvino could not figure out what was happening. In his panic, Suneja even referred to his own flight as 650 instead of 610.

Suneja asked Harvino to take control once again. Harvino pushed the plane's nose up and said, 'I have control.' He kept pointing the nose up. The automatic system activated twice in the next twelve seconds. Suneja asked the controller to clear all planes from 3,000 feet above and below the plane to avoid collisions.

Harvino told Suneja that the plane was flying downwards.

'It's okay,' said Suneja.

The automatic system activated again. The plane's rate of descent jumped from 1,920 ft per minute to 10,000 ft per minute, giving Suneja and Harvino only seconds to avoid hitting the Java Sea.

At 6.31 a.m., the system activated one final time. Air traffic control tried six times to contact the pilots[291].

Lion Air Flight 610 killed 186 adults, one child and two infants[292].

The aftermath

Following the tragedy, news reports were pointing fingers at the country, the airline and the pilot[293]. As Indonesia's low-cost carrier that was previously banned from flying to Europe and the US, Lion Air did not have the best reputation. Some news reports also accused the airline of not providing sufficient pilot training for the 737 Max.

People were also questioning the pilot's credentials, even saying that this tragedy would not have occurred with an American pilot[294]. Ironically, Captain Suneja was trained in the US[295].

Once Indonesian authorities retrieved both black boxes and started investigating the events of the flight, the evidence began to point towards possible faults with the aircraft. A single faulty sensor was found[296]. Yet, altitude readings showed that the plane was careening up and down and audio recordings revealed that the pilots were wrestling with the plane for control for the whole twelve minutes of the flight. It did not make sense. How could one faulty sensor cause such a catastrophe?

The world's attention was slowly shifting to the airplane's manufacturer—Boeing. The company responded by issuing additional bulletins to operators and pilots, redirecting them to existing flight procedures to handle similar conditions[297].

The scale of the tragedy still was not explained. Pressure was mounting on Boeing to provide a plausible explanation.

Finally, Boeing released a statement acknowledging that the Lion Air plane had an MCAS malfunction[298]. MCAS was not a widely known term, even among pilots. Only when pilots went back to the Max's manual did they find 'MCAS' in the 'Abbreviations' section, the only mention in the entire operating manual[299]. It stood for 'Maneuvering Characteristics Augmentation System'. Suneja and Harvino had no idea that MCAS was what they were wrestling with the entire time.

Taming the unions

Pilots were not made aware of a software that could potentially kill them.

In an unprecedented move, Boeing's senior executives, including a senior test pilot and a lobbyist, went down to the Allied Pilots Association's headquarters in Fort Worth, Texas, on November 27, supposedly for a briefing on MCAS[300].

The meeting did not turn out to be a safety briefing. There were no PowerPoint presentations, no documents[301]. Just a promise that Boeing will have a software fix in six weeks. In the meantime, the 737 Max aircrafts would continue flying.

For pilots, this was not enough. They were angry that Boeing did not include MCAS in the training manual.

'I would think that there would be a priority of putting explanations of things that could kill you,' a pilot told Boeing executives[302].

But beyond that, they wanted to know their aircraft better, as would any pilot. And the fact that Boeing concealed the existence of MCAS made pilots wonder if Boeing was still withholding other information[303].

'I don't know that understanding this system would've changed the outcome. In a million miles, you're going to maybe fly this airplane, maybe once you're going to see this, ever,' said a Boeing executive[304].

The pilots could not believe their ears. Why was Boeing not treating the crash as an emergency? They did not give a safety briefing, made a promise that seemed impossible to fulfil and refused responsibility for the crash because 'no one has yet to conclude that the sole cause of this was this function on the airplane'[305].

Boeing's then-President and CEO Dennis Muilenberg even went on national television to say that 'the 737 Max is safe'[306].

The 737 Max is not safe

Five months after the Lion Air tragedy, Ethiopian Airlines Flight 302 carrying 149 passengers and 8 crew members took off at 8.38 a.m. on March 10, 2019.

Unlike Captain Suneja and First Officer Harvino, twenty-nine-year-old Captain Yared Getachew and his crew knew that MCAS was operating in the background. Captain Getachew had been flying for almost nine years and had logged a total of 8,122 flight hours, half of which were on the Boeing 737. When he realized that MCAS had been activated, Captain Getachew disabled the MCAS software by shutting down the electrical trim tab system, just as Boeing had said[307].

But in doing so, he had also shut off the ability to trim the stabilizer on the plane's tail into a neutral position and the pilots had to do it manually[308]. But because the pilots had left the engines on full take-off power, the plane was accelerating too quickly and there was too much pressure on the stabilizer.

The air traffic controller had earlier given them permission to return to the airport and had cleared other flights. Captain Getachew asked his first officer to turn the electrical trim system back on in hopes that it will allow him to return the stabilizer to its neutral position. But turning on the electrical trim system also reactivated MCAS, which pushed the plane's nose further down[309].

Six minutes later, the 737 Max dove into the ground and killed all 157 on board, leaving a crater 33 ft deep[310]. The 737 Max had now caused the deaths of 346 people in just five months.

Now an emergency?

The fact that two crashes of the same aircraft occurred within five months of each other is unthinkable in modern aviation technology.

As the governing body which oversees the Boeing Company, the US Federal Aviation Authority had the power to ground the Boeing 737 Max aircrafts. They did not.

Instead, the Chinese grounded the aircraft on their own volition the day right after the Ethiopian Airlines crash[311]. Soon after, several countries across Asia, Europe and the Middle East followed suit[312]. Eventually, satellite data showed that the aircrafts were only flying over North America, where former US President Donald Trump's administration and the FAA still deemed it safe[313]. Faced with international pressure, Trump finally ordered the 737 Max to be grounded. It is the only airplane ever grounded by a US president.

Fading into the shadows

Even after two deadly crashes that clearly involved a design flaw in the aircraft, Boeing was still trying to shove the blame. Like their response to the Lion Air crash, they were pointing fingers at 'foreign' pilots and incapable crews. During a news conference, then-CEO Dennis Muilenburg said, 'Procedures were not completely followed.'[314] Later on, it was discovered that pilots had only ten seconds to react to the situation before they were doomed[315]. Boeing's disregard for the safety of the pilot, the flight crew and the flying public was startling.

What happened to the Boeing that was known for its culture of safety, integrity and 'engineering first'?

A culture shift?

Right from the start, Boeing was an engineering-first company. It was founded in 1916 by American lumber industrialist William E. Boeing in Seattle, Washington. At its core, Boeing was engineer-led and produced designs that its engineers were proud of. Employees enjoyed a family-like culture that operated on a 'go-for-it-and-damn-the-expenses—but not damn the quality' philosophy. And it served Boeing well. Passengers were fond of saying, 'If it ain't Boeing, I ain't going.'

Did all this begin to change in 1997? In a $14-billion deal that year, Boeing acquired McDonnell Douglas, a Missouri-based aerospace company[316]. Harry Stonecipher, CEO of McDonnell Douglas, was made Chief Operating Officer of Boeing. Stonecipher and John McDonnell, the former chair of McDonnell Douglas' board, were now the two largest individual shareholders of the merged companies[317].

Boeing's management suddenly became dominated by former McDonnell Douglas executives and Boeing's focus and strategy shifted. Stonecipher became CEO of Boeing just four years in, in 2001. Stonecipher was laser focused on cost control and profit maximization. Planes had to be made cheaper and faster. According to Boeing's former quality manager and whistle-blower Cynthia Kitchens, quality managers and inspectors were laid off so mechanics could finish their job more quickly. Where there used to be about fifteen quality managers in a building per shift, there now was one[318].

In 2001, Boeing moved its headquarters from Seattle, where it had been since the company's founding in 1916, to Chicago[319]. The move was particularly disorientating for Boeing's long-serving employees.

Boeing's history had been written on the same runway from the beginning, at the Boeing Field.

Quality began to dip. According to a *New York Times* report, Boeing 'often valued production speed over quality' and that workers at the plant have routinely left metal shavings, tools and other potentially hazardous debris near electrical wiring in planes coming off the assembly line[320]. Once, a ladder was found near the jackscrew at the plane's tail after a test flight of a 787. The ladder just needed to drop and the plane would have gone down[321].

Given the tradition of Boeing's quality-first culture, several employees had raised their concerns to management. But the open culture was no more. William Hobek, a quality manager at Boeing's 787 plant in South Carolina, sued Boeing in 2016, claiming that he was fired after reporting defects multiple times[322]. As reported in the Netflix documentary *Downfall: The Case Against Boeing*, management had reportedly said they did not want any problems in documentation[323]. Dr Amy Edmondson, Novartis Professor of Leadership and Management at Harvard Business School, described Boeing's production facilities as a 'textbook case of how the absence of psychological safety . . . can lead to disastrous results'[324].

Competition with Airbus

Against this backdrop, it's probably safe to assume that Boeing had rushed the production of the 737 Max, especially as its main competitor Airbus threatened its market share.

After a series of mergers and acquisitions in the 1990s, Airbus and Boeing dominated the aircraft manufacturing industry. In 1996, Boeing took about 60 per cent of the industry's new commercial aircraft orders. Airbus was far behind it, at about 35 per cent[325].

Boeing was still holding a comfortable proportion of the market share until 2005 when Airbus overtook Boeing. In 2008, Airbus delivered 482 planes, while Boeing delivered only 375[326]. In 2011, American Airlines, Boeing's exclusive customer for over a decade, was ready to order hundreds of new, fuel-efficient jets from Airbus—the A320neo. The chief executive of American Airlines told Boeing's then-CEO, W. James McNerney Jr., that Boeing had to move more aggressively if it wants the business[327].

As Boeing's CEO without any aviation background, McNerney made the executive decision to create an upgraded version of the 737 instead of designing a new plane[328]. Developing a new plane would have taken a decade but updating the 737 would take just six years[329]. It is no surprise that under Boeing's new leadership, it opted for the latter. This tactic succeeded to some degree—American Airlines made deals with both Airbus and Boeing.

Inside Boeing, the manufacturing process was frenetic. Engineers and designers were working at twice the normal rate. Designers were producing sixteen technical drawings a week and at this speed, they could not afford to provide all the details necessary[330]. The internal assembly designs left out the usual, intricate instructions like specifying the tools to use to install a certain wire, a situation that could lead to a faulty connection[331].

Crucial to getting the Maxes to airlines was also removing any roadblocks to approval from the relevant authorities. Key to this was ensuring that the new model was similar to the earlier 737 models, which had already been approved by the FAA and the European Union Aviation Safety Agency. By keeping to a variation of an older model, airlines could also save on pilot training, making the Max a price-competitive option. The 737 Max had to basically be a ground-breaking, 21st-century enhancement that flew like the original 737 from 1964 and the 737 Classic from 1980[332].

The development of MCAS

Boeing was limited by the original 737 frame in its bid to compete with the more fuel-efficient A320neo. Because the 737 was designed for airports in the 1960s, its design meant that the newer, bigger, more fuel-efficient engines had to be moved forward and upward whereas the 737's engines would traditionally hang under the wings[333].

During an internal flight test using a scale model with the wingspan of an eagle, results showed that there was a tendency for the plane's nose to pitch upward during an extreme manoeuvre. To certify an airplane, the FAA requires pilots to safely execute this manoeuvre[334].

This was a problem. The larger engines changed the aerodynamics of the plane, altering the handling of the plane in a way that did not meet the FAA's requirements. After attempts at a physical fix failed, Boeing resorted to installing MCAS, despite its aversion to such automated fixes that might seize control of a situation from the pilot[335].

Conceptually, MCAS was a simple fix. When it sensed that the nose was pitched too high up, it would push the nose down by manipulating the plane's horizontal tail. With this software operating in the background, pilots could handle the Max like it did any other 737.

But engineers still wanted to give MCAS as little power as possible, so the MCAS required both a high angle of attack—the pitching of the nose—and high G-force for it to activate. Even then, engineers limited the change that MCAS could command.

After MCAS performed exceedingly well in a simulator, Boeing was prepared to get the Max certified by the FAA. It detailed its plan for MCAS in documents for the FAA, including a safety assessment of the MCAS. In its submission to the FAA, Boeing calculated and categorized the effect of possible MCAS failures. These categories determine the level of redundancy needed to be built into the MCAS. Only one instance of an MCAS failure was classified as 'hazardous', defined as an event causing fatal injuries to a small number of people[336]. Such events demanded more than one sensor for redundancy, except when they are unlikely to be encountered.

In this case, Boeing calculated that the hazardous MCAS failure was almost 'inconceivable'[337]. This meant that MCAS did not need to have redundancy built in and could be activated by just one sensor in all circumstances despite needing two types of information to activate.

MCAS undergoes changes

According to *The Seattle Times,* Boeing was about a third of the way through flight testing in 2016 when they found another problem[338]. The Max's handling not only changed in extreme manoeuvres but under certain low-speed conditions as well.

Boeing's engineers then decided to expand the scope and power of MCAS, increasing the degree of change that the MCAS could command and removing the G-force requirement needed for MCAS to activate. The MCAS had essentially become a lot more powerful than when it first started out. Despite making such drastic changes, Boeing did not inform the FAA.

Instead, they conducted their own safety analysis and concluded that there was not any added risk to the previous analysis they had submitted. Unsurprisingly, discussions around the new MCAS design were also limited during flight testing. Boeing was in a rush to complete the 737 Max to catch up with its competitor, the A320neo. Former Boeing test pilots described a culture of pressure inside the company to limit flight testing since it could delay projects, costing Boeing money[339].

FAA certification of the 737 Max

'Would you put your family on a Max simulator trained aircraft? I wouldn't,' wrote a Boeing employee in a February 2018 message exchange[340].

On March 9, 2017, the 737 Max gained FAA certification[341]. But how?

As we learned earlier, the FAA was kept in the dark about the drastic changes in MCAS. Because the FAA relies on the manufacturer to identify the significant changes from previous aircraft models, it missed MCAS because Boeing did not flag it[342].

It is important to note that Boeing was not technically in violation of any FAA guidance by not directly informing FAA certification engineers of the changes to MCAS. While these changes were included in internal coordination documents, the FAA did not require these deliverables[343].

More crucially, FAA certification engineers delegated an increasing amount of the Max's certification work to Boeing's own engineers during the 2012 to 2017 certification. Near the end of the process, as much as 87 per cent of certification plans had been passed back to Boeing[344]. While FAA managers said that it was typical for delegation to increase over time as the agency gained confidence in Boeing's capabilities, it was clear that this confidence was misplaced and that the FAA needed more independence from the company it was overseeing. By delegating the inspection functions to Boeing, the FAA inevitably created conflicts of interest that corrupted the system meant to protect the safety of the flying public[345]. An internal FAA survey even found that many employees of the agency's safety arm were 'overly concerned with achieving the business-oriented outcomes of industry stakeholders'[346].

No pilot training to save costs

Another factor that emerged in the investigations following both accidents was the lack of pilot training. Right from the beginning, Boeing intended for the A320neo's competitor to be an enhanced variation of its highly popular 737.

For airlines, this represented huge cost savings. An improved version of an old plane would mean that it saves pilot training costs. Pilot training was the second major cost for airlines, after fuel. And Boeing harped on that in its marketing to airlines. It insisted that no simulator training was required for pilots. Boeing's tactic worked. As of early 2019, it sold over 5000 Maxes, the fastest-selling aircraft in Boeing's history[347].

But internal investigations would show that there were orders from Boeing's top management to insist that no training was required for pilots, even though with the installation of the more powerful MCAS, the Max was different from the older 737s[348].

An email between unnamed Boeing employees in June 2013, during the early developmental stages of the MCAS, included meeting minutes that stated: 'If we emphasize MCAS is a new function there may be a greater certification and training impact. Treat as addition to Speed Trim.'[349] Speed Trim was an existing system that pilots were familiar with.

If the FAA required pilot training for the new MCAS software, the Max would be less competitive for airlines. It would also mean that the Max could take longer to get certified since it may not be considered as a variant of the 737 anymore.

Without simulator training, all that the pilots needed was a fifty-six-minute iPad refresher course, which left out any mention of MCAS[350]. Ironically, Lion Air had considered putting its pilots through simulator training before flying the Max[351].

According to a *Fortune* magazine article, an employee wrote in June 2017, 'Now friggin Lion Air might need a sim to fly the MAX and maybe because of their own stupidity. I'm scrambling trying to figure out how to unscrew this now! idiots.'[352]

A change from the inside

This whole debacle unfolded right under the CEO's nose. Dennis Muilenburg was fired by the board on December 23, 2019[353].

'Mr Muilenburg is not entitled to—and did not receive—any severance or separation payments in connection with his retirement after more than 30 years with the Company,' wrote Boeing[354].

Since the tragedies, Boeing has been on a path to renew its safety culture. The company's Chief Aerospace Safety Officer Mike Delaney is leading a new safety programme that will use analytical data from airlines, suppliers and Boeing's factories to highlight risks. Employees will also be encouraged to speak up when they notice safety issues[355].

Boeing's engineering teams have done root-cause analysis to dig deeper into the 737 Max tragedies. The company's design practices have been changed to take more account of pilot reactions and to ensure that automatic flight controls like MCAS have limited authority and sufficient sensors to ensure redundancy in case of a failure[356].

Reflection questions

1. What led to the decline in Boeing's culture, which was once known for its focus on quality and safety?
2. What elements of the Steward Leadership Compass stood out? Why?
3. What elements of the Steward Leadership Compass were weak or missing altogether?
4. What lessons can we learn from the story?

Chapter 11

Volkswagen: When the Mighty Stray

This story is collated entirely from publicly available information about the VW Emissions Scandal.

In a clearing in the hills of West Virginia stood an unsuspecting shed made of corrugated iron[357]. It was here in 2012, at the heart of West Virginia University's mechanical engineering faculty, that a professor and three of his students uncovered a $30-billion multi-year fraud.

Dr Daniel Carder, head of the West Virginia University Center for Alternative Fuels, Engines and Emissions, had just received a $69,000 grant from the International Council on Clean Transportation to test diesel emissions[358]. The ICCT is an independent, non-profit organization that aims to provide objective research and scientific analysis to environmental regulators[359]. The team of gearheads were ecstatic. They had always been fascinated by the oxymoronic 'clean diesel' that German car manufacturers were touting[360].

An accidental discovery

Dan and his team got their hands on a Volkswagen Jetta, a VW Passat and a BMW X5[361]. The goal was to find out why diesel cars in the US were supposedly much less polluting than those in Europe. The ICCT hoped that by proving diesels could be clean by testing them in the US, they could take this data to Europe and show that they should be doing it too[362].

It was widely known that the Environmental Protection Agency in the US had stricter regulation standards than Europe[363]. While Europe focused on reducing the effects of global warming by limiting greenhouse gases, the US focused on clean air. This meant that the US' emission standards not only included carbon dioxide and greenhouse gases but extended to nitrogen oxides as well. Nitrogen oxides are a key component of smog and can cause various respiratory illnesses and various cancers and heart problems[364].

For Arvind Thiruvengadam, one of Dan's three students, this opportunity was perfect. He was a specialist in emissions testing and had years of experience working with diesel engines[365]. He was passionate about the environment and was also looking for ways to reduce emissions from vehicles. Dan, on the other hand, was a skilled engineer and was known for his expertise in finding a way to reduce emissions from diesel engines and make vehicles more environmentally friendly.

The results came as a complete shock. The hypothesis the team was working on was that the vehicles were clean, but the tests showed otherwise. Volkswagen's cars were outstanding in the lab, delivering fuel economy and optimal performance while producing low emissions. But on the road, nitrogen oxide emissions were through the roof. Nitrogen oxide emissions from the Jetta exceeded EPA standards by fifteen to thirty-five times, while that of the Passat was five to twenty times the standard[366]. The discrepancies were only found in Volkswagen's vehicles—the BMW was generally at or below the standard[367].

The results were so unexpected that Dan, Arvind and the team kept double checking their procedures, thinking that there was something wrong with their instruments or process[368]. But the results remained the same. Just as they have done for other emissions tests, Arvind and the team diligently wrote the report and handed it to the ICCT. They did not think much of it then, especially not the fact that this report would later result in a cascade of charges against the automaker.

Defeat devices

To the ICCT, there was only one possibility that could explain the huge discrepancy in the results—Volkswagen was using a defeat device, a software or mechanism that can change vehicle emissions levels[369]. This was not new to the industry or Volkswagen for that matter.

In 1974, Volkswagen Group and its American subsidiary paid a $120,000 fine to settle a complaint filed by the US Environmental Protection Agency[370]. Volkswagen failed to report to US regulators that it had included temperature-sensing devices on certain vehicles that would disable systems that controlled emissions at low temperatures[371]. Although they paid the fine, Volkswagen denied any wrongdoing[372].

About twenty-five years later in 1999, Audi, a brand under the Volkswagen Group, had developed a software to reduce the noise of a diesel engine at idle[373]. To achieve that, the software increased emissions. This time, there were no consequences. This software would later serve as the basis for Volkswagen's defeat devices[374].

A bold ambition

But the question remains: Why would Volkswagen's engineers cheat emissions tests?

It all started in the early 2000s when the US Environmental Protection Agency introduced standards that required manufacturers to reduce nitrogen oxide emissions by 70 per cent[375]. This posed a monumental challenge to automakers looking to offer fuel-efficient diesel vehicles in the US. While diesel engines could offer better performance than most gasoline engines, they emit more nitrogen oxides[376]. This led to most automobile manufacturers, including Volkswagen's main competitor Toyota, investing in hybrid cars and other more environmentally friendly options of internal combustion engines[377].

But where other manufacturers saw an obstacle, Volkswagen saw an opportunity. They decided to face the challenge head on and develop a diesel engine that would meet the stricter EPA standards, establishing a competitive advantage for them in the US market[378]

Volkswagen was desperate to expand its market share in the US, especially during the tenure of the ambitious Martin Winterkorn. In December 2007, Winterkorn took over as CEO of Volkswagen Group. Winterkorn was no stranger to Volkswagen. He started out as an assistant to the member of the board for quality assurance at Audi in 1981, having been handpicked and groomed by Ferdinand Piëch, the grandson of Ferdinand Porsche, founder of the Porsche sports car company[379].

Ferdinand Piëch became Volkswagen Group's Chief Executive in 1993 and Chairman in 2002[380]. An engineer by training, he was notorious for his cutthroat management style and intolerance of failure—a culture that sowed the seeds for the $30-billion Dieselgate scandal[381]. 'It was like North Korea without labour camps,' was *Der Spiegel* magazine's infamous description of Volkswagen's automobile factories under his leadership[382].

Winterkorn was Piëch's protégé in the earlier years of their relationship and he later became the CEO of Volkswagen Group in 2007, where he successfully remained in power until he stepped down in the wake of Dieselgate[383]. A hands-on, perfectionist executive like Piëch, Winterkorn was known to carry a gauge in his jacket to measure the gaps between car doors and bodies, which he considered an indicator of quality[384]. He was also known for publicly berating subordinates and banging car parts on tables to emphasize a point[385].

Strategy 2018

Like Piëch, Winterkorn was also ambitious. Soon after he became CEO, Winterkorn set aggressive targets, culminating in 'Strategy 2018', a growth strategy launched in December 2007[386]. Speaking with Forbes in 2013, Winterkorn said the goal of Strategy 2018 was to make Volkswagen 'the world's most profitable, fascinating and sustainable automobile manufacturer'[387].

So, while most manufacturers turned away from diesel engines when the US EPA tightened its emissions standards, Winterkorn saw that as an opportunity to overtake Toyota, its biggest rival in the US market.

As Toyota worked on its hybrid technology, Volkswagen made a huge bet on 'clean diesel'. Investing in this concept was a logical move for Europe, where emission standards were easier to meet and where diesel engines were more common[388]. But Volkswagen's engineers were faced with an insurmountable problem in the US and were scrambling for a way to deliver performance while meeting the new emission standards and staying within budget[389]. Unfortunately, the pollution control technology they adopted did not deliver the performance and low emissions advertised by Volkswagen.

In a multi-million-dollar campaign that included Super Bowl ads, online social media campaigns and print advertising, Volkswagen's marketing team touted the environmental benefits and impressive performance by its diesel vehicles[390]. The advertisements promised that drivers could have their cake and eat it too—high performance, low emissions.

Behind the scenes, the engineers did not have time to come up with a proper fix. It would take a few more years before they developed the equipment sufficient to meet EPA's diesel regulations.

Yet, admitting that they could not overcome the technical challenge of achieving both performance and low emissions was not an option if they wanted to keep their jobs. Winterkorn's perfectionist tendencies and abhorrence of failure had perpetuated a culture of micromanagement and concealment, where subordinates were afraid to admit failure or contradict superiors[391]. A consultant who had worked with Volkswagen reported that the pressure from management was intense[392]. Engineers feared for their jobs and felt that they could not voice any problems they encountered[393]. The only way forward? The infamous defeat devices.

They adapted Audi's defeat device from 1999 and enhanced the software to monitor speed, engine operation, air pressure and even the position of the steering wheel to determine if the vehicle was being tested[394]. Once the defeat device detected that the vehicle was being tested, it would enter a safety mode with decreased power and performance, temporarily reducing nitrogen oxide emissions and meeting the strict US EPA standards[395].

Volkswagen succeeded. They sold more than 12 million vehicles, including about 500,000 in the US. Volkswagen's Jetta model year 2006 even won the 'Green Car of the Year' award at the Los Angeles auto show in 2008[396]. By 2014, Volkswagen Group had already achieved its goal of selling more than 10 million units, more than half of which were attributed to the Volkswagen Passenger Cars brand[397].

The revelation

Volkswagen was riding the waves of its success until the ICCT turned the report over to the US EPA and the California Air Resources Board (CARB) in May 2014[398]. CARB had even stricter standards than the EPA as California was trying to limit smog in Los Angeles.

When CARB approached Volkswagen to explain the discrepancies in the tests, the company denied any wrongdoing, attributing the excess emissions to 'various technical issues' and 'unexpected' real-world conditions[399]. In December 2014, it issued a voluntary recall of about 500,000 vehicles in the US, allegedly to implement a software patch[400].

But CARB was not satisfied. Together with the EPA, CARB said it wanted to do 'confirmatory' tests, running those from May 2015[401]. Two months later, CARB informed Volkswagen that the test vehicles still produced emissions exceeding state and federal limits[402].

In July 2015, US regulators threatened not to certify Volkswagen model year 2016 vehicles for sale in the US[403]. This sent Volkswagen into a frenzy. Several senior Volkswagen executives and engine development department employees convened at what was internally known as the 'damage table meeting' chaired by Winterkorn at the company's headquarters in Wolfsburg, Germany[404]. At this meeting, attendees and Winterkorn, especially, were informed of exactly how Volkswagen was deceiving US regulators.

It turned out that not everyone agreed with Volkswagen's decision to cheat the emissions tests. In a damning move, a VW employee revealed—against explicit instructions from his superiors—that Volkswagen had used illegal software in its 2.0-litre diesel vehicles to cheat US emissions tests[405].

The cat was officially out of the bag. On 3 September 2015, Volkswagen admitted that it had installed defeat devices in various 2.0-litre diesel vehicles sold in the US[406].

Eleven million vehicles were affected worldwide[407].

Immediately following the revelation, Volkswagen's shares plummeted over 20 per cent and reached its lowest in more than three years[408].

On 23 September 2015, Winterkorn resigned, saying that he was 'stunned' by the events over the past few days and that he was 'not aware of any wrongdoing on my part'[409].

Since then, Winterkorn has been faced with a slew of charges from both US and German prosecutors. He was charged in the US with three counts of wire fraud and for conspiring to defraud the US and VW customers to violate the Clean Air Act. In 2019, German prosecutors charged him with serious fraud, embezzlement and violating competition law and in 2021, he was charged with giving false testimony in the German parliament[410].

If convicted, Winterkorn faces up to twenty years in prison and a $25,000 fine for his wire fraud charges in the US. For conspiring to violate the Clean Air Act, he could be jailed up to five years and be fined up to $250,000[411]. He could also face a maximum of ten years in prison for his charges in Germany[412].

The bare minimum

How did one individual wield so much power over the company's culture and people? Unlike most US companies, German companies have not one, but two boards—the management board, led by the Chief Executive, and above it the supervisory board, to which the CEO reports. Theoretically, the supervisory board can hire and fire management board members and must sign off on major decisions.

The reality at Volkswagen was somewhat different. Half of Volkswagen's twenty-seat supervisory board is held by German workers in accordance with legal requirements[413]. The other half is for shareholders. Of the remaining ten seats, the firm's home state of Lower Saxony gets two. Here is the issue—representatives from Lower Saxony and the workforce share the common goal of protecting jobs at one of the state's biggest employers[414]. This meant that the interests of management, union employees and the government were aligned[415].

Four of the ten seats reserved for shareholders are also held by members of the Porsche and Piëch families, who own more than half the voting shares and tended to vote as a single bloc[416]. According to a former board member, Volkswagen was a 'dictatorship' under Winterkorn, where dissent was not allowed[417].

The breadth of deceit

Despite abiding by the law in their board composition, Dieselgate had cost Volkswagen a total of $25 billion in fines, penalties, civil damages and restitution in the US[418]. Volkswagen also either repurchased the affected diesel cars or gave cash payouts to owners if they preferred having their vehicles fixed[419]. In 2017, they pled guilty to three US charges, including fraud[420].

On the other hand, Europe received minimal compensations in the immediate aftermath of Dieselgate. Volkswagen insisted that the affected cars could just have the software tweaked to meet Europe's less rigorous emissions standards. And only in May 2022, seven years after the outbreak of the scandal, did Volkswagen pay out €193 million to drivers in England and Wales[421].

In total, the group had paid out more than €30 billion worldwide[422].

Dieselgate had not only exposed Volkswagen's moral failure but that of several others in the industry as well.

Following Dieselgate, US authorities stepped up their scrutiny of diesel vehicles and several others were also fined[423]. Fiat Chrysler agreed to a $515-million settlement in the US over charges that its diesel vehicles had 'undisclosed emission controls' that allowed them to emit higher levels of pollution on the road[424].

German prosecutors also fined BMW €8.5 million over diesel cars with higher harmful emissions than allowed and Porsche agreed to pay a fine of €535 million in Germany while Daimler paid €870 million[425].

Even Bosch, one of the world's largest auto suppliers, was slapped with a $327.5 million fine in the US for its role in devising the software[426]. As early as 2006, Bosch agreed to write the necessary code to execute Volkswagen's plan for adapting the software that would become the defeat devices. Bosch even helped to delete text from software documentation that might have caused suspicion[427].

While key executives and engineers involved were jailed or charged with fraud and Volkswagen is still paying millions in damages years after their crimes were exposed, the massive extent of cheating throughout and across the industries points to a more fundamental problem—rules and regulations alone often fail to prevent moral failures[428].

Reflection questions

1. Could better and more stringent regulations have prevented VW from gaming the system? Why or why not?
2. What elements of the Steward Leadership Compass stood out? Why?
3. What elements of the Steward Leadership Compass were weak or missing altogether?
4. What lessons can we learn from the story?

Chapter 12

Theranos, the Unicorn: A Case of Purpose-washing?

'A world in which no one has to say goodbye too soon.'[429]

Clad in her black turtleneck underneath an all-black suit, commanding the ears of the audience in her unnaturally baritone voice and staring them down with her unblinking blue eyes, Elizabeth Holmes sold her vision to a room full of hopefuls at her TEDMED talk in 2014.

This was the same future that Elizabeth Holmes sold to investors, business partners and patients. Back in 2004, nineteen-year-old Elizabeth Holmes dropped out of Stanford after two semesters and founded Theranos—a portmanteau of 'therapy' and 'diagnosis'—a healthtech startup that promised to revolutionize the $75-billion blood-testing industry by changing the way blood tests were conducted[430]. Instead of drawing vials of blood using a long needle, Theranos' technology would enable blood tests to be done with just a few drops of blood from a finger prick. Blood tests would be cheaper, faster and more accessible.

This was not just the ambition of a naïve Stanford dropout. Theranos received more than $400 million in investments and, at its height, the company was valued at $9 billion[431]. The investors themselves were of impressive stature, including former US Education Secretary Betsy DeVos, media mogul Rupert Murdoch and the Walton family of Walmart[432].

Eighteen years after its founding, Elizabeth was sentenced to eleven years and three months in prison after being found guilty on four charges of defrauding investors[433]. Her deputy Sunny Balwani was convicted of twelve counts of wire fraud and conspiracy to commit wire fraud[434]. He was sentenced to twelve years and eleven months in prison[435].

How did this company, founded on the desire to create a better world for humanity and backed by so many high-profile investors, go down as one of the greatest scandals in Silicon Valley?

The disruptors

Blood testing is often used to inform medical decisions by doctors. In the US, the $75-billion blood-testing industry is dominated by Laboratory Corporation of America Holdings, commonly known as LabCorp and Quest Diagnostics[436]. Both companies can run 3,000 to 4,000 types of tests and are well integrated into the healthcare system in the US[437]. LabCorp and Quest usually collect a vial or more of blood using venipuncture, a process by which a needle is inserted into a vein, usually in the arm.

Unlike this painful and invasive procedure, Theranos was built on the idea of finger pricking. Instead of extracting vials of blood to run the tests, Theranos' technology only needed a few drops of blood obtained by pricking the finger. The blood would be stored in a 'nanotainer', a small container that would be fed into an analysis machine called the Edison. It was named as such after American inventor Thomas Edison, who famously said, 'I've not failed. I've just found 10,000 ways that won't work.' Prior to the Edison, Theranos had tried several versions of an analysis machine and even tried inventing a medical patch that could detect infectious diseases in blood and administer antibiotics[438]. To Elizabeth, the Edison was their first shot at success.

The genesis

According to Elizabeth, her fear of needles inspired her to build Theranos[439]. She recognized that blood tests were important in diagnosing a variety of medical conditions, but a phobia of needles made patients reluctant to get them. By using a tiny needle to draw blood, Elizabeth believed that more people would be willing to get their blood tested, leading to earlier diagnoses and potentially saving lives[440].

She also shared the story of her uncle's death at the TEDMED conference in 2014, eleven years after she started Theranos. 'I remember his love of crossword puzzles and trying to teach us to play football. I remember how much he loved the beach. I remember how much I loved him. He was diagnosed one day with skin cancer, which all of a sudden was brain cancer and in his bones. He didn't live to see his son grow up and I never got to say goodbye.'[441] Like many entrepreneurs in Silicon Valley, Elizabeth excelled at selling stories. She captured the hearts of her TEDMED conference audience.

But she was not that close to her uncle, at least not close enough to warrant his death being an inspiration to the founding of the company. John Carreyrou, the journalist from *The Wall Street Journal* who wrote the first exposé on Theranos in 2015, writes in his book *Bad Blood*, 'To family members who knew the reality of their relationship, using his death to promote her company felt phony and exploitative.'[442]

Theranos' muddy purpose was not the start-up's only red flag.

The Edison

To the engineers who created the Edison, Elizabeth's hopes in what they coined the 'gluebot' were premature. The Edison could only execute a blood-testing technique called the chemiluminescent immunoassay, which was not a new technique. It was first invented in the 1980s by a professor at Cardiff University. The Edison had just automated an existing process.

Merely automating a manual process was not the main issue. The bigger problem with the Edison was its inability to produce consistent, accurate results. Elizabeth's insistence on using just a few drops of blood to test a wide range of conditions ignored technical and scientific constraints. Using such a tiny amount of blood would not provide an

accurate reading for markers of infectious diseases[443]. The tiny drops
of blood would also quickly dry up in the nanotainers[444].

Investors

Even though Theranos' purported proprietary technology did not
work, Elizabeth successfully garnered financial support. Her bold
vision, coupled with her confidence, passion and charisma, appealed to
high-profile investors. By the end of 2005, Elizabeth had raised nearly
$6 million from an array of investors including venture capitalist John
Bryan and Stephen L. Feinberg, who was on the board of Houston's
MD Anderson Cancer Center[445].

Getting $6 million in the first round of investments was just the
start of Elizabeth's persuasive prowess. She eventually got men of high
standing on her Board of Directors, including former US secretaries
of state George Schultz and Henry Kissinger; James Mattis, former
four-star general in the US Marine Corps; and later David Boies, a
lawyer of national prominence who succeeded in the US government's
prosecution of Microsoft. Oddly enough, only two of the twelve board
members had any form of medical expertise: William Frist, heart and
lung transplant surgeon and former US Senator; and William Foege,
former Director of the Centers for Disease Control and Prevention[446].
Theranos' board composition was highly unusual for a health company.

The trickle-down effect

For a company ambitiously aiming to revolutionize the health industry,
its management team did not seem the least bit qualified. Two years
after Theranos came up with the Edison, Ramesh 'Sunny' Balwani
joined the company as its Chief Operating Officer. Throughout his time
at Theranos, Sunny played a key role in shaping the company's culture.

Sunny's management style fostered a culture of fear. When he
joined the struggling start-up, he took on the role of firing employees.
Those who were laid off were usually escorted out by security silently,
with no explanation given to the rest of the employees. Anyone could
be here one day and gone the next. Sunny was also condescending
towards employees, publicly berating or barking orders at them.

Elizabeth herself had no regard for her employees. At one point, she wanted to run the engineering department 24/7 to accelerate development. The engineers were already working overtime and the head of the engineering department felt that Elizabeth's proposal would only make his small team burn out faster. He pushed back. Elizabeth said, 'I don't care. We can change people in and out. The company is all that matters.'[447]

Elizabeth and Sunny were also so paranoid about technology leaks that in one instance, Sunny called the police to chase down an employee who had just been laid off. Sunny thought that the employee was not working long-enough hours and even reviewed security footage to track the employee's comings and goings. Just as the employee was about to leave the company premises on his last day, Sunny and Elizabeth insisted that he sign a nondisclosure agreement before leaving. The employee refused. He had already signed a confidentiality agreement when he was hired, just as all other employees had. The employee ignored them and drove off. Enraged, Sunny called the police. When they arrived, he told them that an employee had '(stolen) property in his mind'[448].

Head up in the clouds

Despite the limitations of the Edisons, Elizabeth claimed that it could run more than one thousand tests. And this was the story she sold to investors and partners. In her email to Walgreens, the US' second-largest drugstore chain, Elizabeth stated that Theranos could run any blood test from a few drops of blood obtained from pricking a finger and for less than half the cost of blood tests from traditional laboratories.

In January 2010, Elizabeth approached Walgreens to propose a collaboration between the two companies. Elizabeth said that Theranos could run 95 per cent of all conventional lab tests on its Edisons and the results would be ready in less than thirty minutes[449]. Walgreens signed a preliminary contract, under which the drugstore chain committed to prepurchase up to $50 million worth of Theranos cartridges and to loan it $25 million[450].

To ensure that the deal was sound, Walgreens hired Kevin Hunter, who headed a small lab consulting firm. During the meeting with Elizabeth and Sunny at Theranos' Palo Alto office, Kevin started noticing red flags—the extreme secrecy that bordered on paranoia, the refusal to show Kevin the laboratory and the failure to produce the test results of Walgreens' executives.

Kevin's suspicions were not unfounded. Elizabeth and Sunny were indeed concealing the failure of the Edisons from him and other Walgreens executives. Not only that, but the documents they used to prove that their technology was vetted were forged. In his testimony during Elizabeth's trial, Walgreens' Chief Financial Officer Wade Miquelon said that Elizabeth shared a document carrying the Pfizer logo, suggesting that the drug company supported Theranos' technology. But Pfizer never wrote the document nor gave its permission to put its logo on it. During her trial, Elizabeth herself admitted to manipulating the documents 'because this work was done in partnership with those companies and I was trying to convey that'[451].

Walgreens was not the only retail partner Theranos was courting. Safeway, an American supermarket chain, had also signed a deal with Theranos. Safeway promised to loan Theranos $30 million and pledged to undertake a massive renovation of its stores to make room for sleek new clinics where customers would have their blood tested on the Theranos devices. The startup requested that these clinics be called 'wellness centres' and need to look 'better than a spa'. Safeway shouldered the total renovation cost of $350 million[452].

The miniLab

Elizabeth had oversold the Edisons. The fact that they could only execute chemiluminescent immunoassays meant that they could not deliver on the hundreds of other tests Elizabeth had promised Walgreens and Safeway they could do. Theranos needed a new machine. The miniLab was created.

The miniLab essentially miniaturized four types of existing blood-testing technology and fit them all in a portable machine. But it could only process one sample at a time and would not be able to handle all the patient samples that would stream in from the clinics in Walgreens and Safeway.

The development of the miniLab was taking too long and Theranos had already missed the deadline to launch its services with Walgreens by February 2013[453]. Elizabeth risked losing the Walgreens partnership if Theranos did not deliver soon.

With the miniLab in no state to be launched, Elizabeth and Sunny decided to pull out the older Edisons. The pair was bent on making the Walgreens partnership work come hell or high water. Because the Edisons could not run more than three tests on one finger-stick sample, Sunny decided to predilute the samples before they were run through the device. But this additional dilution increased the already high error rate.

To several employees, it was clear that neither the miniLabs nor the Edisons were ready to be deployed for real-life patient testing. When an employee asked Elizbeth why she did not want to wait until the miniLabs were ready, Elizabeth said, 'Because when I promise something to a customer, I deliver.'[454] But were the drugstore and supermarket chains really Theranos' ultimate customers? To some of Theranos' employees, their customers were the patients who would make real, consequential medical decisions based on the data they received from the company.

Modifying commercial analysers

At the same time Theranos was trying to resuscitate the Edisons, another group of engineers working on the miniLabs began tinkering with the Siemens ADVIA 1800, one of the laboratory's commercial analysers that specialized in general chemistry assays. Such assays accounted for about two-thirds of doctors' orders.

Because these analysers were made to handle larger volumes of blood, the engineers had to adapt the ADVIA to work with Theranos' smaller samples. The process they settled on involved diluting the blood twice, which meant that the ADVIA was not used in a way that Siemens or the FDA approved of. The results generated by the ADVIA were consequently unreliable.

Despite the lack of scientific rigour that went into the development of the machines, Elizabeth forged ahead with the partnerships. In the end, Theranos machines were not placed in either Walgreens or Safeway. Instead, phlebotomists were stationed there to draw the patients' blood and in more cases than not, venipuncture was used in addition to Theranos' signature finger-stick[455].

As a beta run before the full launch, Theranos took over the blood testing at one of Safeway's employee health clinics. Once the employees' blood samples had been taken via venipuncture or finger-stick—or both—the samples were transported to a one-story building in Palo Alto, where Theranos had built a little lab containing more than a dozen commercial blood and body-fluid analysers. These analysers came from Chicago-based Abbott Laboratories, Germany's Siemens and Italy's DiaSorin.

Although Theranos had given the impression that its test results were almost instantaneous, some Safeway employees waited two weeks for their results. The most alarming thing was the fact that some of them were receiving abnormal results. A senior Safeway executive received a result indicating that he almost certainly had prostate cancer, but when he got retested at other labs, his results came back normal.

The whistleblowers

Of course, neither Walgreens nor Safeway knew for sure that Theranos was not using its technology. Back at Theranos' headquarters, scientists were holed up in the basement, where the Edisons and modified commercial analysers were kept. Erika Cheung, a fresh graduate out of UC Berkeley, was one of the scientists working on the Edisons. Erika was tasked with retesting blood samples on the Edisons to measure the variation of the results. The data was used to calculate the Edison blood test's precision.

But she discovered that data runs that did not meet the numbers were simply discarded and the experiments were repeated until the desired number was reached[456]. Yet, even with 'good' data runs, some values were deemed outliers and deleted. No one could give Erika a straight answer as to how an outlier was defined.

Erika kept these suspicions at the back of her mind, but it was not until she ran quality-control checks on the Edison devices that she seriously questioned the morals that underpinned Theranos' operations. In November 2013, Erika received an order from the Walgreens store in Palo Alto for a vitamin D test. As usual, she ran a quality-control check on the Edison before testing the patient sample. In laboratories, quality-control checks are a basic safeguard against inaccurate results and are a mainstay in most laboratories. The first quality-control check that Erika ran failed. So did the second one. After emailing an emergency helpline the company had set up and trying a slew of proposed solutions, an employee from the research and development team came down[457].

Under the protocol Sunny and a project manager had established, patient samples were processed using three different Edisons. Each device would generate two values, so in total, the three Edisons would produce six values. The median of these six would be the final result Theranos sent back to the patients.

Since Erika had tested two samples, there were twelve values. When the employee from the research and development side came down, she deleted two of those values and declared them outliers. The employee had not bothered to explain the rationale and went on to test the patient sample and sent out a result. Erika was shocked. For one, the repeated quality-control failures would usually call for the devices to be taken offline and recalibrated. Secondly, the employee was not even authorized to be in the clinical lab, let alone process patient samples.

Erika was not the only one who disagreed with Theranos' testing of patient samples. Tyler Schultz, whose grandfather George Schultz sat on the board, thought that this method was conceived to make up for the imprecision of the machines. There would not be a need to disregard the other values and only take the median if the Edisons were reliable to begin with.

Cheaters are going to cheat

Such irresponsible laboratory practices were not the only instances that made Erika doubt the moral nature of the work she was doing. Less than a week after this incident, an inspector from the Laboratory Field Sciences division of the California Department of Public Health went down to Theranos. It was time for the Theranos' lab's CLIA certificate to be renewed and that required an inspection of the lab. Theranos actually had two labs in its premises: 'Jurassic Park', the CLIA-certified lab which contained commercial analysers; and 'Normandy', which contained the modified Siemens machines and the Edisons. Normandy was also the lab Erika and Tyler were assigned to.

Before the inspector arrived, Sunny warned employees not to enter or leave Normandy during the inspection. The stairs that led to Normandy were hidden behind a door that needed a key card to be opened. Clearly, Sunny did not want the inspector to know of Normandy's existence.

In the end, the inspector spent several hours in Jurassic Park and only found minor problems that the lab director committed to fixing. And she was gone. Erika and other Theranos employees could not help but feel like the inspector was misled.

Proficiency testing

Misleading federal inspectors was not the only questionable act that Theranos had taken. The start-up was also cheating in tests. In the US, all clinical labs must submit to proficiency testing three times a year. Proficiency testing is an exercise to smoke out labs with inaccurate tests.

In its first two years of operation, Theranos had always tested its lab samples on commercial analysers. But since they were using the Edisons for some of their tests, lab director Adam Rosendorff got Erika and other lab associates to split the proficiency-testing samples and run a part of it on the Edisons and the other on the Siemens and DiaSorin analysers. The results differed significantly, especially for vitamin D.

When Sunny found out about the 'experiment', he immediately quashed it and made them report only the Siemens and DiaSorin results. Tyler suspected that this was not the way proficiency testing should be carried out.

Tyler wrote to the New York State Department of Health to confirm his intuition. On 31 March, 2014, he received an email from Stephanie Shulman, Director of the Clinical Laboratory Evaluation Program, who confirmed Tyler's suspicions. Theranos' practices did amount to 'a form of PT cheating' and were 'in violation of the state and federal requirements'[458]. Tyler confided in his grandfather, George Schultz, who was on Theranos' Board of Directors. But George had a very close relationship with Elizabeth and told him to give Elizabeth a chance to explain herself.

In his email to her, Tyler explained the discrepancies he had found and the explanations he had received from more experienced scientists. He even included charts and validation data to illustrate why he was not convinced by these explanations.

He did not hear from Elizabeth. A few days later, an email from Sunny landed in his inbox. With regards to Tyler's points about proficiency testing, Sunny wrote:

> That reckless comment and accusation about the integrity of our company, its leadership and its core team members based on absolute ignorance is so insulting to me that had any other person made these statements, we would have held them accountable in the strongest way. The only reason I have taken so much time away from work to address this personally is because you are Mr. Schultz's grandson . . .

Tyler decided enough was enough. He quit.

Real-life testing

Erika knew that Tyler had quit and was seriously considering doing the same thing. Theranos was just given clearance to test for hepatitis C—an infectious disease—on the Edisons. When a patient order for the hepatitis C test came in, Erika refused to run it. In tears, she told her supervisor Mark that the reagents for the test had expired, the Edisons had not been recalibrated in a while and she just did not trust the devices. The pair devised a plan to run patient samples on commercially available hepatitis kits. When they tried to order a new batch after the kits ran out, Sunny blew his top.

That afternoon, at about the same time Tyler walked out of Theranos, Sunny called Erika to his office. Sunny had looked through Tyler's emails and figured out that Erika had been the one who sent him the proficiency test results. Sunny berated her when she brought up the quality-control failures in the lab.

It was clear to Erika that the leaders of the start-up knew about the unethical practices going on under their noses. She was sickened, knowing she was complicit in the total disregard Theranos had for its patients' well-being.

Erika met with Tyler after her shift and, at his suggestion, they went to George Schultz's house for dinner, hoping that Erika's account—together with Tyler's—could make headway with the board member. They tried to convince George that Theranos' devices were not working despite the stories that Elizabeth had told. But George's unwavering belief in Theranos and Elizabeth could not be shaken. Erika and Tyler had no choice but to heed George's advice and to leave Theranos behind.

Erika quit the next day.

Stalking and intimidation

Even after Erika had left the company, she still felt uneasy, knowing that Theranos was still testing patient samples and giving inaccurate results. She had heard that John Carreyrou, a journalist from *The Wall Street Journal*, was poking around Theranos. She decided to approach him.

A few days later, Erika received a letter from a man who had waited in the parking lot of her new workplace for a few hours. Erika stopped short when she saw the address. It was the address of her colleague's apartment, where Erika was staying temporarily. Not even her mother knew about this address. Erika was sure she was being watched.

She read the letter. It was signed by David Boies, the lawyer of Microsoft fame whom Elizabeth had hired. Theranos had a long-standing working relationship with David. The pair met in 2011 after an early Theranos investor asked him to represent her. Impressed by Elizabeth's intelligence and commitment, David took half of his and his firm's fees in Theranos stock. At Theranos' peak, the stocks were worth $7 million[459].

In the letter, Erika was threatened with legal action if she did not submit to an interview with Boies Schiller attorneys and reveal the information she had disclosed about Theranos and to whom.

Erika was shaken, without a doubt. But she refused to let a tyrant bully her into silence. She gathered her courage, put her hands to the keyboard and wrote:

> Dear Gary,
>
> I've been nervous to send or even write this letter. Theranos takes confidentiality and secrecy to an extreme level that has always made me scared to say anything . . . I'm ashamed in myself for not filing this complaint sooner . . .[460]

Erika had written to Gary Yamamoto, a veteran field inspector for the Centers for Medicare and Medicaid Services. At the end of the email, Erika wrote that she had resigned from the company because she could not live with herself knowing that she could 'potentially devastate someones (sic) life by giving them a false and deceiving result'[461].

The patients

A major stakeholder missing from Theranos' considerations in its operations, ambitions and strategies was the patients. And it was this very group, the unseen throughout this entire debacle, that spurred so much unease among Theranos' employees. They knew that their work had real consequences for patients who not only had to make medical decisions about their lives, but also suffer through the unnecessary emotional turmoil of the results they had received.

Imagine the rollercoaster of emotions the senior executive from Safeway experienced when his results showed that he had prostate cancer. He was not the only victim. Erin Tompkins' test misdiagnosed her as having an HIV antibody[462]. Brittany Gould's results indicated she had suffered a miscarriage[463].

Did Elizabeth really want to create a future where 'no one had to say goodbye too soon'? Or was she enamoured by the promises of Silicon Valley?

The downfall

At its height in 2014, Theranos was valued at $9 billion and Elizabeth was named one of the richest women in America by *Forbes*, owing to her 50 per cent stake in Theranos[464].

But an empire built on blood money had to come crashing down.

In October 2015, John Carreyrou from *The Wall Street Journal* published a damning exposé on Theranos. In the article, he highlighted the inaccuracies of the Edisons and revealed that as of the end of 2014, less than 10 per cent of Theranos' tests were done on the Edisons. This amounted to only fifteen tests being performed on the Edisons. On the other hand, sixty tests were done on the commercial machines using the diluted samples. The remaining tests—about 130—were run on traditional machines using samples obtained through venipuncture[465].

The slew of investigations that opened up after the news broke led to Theranos voiding two years of test results from its Edison devices from 2014 to 2015 and issuing tens of thousands of corrected results to doctors and patients[466]. The seven-year-long drawn-out battle culminated in Elizabeth's and Sunny's criminal convictions and the collapse of Theranos.

Reflection questions

1. What role did the board play in the collapse of Theranos, if any?
2. What elements of the Steward Leadership Compass stood out? Why?
3. What elements of the Steward Leadership Compass were weak or missing altogether?
4. What lessons can we learn from the story?

Part Three

Steward Leadership Measurement
and Applications

Introduction to Part Three

If you have come this far in the book, by now you are hopefully convinced about the need for stewardship and the power of steward leadership. However, one question that comes up a lot when we discuss the shift from ESG to ESL is that of measurability.

The proponents of ESG say that it is easy to measure. There are a lot of science-based measures already in place for E. While S might be more subjective, the G can be quite tangible and therefore quantifiable. So, two of the three elements are easily measurable, they say. They worry that a move towards ESL will leave only the E as measurable, leaving two of the three elements to subjectivity.

Chapter 13 attempts to address these concerns and provides a framework for boards and management to keep track of their progress with steward leadership.

The next two chapters shine a light on two additional aspects of creating value that are becoming increasingly important in current times: Business Ecosystems and Diversity, Equity and Inclusion (DEI). Chapter 14, written by Arnoud De Meyer, discusses steward leadership in business ecosystems. It establishes the fact that today's complex problems cannot always be solved by single companies and that an ecosystem of partners is better positioned to do so. It further argues that value creation through an ecosystem is harder than doing it all by oneself and therefore requires strong steward leadership.

Finally, Chapter 15, written by Vinika Rao, challenges conventional wisdom about DEI and offers powerful new ways of looking at the topic. It argues that diversity goes well beyond gender, ethnicity and racial differences; equality is not equity; and inclusion cannot just be token.

Chapter 13

Is ESL Tangible and Measurable Enough?

Starting with Chapter 1, we have been making the case that ESG as a framework needs to be upgraded to ESL. Even after they agree that the argument makes sense, it makes some people uncomfortable because of the perceived lack of ESL measurability. The E and G of ESG are measurable in specific terms, they say, leaving only the S as harder to measure. If we move to ESL, the only element that will remain specifically measurable will be E, they worry.

But is specific measurement the ultimate gold standard? We saw in Chapter 1 what harm an obsession with measurement can do. Does everything need to be reduced to a mathematical formula? Or are qualitative, directional measures equally effective in some cases?

The answer will depend on what the board and management want to achieve and where they want to be on the E/S spectrum that we discussed earlier. We are by no means denying that there is a degree of truth and merit in the cliched phrase 'what gets measured gets done'. But the implied trap is that '*only* what gets measured gets done', often at the expense of all other and sometimes more critical initiatives. Fanatical obsession with metrics, benchmarks and numbers leads us to focus on 'what we need to do' and not 'what is possible'. Steward leadership is more art than science, so we posit that qualitative measures are equally effective. In fact, attempting to reduce everything into a scientific/mathematical formula often inhibits innovation and creativity, particularly in human-centred pursuits such as management, leadership and governance.

Keeping this in mind, we have developed a tool that can help management teams and boards understand the strengths and weaknesses of their organizations' steward leadership culture. Called the Steward Leadership Quotient (SLQ), it is based on the Steward Leadership Compass presented earlier and aims to help boards and senior management understand employee perceptions about whether the organization's attempts to lead the business with stewardship values and purpose are genuine or not. As we explain later in this chapter, SLQ is not a benchmarking tool. Instead, it is a 'reflection' tool for the senior leadership and boards to understand how strongly stewardship values and purpose manifest in day-to-day decisions within the organization.

Steward Leadership Quotient (SLQ)

Generally, the first people to find out if an organization walks its talk on stewardship or not will be its employees. So, SLQ is designed to gather employee feedback on each of the four values of the Compass and on organizational purpose. Specifically, it presents twenty-five statements to employees and asks them to indicate their agreement or disagreement on a 1–6 scale, where 1 = strongly disagree, 2 = disagree, 3 = slightly disagree, 4 = slightly agree, 5 = agree and 6 = strongly agree. The statements are given below:

I. Interdependence (Does the organization view the world as an interconnected system in which success of the organization depends on the success of others?)

1. Our organization believes that the well-being of employees is integral to its success.
2. Our organization believes that in order to succeed, its products and services must not compromise societal well-being.
3. Our organization takes into consideration both collective and individual accomplishment when evaluating performance.
4. Our organization's business strategy seeks to create a positive impact on the community.
5. Our organization strives to address the needs of our external partners in difficult times.

II. Long-term view (Does the organization create sustained value for both current and future generations?)

6. Our organization aims to create long-term business growth without compromising the well-being of future generations.
7. Our organization is committed to the responsible use of natural resources as part of its long-term strategy for sustainable growth.
8. Our organization takes a long-term approach to drive business growth.
9. Our organization plans ahead to ensure smooth leadership transition and succession.
10. Our organization is willing to delay instant gratification to enhance long-term positive impact.

III. Ownership mentality (Does the organization and employees take proactive responsibility to make stewardship happen?)

11. In our organization, employees do not hesitate to speak up if they have concerns.
12. In our organization, employees have autonomy in making decisions that are in line with the organization's values and purpose.
13. Our organization accepts who I am as an individual.
14. Our organization's culture enables me to feel personally accountable to its objectives.
15. In our organization, employees are empowered to make a difference through the work they do.

IV. Creative resilience (Does the organization encourage employees to develop tenacity to find innovative solutions to disruptive challenges?)

16. Our organization's culture encourages experimentation to accelerate innovation.
17. Our organization strives to find solutions to difficult challenges without giving up easily.

18. Our organization encourages us to question assumptions to foster continuous improvement.

19. Our organization encourages us to reflect and learn from mistakes and problems.

20. Our organization is able to turn crises into opportunities.

V. Stewardship purpose (Does the organization aspire to create a collective better future for a variety of stakeholders, society, future generations and the environment?)

21. Our organization's purpose incorporates the broader needs of external stakeholders.

22. Our organization's mission is to make a positive impact on the world.

23. Our organization's business activities are driven by a purpose that takes into account the needs of a wide variety of stakeholders (in addition to shareholders).

24. Our organization's purpose aims to create a better future for a wide variety of stakeholders, including employees, shareholders and society at large.

25. In our organization, there is alignment between senior leaders and employees on the need for a purpose that considers the well-being of a wide variety of stakeholders (in addition to shareholders).

The SLQ is designed to help senior leadership teams understand the extent and consistency to which the mindset and practice of steward leadership are applied within their organizations. It can be used for the organization as a whole, a department, function or any sub-team therein. Unlike an employee engagement survey that asks employees to indicate how satisfied they are with their employment, SLQ seeks employee feedback on how well stewardship values and purpose are embedded in business strategy, execution and organizational culture. Individual responses are fully confidential; all data is aggregated during reporting.

SLQ is a result of several years of research efforts. The twenty-five statements are arrived at after exhaustive primary and secondary research and a rigorous validation process. The research team curated the initial set of statements based on existing literature on steward leadership values. Subsequently, the statements were put through a rigorous multi-stage testing and validation process, comprising cognitive interviews and quantitative methods, to test inter-rater reliability (degree of agreement among independent experts) and scale validity (to check if it measures what it intends to measure). The initial statements or questions went through multiple rounds of editing and fine-tuning to arrive at the final twenty-five-statement set presented in this chapter.

An example might help us understand the application of SLQ.

The leadership team at a large multi-national FMCG company, let's call it Alpha Inc.[467], which prides itself on being a champion of sustainability and its strong sense of purpose, used the self-assessment tool. Note that Alpha Inc.'s sustainability strategies have been acclaimed as best practices within their industry, winning accolades for their leadership and sustainability efforts. In their recent engagement surveys, Alpha Inc. employees generally reported a high level of workplace satisfaction, with several employees particularly noting good workplace practices such as flexible work arrangements, fair employment practices, managing diversity and best sourcing initiatives according to industry standards.

Alpha Inc. adopted a three-step approach as they rolled out the SLQ tool.

1. They collected employee responses by administering the SLQ survey across the entire company.
2. Next, at an offsite meeting, the leadership team filled out the survey by placing themselves in the shoes of employees, i.e., they tried rating each item as an employee of the company would.
3. Finally, the leadership team compared their self-assessment with broader employee data, discussed what was working and

not working and debated how they could further strengthen their steward leadership culture.

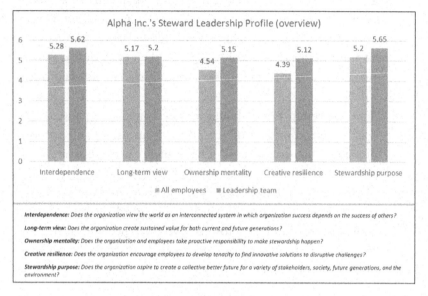

<figure>
Interdependence: Does the organization view the world as an interconnected system in which organization success depends on the success of others?

Long-term view: Does the organization create sustained value for both current and future generations?

Ownership mentality: Does the organization and employees take proactive responsibility to make stewardship happen?

Creative resilience: Does the organization encourage employees to develop tenacity to find innovative solutions to disruptive challenges?

Stewardship purpose: Does the organization aspire to create a collective better future for a variety of stakeholders, society, future generations, and the environment?
</figure>

Figure 23: A summary snapshot of SLQ scores for all employees (excluding the leadership team) and the leadership team. Source: Stewardship Asia Centre.

Note that since the twenty-five statements under the 'values' and 'purpose' categories are all positively worded, the closer the score is to '6', which is 'strongly agree', the stronger the indication or more numerous the instances that key stakeholders (employees in this case) see the stewardship value in action in day-to-day operations and decision-making. While there is no good or bad score, the skyline does indicate potential stewardship values (the ones with a comparatively lower score) that the organization may want to reinforce. For instance, in Figure 23, ownership mentality and creative resilience scores indicate that, on an average, employees only 'slightly agree' that these values manifest in day-to-day operations, while for the other two values—long-term view and interdependence—employees 'agree' (comparatively a more convincing response) that they play out more frequently in a regular work environment.

Observations

- At first glance, Alpha Inc. seems to be demonstrating a relatively strong steward leadership culture in general, attaining an aggregated SLQ score of 4.92 out of 6 for all employees and 5.35 for the leadership team. This indicates that majority of the employees generally agree that their company genuinely practises stewardship values and purpose in its day-to-day operations.
- The leadership team, though a much smaller sample, seems much more confident of the stewardship values and purpose at play in the organization. It has a higher average score on all five pillars.
- For the employee population, in contrast with high scores on interdependence, long-term view and stewardship purpose, the scores of 4.39 and 4.54 for creative resilience and ownership mentality respectively warrant greater scrutiny for possible areas of improvement.

Figure 24 further slices the employee data, with each bar representing the aggregated score of each single statement within the five elements (four stewardship values and overall stewardship purpose). The SLQ statements are reproduced below the figure for easy reference.

- While the creative resilience value has the lowest aggregated score among the five elements of the Compass (Figure 25), the first statement under the value of ownership mentality— *In our organization, employees do not hesitate to speak up if they have concerns*—stands out with an overall lowest individual statement score of 3.73 (Figure 24).
  - o What might be causing this low score?
  - o Does the culture of not speaking up point towards low psychological safety in the organization or does it indicate that deep within, the organization has a command-and-control culture? Or is it a knee-jerk reaction to any recent

stress or disruption that the organization may have gone through?

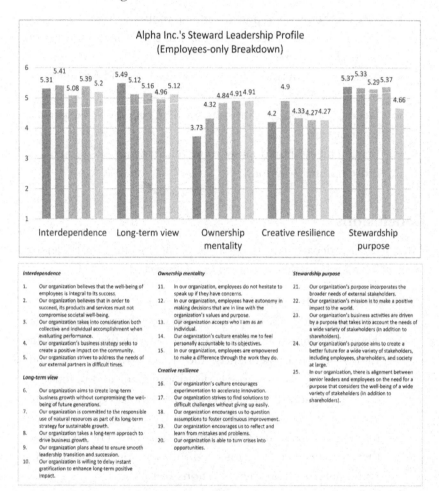

Figure 24: Alpha Inc.'s steward leadership profile of employees-only breakdown.
Source: Stewardship Asia Centre.

- While Alpha Inc. exhibits a strong sense of stewardship purpose, the statement, *'In our organization, there is alignment between senior leaders and employees on the need for a purpose that considers the well-being of a wide variety of stakeholders (in addition to shareholders)'* is rated relatively low at 4.66.

Additionally, employees also shared the following qualitative inputs via verbatim comments as suggested areas of improvement:

- Need to better align purpose and execution.
- Better alignment needed across teams and ranks to address the issue of inconsistency.
- Stronger commitment to common goals would further boost overall success.
- Need to develop an atmosphere where everyone can speak up without fear.
- Management should allow more 'challenging up' to arrive at more optimal solutions.

Conclusions

After rigorously debating the issues at the offsite meeting, the leadership team at Alpha Inc. made the following conclusions:

1. Based on the skyline across five pillars, directionally, the employee and leadership team survey results are quite similar. The leadership team and employees agree that stewardship values of 'interdependence' and 'long-term view' are quite evident in regular day-to-day decision-making and functioning of the organization. However, the employees' scores for 'ownership mentality' and 'creative resilience' values dip more than the leadership team's estimation. The two values therefore need to be reinforced through appropriate internal communications and actual actions from leaders.

2. There needs to be better alignment with the purpose of the organization, especially as it relates to the well-being of diverse stakeholder communities. The leadership team agreed that they must use the purpose 'filter' more often in their decision-making and encourage their direct reports to follow suit. Perhaps there needs to be better communication across the organization around why some decisions are made and how they (positively) impact broader stakeholder well-being.

3. People are not speaking up or, at the very least, they are holding back their opinions and that needs to be addressed. One of the possible root-causes might be the recent 'stress' the organization had experienced during the Covid-19 pandemic, which led leaders to embrace a command-and-control attitude. With the worst of the pandemic hopefully over, the leadership team now needs to 'soften' the top-down approach and ease some of the crisis era controls.
4. Low scores on ownership mentality items were driving the low scores on creative resilience. Specifically, perceptions around the fear of speaking up and the lack of empowerment are inhibiting creativity and innovation. To spur innovation, this needs to be addressed urgently.

The management team at Alpha Inc. took these messages away from the exercise and came up with appropriate action steps to be integrated with the talent management and communication strategy for the following year. At a high level, they agreed to:

1. Look into the creative resilience value, explore potential psychological safety issues and evaluate alignment between the leadership team and employees. The team agreed to conduct small group meetings within their own businesses and functions and report back the key takeaways in the subsequent leadership meeting scheduled three months later. They also decided to partner with HR to conduct a series of focus group sessions to further analyse root causes and key challenges around alignment, (lack of) trust/psychological safety and potential values dilution.
2. Encourage better organization-wide communication and promote honest conversations across levels and departments. The team agreed to host mini-town hall meetings every quarter at various business locations. In their first round of mini-town halls, they all agreed to share the SLQ survey results and response action steps initiated by the leadership team.
3. Incrementally delegate decision-making and encourage their direct reports to do the same. They agreed to closely track the

employee response on 'delegation' in the subsequent year's employee engagement survey.

At the end of the day, only time will tell how well Alpha Inc. is able to address the issues highlighted. Success will depend on the sincerity and consistency of efforts put in by management.

Our experience tells us that just like Alpha Inc., progressive companies and evolved leadership teams routinely use tools like the SLQ to objectively reflect upon aspects of their culture to understand and address what may be holding the company back from achieving its full potential.

Figure 25 below lists what the SLQ is and what it is not.

What It Is	What It Is Not
Internal feedback instrument for organizations to self-assess and reflect on their steward leadership culture.	A rank-and-rate exercise to externally measure or publish an organization's ESG performance.
First questionnaire for organizations that seek to break down the concepts of steward leadership into measurable constructs.	A check-the-list tool to benchmark against other companies or indices.
A tool that helps enhance steward leadership based on stewardship values, purpose and behaviours.	An exercise to name and shame organizations based on reporting disclosures.
A 360-degree anonymous feedback of employees' perception of the organization's stewardship traits.	• An annual survey to understand employee satisfaction and engagement. • A psychometric assessment of personality traits.

Figure 25: What SLQ is and is not.
Source: Stewardship Asia Centre.

Used appropriately, SLQ is a powerful tool that can help leaders unpack how stewardship manifests in an organization through values and purpose in action; and identify key areas that boards and management teams must reinforce or attend to.

SLQ and governance (From ESG to ESL)

Corporate boards have two responsibilities—value preservation and value enhancement. SLQ can be helpful in fulfilling both.

Value preservation: As we discussed in Part One, boards spend most of their time on risk management and regulatory compliance. This is certainly one way to preserve value. However, we also saw from some of the stories in Part Two how, despite such disproportionate focus, many boards have been unable to avert massive value destruction. Why? Perhaps because governance focuses too much on the letter rather than the spirit of the law. Before rules or laws are broken, values are compromised. Only with compromised values can one justify wrongful behaviour in one's mind. SLQ can help boards see early signs of values breakdown or purpose blindness (e.g., in the case of Theranos).

Value enhancement: Progressive boards look beyond their fiduciary duty to preserve value. They focus equally on value enhancement. While evaluating business plans and key initiatives, the best boards seek to understand how values and purpose align with overall strategy. SLQ deployment and analysis of key findings can help boards fulfil this responsibility without micro-managing the management team.

Companies can deploy SLQ in a couple of ways:
- Mandate an enterprise-wide deployment of the survey.
- Roll it out at a department, division or function level.

As long as the sample set is statistically valid, SLQ data will provide useful information.

A steward leadership tool for real steward leaders

Finally, we must add that SLQ will make some leaders very insecure. Only those leaders who are very confident of their own steward leadership will eventually embrace it. Bosses whose efforts towards stewardship are not 100 per cent genuine, i.e., those who are trying to greenwash or window-dress, will find it difficult to use SLQ. The 'bravehearts', those who have *genuine desire and persistence to create a collective better future*, will not only find the tool useful, but they are also likely to share the data with key stakeholders without fear. It is certainly not a tool for the faint-hearted.

Chapter 14

Steward Leadership in Business Ecosystems

Dr Arnoud De Meyer

Chair, Stewardship Asia Centre
Professor Emeritus, Singapore Management University (SMU)

Introduction

As pointed out in prior chapters, the existential challenges we face today are both complex and daunting. To address them, we will need a higher level of steward leadership to augment ground-breaking innovation. But are today's business organizations geared and structured in a way that maximizes innovation? Do today's organizations have everything it takes to adequately address the challenges?

Leading economists have often classified two ways in which firms or non-profit institutions organize themselves to solve business or societal challenges—markets in which providers of expertise and products trade with each other and hierarchical organizations where specialists come together to coordinate their efforts to tackle problems. Recently, management scholars have pointed out that there are several alternative, hybrid approaches that have characteristics of both markets and hierarchies[468]. Some of these hybrid solutions have been labelled business ecosystems, as they are akin to biological ecosystems where living organisms cohabit within their physical environment and are linked through nutrient cycles and energy flows.

The core message of this chapter is that business ecosystems are better adapted to cope with high levels of uncertainty in the environment and that with the appropriate collaborative leadership, they have a lot in common with organizations that commit themselves to steward leadership.

Socioeconomic challenges may require new types of organizations

For over fifteen years now, my co-author Peter J. Williamson and I have studied how organizations innovate when they are confronted with a high level of uncertainty or when they have to operate in an environment that is characterized by VUCA conditions, i.e., the combination of a high level of volatility, uncertainty, complexity and ambiguity[469]. It all started when we observed in 2008 that entrepreneurs and innovators operating around the University of Cambridge (United Kingdom) behaved quite differently from what we had learned about entrepreneurship in, for example, Silicon Valley. We noticed that these often-smaller companies would share resources with each other and with the university, would help each other in managing the business, would develop solutions and innovate together and this without lots of formalized contracts or necessarily having a very visible entrepreneur leading all this. This was quite in contrast with what we learned about the heroic entrepreneurs one often hears about in the United States. These often-serial UK entrepreneurs would have a seat on each other's boards and would help each other out in difficult times.

The icon of this approach was a company called ARM, a designer of RISC processors[470] used in smartphones and Internet of Things (IoT) applications. ARM, which is a pure IP player, was orchestrating its value chain from the design of these processors, over chip design and production, the design of appropriate machinery and test equipment, to application by Original Equipment Manufacturers (OEMs) like Apple, Huawei or Samsung, all the way to software developers for smartphone apps. And they had an overwhelming worldwide market share, close to 98 per cent. How could a relatively small company with barely 2,000 employees and almost no physical assets orchestrate a value chain with behemoths like TSMC, ASML,

Apple, Samsung and Huawei? We have documented the details of this elsewhere[471], but ARM was in essence successful because they developed and managed a loosely coupled network of partners deep into their value chain. They were focused on creating value for the end consumer of smartphones and did so by understanding not only the requirements of their customers but also that of their customer's customers and partners further down in the value chain. The ultimate value of this approach was illustrated when Softbank took the company private in 2016 for a price of $32 billion and that too for a company with only its IP as assets and about 2,000 employees. In our opinion, Softbank paid the hefty price because they were buying precisely that loosely coupled but influential network.

In our early research, we were intrigued whether this was an idiosyncratic organization for a small group of companies in Cambridge or whether this could be generalized. Soon, we discovered and documented quite a few other successful organizations that had innovated by leveraging such loosely coupled networks or business ecosystems, as we started to call them. Companies as diverse as Dassault Systèmes, a large European software developer, Alibaba in China and Amazon Web services (AWS), the large Chinese white goods producer Haier, *The Guardian* news site and paper or athenahealth, a US-based service provider for medical practices and clinics, adhered to the same practice of working in such ecosystems.

We also found quite a few non-profit applications adopting a similar approach. The VentilatorChallengeUK consortium was one such example[472]. At the start of the Covid-19 pandemic, over 100 firms from diverse industry sectors pivoted, collaborated and pooled their resources to develop a new ventilator in twenty-one days and launch scale production in four weeks. Under normal circumstances, this would have taken several years.

The Building and Construction Authority in Singapore uses an ecosystem of developers, architects, engineering and construction companies to enhance productivity and innovation in Singapore's Built Environment sector[473]. Their aim is to reduce the reliance on cheap migrant workers in the construction industry and implement innovations such as new materials like mass engineered timber. All these innovations exist everywhere, but the whole built environment industry in Singapore has to transform to overcome the addiction to cheap labour and adopt these new practices.

Over the years, we have concluded that leveraging such a loosely coupled network may well be a preferred approach to innovate in the face of uncertainty. While it may not be the most efficient approach, it appears to be the most effective.

Defining business ecosystems

In a little-noticed 1993 article in *Harvard Business Review*, a biologist, James Moore, had made the case for learning from nature and organizing businesses as an ecosystem. Paraphrasing him, we define an ecosystem as 'a network of organizations and individuals that co-evolve their capabilities and roles and align their investments so as to create additional value and/or improve efficiency'[474].

Three elements in this definition are important. Firstly, it is about additional value creation and a deep belief that to do so one requires collaboration with a wide range of partners.

Secondly, it focuses on a non-hierarchical network of partners and sometimes individuals. Business ecosystems are very different from a strictly controlled supply chain, where a major principal controls significant parts of the value-added chain. There is nothing wrong with supply chains in themselves. They can be very important and applicable when there is less uncertainty and the focus is on efficiency and productivity. But as always, it is a matter of horses for courses. To innovate, such supply chains will lose out compared to ecosystems.

And thirdly, these partners may work quite independently from each other, but they do align their investments. Returning to the case of ARM, we described how this company regularly organized workshops with representatives from all its partners, where they discussed the future of RISC processors. While these representatives may not have returned home with contracts or very detailed specifications, they did bring back a roadmap of how these processors would evolve and they could determine their own investments and develop their technical capabilities in line with this roadmap.

Through our many case studies, we realized very early on that managing such ecosystems was not a sinecure. It is easy to understand that managing a business ecosystem requires a lot of active interaction with the partners, if not handholding, the resolution of conflicts, the alignment of different goals and objectives and the reduction of potential transaction costs. Later in this chapter, I will return to how one makes it work.

But there are clear advantages and benefits associated with these complex organizations and networks. One of the significant benefits is the ability to learn jointly by bringing together partners with diverse capabilities. You do not need to have all the capabilities in-house, nor do you need to own all the physical assets necessary to deliver the value. Like the network in Cambridge, you can share many such assets. Or in some cases, you can go much faster when you do not need to develop the much-needed assets and capabilities. Take for example the Chinese platform Alibaba[475]. Originally, it was a copy of eBay adapted to the Chinese market. But unlike eBay operating in industrialized economies, Alibaba did not have good payment systems like PayPal or credit cards. They could not count on delivery organizations like UPS or FedEx. In fact, they had to develop these capabilities, as well as doing well in their core business. Frankly speaking, they could not. They neither had the financial resources to develop these nor the competencies. The solution was to build an ecosystem of service providers such as China Post, which helped them to build a performing payment system—Alipay. Others developed the distribution system and the last mile delivery. And once Alibaba was committed to working in an ecosystem, it was easy for them to work with many other partners providing professional services in marketing, accountancy, etc.

A second benefit is that such ecosystems can be very flexible—new partners can join, others can leave. And partners can adjust their activities quickly according to changing circumstances. Thirdly, the cases of Alibaba and other large Chinese providers of super-apps, show that ecosystems enable them to scale up faster. Ultimately, ecosystems enable the ecosystem leader to innovate faster.

These benefits turned out to have even more relevance during and after the Covid-19 pandemic, when we saw and still see the acceleration of existing changes in the business models—the transformation of our very efficient and lean supply chains to become more resilient and robust and when the geopolitical environment is changing and perhaps becoming more hostile.

As I mentioned earlier, these benefits are precisely the reason why business ecosystems are good at innovating in the face of uncertainty. What they are not as good at is the efficient production and delivery of value when the environment is relatively stable. An interesting case to illustrate this is Amazon, the US-headquartered retail giant. In its cloud hosting business, it is operating as a business ecosystem, offering only the global infrastructure and the foundation services needed by the users of its cloud hosting. Many of the other technological or commercial services are offered by thousands of partners worldwide in a marketplace created by AWS. But in its retail business, it operates as a tightly controlled supply chain. Same company, two different approaches!

There is a caveat. We are also convinced that some of these ecosystems will, in the long term, evolve towards more traditional supply chains. When the uncertainty is reduced or when innovation is less needed, it appears logical that the more difficult to manage ecosystems evolve towards efficient and strictly controlled supply chains.

Building and developing a business ecosystem

Today, in 2023, fifteen years after we studied the first business ecosystems in Cambridge, the concept has gotten broad acceptance. There is even a risk that it is becoming a management fad. The question that I get more often today is not about the potential value of an ecosystem anymore, but more about how to build or develop an effective one. Many executives and leaders recognize that they are already, often unconsciously, operating in one or more ecosystems. They wonder how they can move beyond being a partner and how they can exert leadership in them. Through our case studies, we observed six guidelines one needs to apply to be successful in making this transition.

1. Credible ambition

First, as an ecosystem leader, you must ensure that your ambition to establish an ecosystem is credible. There should be no suspicion among your partners that you disguise an ambition to take control of a value chain as a false commitment to an ecosystem of relatively equal partners. This may be difficult for large established companies with a successful track record of acquisitions and internal development. In our book *Ecosystem Edge: Sustaining Competitiveness in the Face of Disruption*, we mention the case of a CEO of a large automotive company publicly expressing the objective to develop an autonomous vehicle through an ecosystem of small and big business partners, universities and research institutes. But its middle management, used as they were to run very efficient 'just-in-time' supply chains, had difficulties in managing the differences in culture and the lack of efficiency of some of these partners. In their attempt to render the collaboration more efficient, they killed the ecosystem. By 2015, their partners did not believe anymore that the company's intention to build an ecosystem was a genuine one.

The good news is that there are examples of established companies that have established their credibility and started a successful and innovative ecosystem. An example is the Singapore-headquartered DBS bank.

DBS used to be a fairly bureaucratic organization until its current CEO, Piyush Gupta, started a major programme of cultural transformation[476]. He wanted to create a bank where everyone acted as an entrepreneur. To develop mobile banking, DBS realized that it required much more than replicating a banking website on a mobile phone. DBS understood that they had to bring together actors in disparate industries to create new offerings or capture value that individual companies may not be capable of creating on their own. They needed the collaboration of more than eighty ecosystem partners like telcos or fintech companies. Thanks to the newly developed entrepreneurial spirit, they were ultimately successful in grooming this ecosystem.

2. Complementary foundation partners

Second, foundation partners, often deep down in the value chain, are key to the successful development of an ecosystem. Such foundation partners are not necessarily the biggest or the most established partners. They are the ones that can give a deep insight into what the real needs of the end consumer are or what some of the new capabilities are that needed to be developed. The case of Dassault Systèmes, the French developer of product life cycle management systems, illustrates this. Their core capabilities rest in a set of algorithms that help in all the activities of design, development, production and documentation of new products. The origins of the company go back to their sister organization, Dassault Aviation, of which they were a spin-off. The company understood that its capabilities could be applied in other sectors than aviation or automobile development, but that they lacked the expertise of how design and development was done in sectors like fashion and pharmaceuticals. Their solution was to work with some of the 'hungry' partners in these sectors, who hoped to gain competitive advantage by having a better product life-cycle management system. They were, therefore, prepared to share how they did their design and development. Examples of this were Gucci in the fashion business and Novartis in pharmaceuticals.

3. Clear roadmap

Third, potential partners need a roadmap of how the ecosystem will develop. This will encourage potential partners to engage and invest. The earlier example of ARM illustrates this. Their workshops with all their partners enabled them to define the contours of the future of RISC processors. Such a roadmap may be quite high level and will be dynamic and evolve over time. But an ambitious ecosystem leader needs to provide some signposts to guide the partners on what role they can play in the ecosystem and what opportunities exist for the individual partners. Such a roadmap provides confidence to the ecosystem partners.

4. Clear value propositions for all partners

Fourth, when joining the ecosystem, potential partners will need to understand what is in it for them. An ecosystem leader often understands very well what capabilities potential partners can bring to the ecosystem. But why would they join? An ecosystem leader needs to articulate a set of value propositions that will entice partners. And there needs to be clarity on how the value will be shared. In this context, it is interesting to note that ecosystems often develop knowhow that is shared within the ecosystem but protected from outsiders. We have called this ecosystem goods. But in the process of sharing, all partners have to reflect on what they need to share and what they need to keep for themselves to ensure they can extract value out of the ecosystem. All partners need to have some element of or activity in the ecosystem that they can own and control and on which the ecosystem's ability to create value for customers depends. That will enable them to get a fair share out of the value that is created together. Such an element has been labelled a keystone[477], similar to the keystone that one finds at the top of an arch or a dome and which is essential to keep the construction together. Partners in an ecosystem can extract value when they control such a keystone. It may be a small element in the whole construction, but one that is essential to create stability for the ecosystem as a whole.

5. Minimizing transaction costs and barriers

Fifth, joining an ecosystem inevitably entails transaction costs for any partner joining. How does one reduce the costs and barriers that might impede partners joining the ecosystem? Developing good and simple platforms for sharing information, as we saw in the case of DBS, can help. DBS developed a middleware and more than 200 application programming interfaces (APIs) to help its ecosystem partners to communicate and work with DBS.

6. Supporting sub-ecosystems

And finally, an ecosystem can be greatly helped by partners who bring a sub-ecosystem along and so help speed up the growth of your ecosystem. The case that comes to mind is that of Rolls-Royce setting up a new factory of turbo engines in Singapore[478]. To run that factory, they needed a flow of skilled employees and engineers with a deep understanding of metallurgical construction and aircraft engines assembly. None of that was readily available in Singapore. An ecosystem of universities, polytechnics and the institutes of technical education was needed to educate and train these skilled workers. To do so, they enlisted the help of the Economic Development Board (EDB) and other government institutions. These organizations brought along the whole-of-government ecosystem in Singapore, which was needed to convince some of the institutions of higher learning to build an ecosystem of educational institutions committed to delivering relevant diplomas and degrees.

Key enablers for success

How do you make a business ecosystem work? Without going into all the drivers and enablers for success, I will highlight four of them here—the relentless focus on value creation, the need to build trust, the commitment to continued learning and preserving fairness in the sharing of the value created by the ecosystem.

Investing in an ecosystem only makes sense when one can create additional value that would not be possible without the partners. As we will mention later, the mindset of an ecosystem leader must be one of a relentless commitment to additional value creation and a deep conviction that one organization cannot do it alone. Growing the pie of value must be the goal. That genuine desire to create value for end customers and society is really the trigger for leveraging an ecosystem.

Once the goal of value creation is established, you need to convince partners to join you and then you need to coordinate them. In a market, the coordination mechanism is price setting. Market participants will ultimately collaborate and work together when they have set the price for the transaction and stipulated the contractual obligations. At the other extreme, in a hierarchical organization coordination comes through authority—the boss tells you and your colleagues what to do and how to interact with each other.

How does one coordinate in a hybrid type of organization? Essentially through building trust. Reflect on the example we started with about the group of entrepreneurs in Cambridge. Their very informal collaboration only worked because they trusted each other. And, frankly speaking, also because if one of them would break the trust, he or she would be ostracized within the community. It is because we trust our partners that we can collaborate with them. And because of the trust we have in each other, transaction costs will be lower and the collaboration will endure and survive temporary conflicts and contradictions.

How does one build trust? Of course, it is helped by the respect we have for each other's capabilities and professionalism and the experience we have of working together. And we can enhance and support such trust by developing good interfaces, by codifying some of the complex and tacit knowledge so that it can be exchanged more efficiently, by having good governance procedures and standards and not hesitating to intervene and penalize bad behaviour when one of the partners would take a free ride within the ecosystem. An anecdote about Alibaba demonstrates this issue of governance and penalizing bad behaviour. Alibaba discovered that a seller of electronic fare such as clickers and remote controllers was promoting its product under the category of women's fashion to have more traffic to their site. Alibaba decided not to act itself, but it created a panel of other trustworthy sellers to judge such deviant behaviour and to propose action. Though it is an anecdote, it is an interesting example of how to use the ecosystem partners in governance and policing. Alibaba signalled very clearly to its partners that 'we are in this together and we need to trust each other'.

A third enabler of an effective ecosystem is the commitment to and the development of joint learning. Ultimately, one brings partners together in this loosely coupled network because you want to learn together and you want to leverage the knowledge generated in the ecosystem to enhance your own innovation activities. Therefore, you need to encourage learning and innovation among partners in the ecosystem. And you may want to orchestrate the accumulation of the 'ecosystem goods' that can benefit the whole ecosystem without disadvantaging individual participants. Such ecosystem goods are most often the knowledge that is developed and shared within the ecosystem and between its partners. An example of that is ARM, which works with all of its partners to share the improvements of the design of RISC processors with all partners in the network. An improvement developed by one of the partners, be it an OEM or a chip fab, can be shared throughout the whole network.

You also need to enable the ecosystem to draw in new knowledge from outside which it can use to fuel innovation. But as was mentioned earlier, ecosystem partners will always need to strike the right balance between sharing knowledge within the ecosystem to help it innovate and keeping some knowledge proprietary to underpin getting your own share of the pie and your profitability.

Finally, partners will stay in the ecosystem and contribute when they are convinced that they get their fair share out of the value that is created together. Dividing up the pie in a fair way is never an easy task. But it is essential for the ecosystem leaders to ensure that every partner experiences fairness if you want to keep getting long-term benefits out of the ecosystem.

Steward leadership and business ecosystems

You have probably noticed how similar the values and characteristics of business ecosystems are to the drivers of steward leadership. As an aside, business ecosystems are often compared to the old forms of collaboration that one finds in villages all over the world and which are often described as commons or a place where the community would collaborate to herd the cattle together. The characteristics of such commons are well aligned with some of the principles of steward leadership like long-term view, interdependence and ownership mentality. Elinor Ostrom, who was awarded the Nobel Prize in economics in 2009 for her analysis of economic governance, especially in such Commons, argued that local property can be successfully managed by local commons without any regulation by central authorities or privatization and it is for the long-term good of the local community.

Let us also examine the components of the Steward Leadership Compass and how ecosystem management relates to it.

Stewardship purpose: As has repeatedly been mentioned in this book, steward leadership starts with that genuine desire to create a collective better future. The joint value creation—which is the ultimate driver of an ecosystem—should, can and will encompass this aspiration for a collective better future. It is easy to imagine how the desire to create new value will be aligned at the same time with goals such as investing in renewable energy, developing closed loop logistics chains and enhancing diversity.

Interdependence: Seeing the world as an interconnected system goes back to the essence of what business ecosystems are all about. It is the DNA of an ecosystem. In an ecosystem, you know that your success depends on that of others. The ultimate value creation will be achieved only if we work together.

Long-term view: This is also part of the ambition of an ecosystem. We are not together in a business ecosystem for short-term gain, but ecosystem partners and leaders believe in long-term collaboration to create value through innovation.

Creative resilience: The same is true for the creative resilience or the tenacity to find innovative solutions to disruptive challenges. As I argued from the start of this chapter, business ecosystems are valuable when you are confronted with huge levels of uncertainty and potential disruption.

Ownership mentality: Perhaps the most important element of ecosystem success is ownership mentality. Please note that I say 'ownership mentality' not 'ownership'. In a hierarchical organization, it is ownership and authority that makes things happen. As I mentioned earlier, in an ecosystem, it is trust and mutual respect. The very reason we opt for an ecosystem over a hierarchy is that today's complex problems cannot be solved by one company alone. I also mentioned that creating value through an ecosystem is harder, but the rewards are often greater. To extract the maximum value for all partners, one must apply an ownership mentality towards making the ecosystem effective, i.e., take responsibility to make the ecosystem a success wherein the whole is greater than the sum of its parts. When one applies the ownership mentality in an ecosystem, one commits to working collaboratively and patiently to make sure all partners get the maximum value possible. More on this below.

Thus, these five elements of the Steward Leadership Compass come naturally to business ecosystems.

Leading an ecosystem: Key skills and mindsets

Providing steward leadership in a business ecosystem is very distinctive from leadership in a hierarchical organization. It requires a very different mindset and distinctive traits.

As I already mentioned, one of the key elements of the mindset of an ecosystem steward leader is his or her deep belief that there is an opportunity to create value and a collective better future and the conviction that no single company can unlock the value opportunity acting alone. This is reinforced by a relentless focus on growing the pie, increasing the value created for the ultimate consumer and the society. And finally, in an interdependent system, a leader must be aware that she or he will need to focus on attracting, engaging and motivating people who are not necessarily their employees, but who work for your partners or are independent actors in your ecosystem.

What are the skills required from a steward leader in a business ecosystem? I see four key ones. First, they need the capacity to listen, both to the employees and colleagues within their own organization but also to weak external signals and messages from partners. Partners may not always tell you what they really think. Or they may not even be capable of formulating their tacit knowledge or perceptions. Steward leaders have to be sensitive to the very weak signals that their partners express. I remember from a conversation with one of the CEOs of a successful ecosystem leader company that he felt this was the most challenging part of his job—to truly listen to partners.

Second, they need to have the ability to nudge the ecosystem to respond flexibly to uncertainty and develop the creative resilience. This does not come easy as they may not have formal authority over the partners and their employees. Therefore, they need to develop their soft power. Such soft power comes from their vision, their credibility and the respect they command from their partners.

And finally, they need to be committed to collaboration or getting things done through a community of peers. But this is not traditional collaborative leadership as you would find within an existing organization. As I mentioned before, it requires you to lead beyond your organization. It is about building consensus among the employees of the partners' organizations and ensuring that a wide group of peers take ownership of most of the decisions you will make. Therefore, the steward leader will probably need to be an active networker, becoming a trusted source of knowledge and information that others in the ecosystem have not yet spotted. It is all about persuasion. And the leader will also need to be ambidextrous, will have to be prepared to embrace diversity and dilemmas, while at the same time, develop an overarching identity and goal for the ecosystem. Conflicts will happen in an ecosystem. One cannot and should not avoid them. But they need to be handled wisely and solved in alignment with the ultimate goal of value creation for customers and society.

Conclusion

Well-managed business ecosystems are better at handling innovation when one is confronted with high levels of uncertainty. But they are not easy to manage. The complexity of the relations between partners or the non-hierarchical, sometimes non-contractual, relationships between the partners render it challenging to manage the collaboration. But it is not impossible. In our research, we have described extensively several successful cases and in very different economic contexts, such as China, Europe or the USA.

It is interesting to note that these successful ecosystems have adopted many characteristics of steward leadership. In business ecosystems, there is a genuine desire to create value to prepare for a better future. The purpose of business ecosystems is to find innovative solutions to disruption and thus foster creative resilience. By nature, they have to be long-term oriented and they recognize the interdependence of the partners in the value chain and in society. And with the right leadership, they can also develop a real ownership mentality.

I hope I have convinced you of my core message—business ecosystems are better adapted to innovate and to cope with high levels of uncertainty in the environment. And with the appropriate collaborative leadership, they have a lot in common with organizations that commit themselves to steward leadership. In fact, good steward leadership is essential to creating successful business ecosystems.

Chapter 15

Steward Leadership and DEI: Leading Inclusively for Sustainable Growth

Dr Vinika Rao
*Executive Director, Emerging Markets Institute, Gender
& Africa Initiative, INSEAD
Asia Director, Hoffmann Global Institute for Business and Society
Advisory Board: European Women on Boards (Europe)
and Nine by 9 (Singapore)
Board of Directors: TiE Singapore and Live With AI
Ambassador: Power Women (India) and She2030 (Europe)
International Advisory Committee: Mody University for
Women & SP Jain Return to Work Programme (India).*

Throughout this book so far, we have made the case to upgrade ESG to ESL. I hope by now you are convinced that L (Steward Leadership) enables much stronger impact on both environmental and social challenges. In this chapter, I explore the current state of play with Diversity, Equity and Inclusion (DEI) and explain how powerful it becomes when applied using the steward leadership spirit.

In the survey Stewardship Asia Centre conducted for this book (see Chapter 2 and the Appendix) in 2023, 81 per cent of responders agreed that business leaders who promote diversity and inclusion create greater sustainable impact *because they engage all to take action.* Future-ready business leaders are increasingly aware that customers will not buy from them, investors will not fund them and employees will not work with them if they fail to be effective stewards of the resources they use and the communities they operate within. Profit must be delivered with purpose and this needs to happen both 'intentionally and inclusively'. When leaders equip their organizations for sustainable growth, they need to engage all their stakeholders in this effort by creating a safe, diverse and inclusive work environment that leaves no one behind. Only then will the organization succeed in creating the collective better future that steward leaders strive to establish.

The connection between inclusion and sustainability

The British Academy's Future of the Corporation Programme emphasizes that corporate purpose involves creating profitable solutions for problems of people and planet and not profiting from these problems[479]. However, corporate activity in recent times has created significant problems for both people and the planet, the consequences of which are felt most by those who can afford them the least and are often excluded from impact assessments. The 'Statement of Purpose of a Corporation'[480], which we discussed in Chapter 3, states that while every company serves its own purpose, they ultimately share a commitment to all stakeholders and foster diversity and inclusion. In its definition of sustainable development[481], the United Nations Bruntland report underscores how the needs of current generations should not be met at the cost of the ability of future generations to fulfil their own. The need to be inclusive towards all populations thus extends beyond current generations to those that will come in future years.

The global workforce is more diverse than ever before in human history. People work longer and retire later, meaning that the so-called veterans and baby boomers are active on one end of the age spectrum, while Gen Z is making its presence felt on the other. A quick review of the number of gender identities recognized today reveals lists of over a hundred categories. Workplaces have been made more accessible for differently abled people, across mental and physical dimensions. Technology has thrown out antiquated post-world war HR practices and introduced more flexibility of time and location. It has broken down geographical barriers and allowed increasing combinations of races and nationalities to work together. And diversity is now extending beyond humankind as artificial intelligence takes its spot in offices everywhere. To create, develop and implement sustainable practices effectively in the workplace of the future, the interests and aspirations of all these diverse participants will need to be considered in order to effectively engage them.

The evolution of DEI: Looking beyond diversity

Much has been said and written about the business case for diversity and its purported impact on firm performance. However, there is increasing evidence that just putting together a group of people who cover the facets of diversity is not enough to positively impact performance. In fact, initiatives focused solely on diversity can even serve to increase biases and inequalities[482], create worries about reverse discrimination[483] or penalize the very minority groups they seek to benefit[484]. The positive ramifications on profit and performance kick in when diversity is enhanced with inclusion, equity, mutual respect and belongingness.

Consequently, in the last two decades, DEI in the workplace has evolved from the erstwhile focus on demographic and economic diversity in workforce representation and the obsession with demonstrating the impact on the bottom line. Creating diverse, equitable and inclusive teams is increasingly accepted as an important capability for firms to adapt to the changing needs of people and planet, identifying innovative solutions and executing impactfully for sustainable growth. Today, the DEI conversation is inextricably linked with the overall focus on environmental, societal and governance issues. It has taken its rightful place as an integral component for the achievement of firm purpose and sustainable growth.

Using gender as a case study

Despite the growing acknowledgement of the importance of DEI measures for sustainable business growth and the measures apparently being introduced by organizations, our business and policy collaborators repeatedly raise concerns on why the needle is moving at a glacial pace despite all the efforts being made. 'DEI fatigue' has set in for many. This essay uses the lens of gender, a key diversity parameter, as a case study for exploration into current DEI issues.

'S.A.D.' state of affairs in DEI

A pre-pandemic research I led at the INSEAD Emerging Markets Institute explored the reasons behind persistent gender imbalance with working professionals across the Asia-Pacific region, with a view to understanding what was working and what needed to be changed[485]. The study involved in-depth interviews with women in senior leadership positions, women in mid-level roles and male leaders who self-identified as allies. The resulting findings on what may be missing in the DEI measures implemented by their firms were summarized into what seemed like an appropriate acronym: S.A.D., with an apology for succumbing to the business school fondness for abbreviations.

Lack of Specificity on which needs are being addressed and for whom, in the context of the larger cultural, societal and infrastructural realities and who has identified these needs as being critical. As one young mother in a high-pressure leadership-track role put it, 'Some of these measures have obviously been designed by men, they overcompensate in unimportant areas and miss out in some important ones.'

Lack of Accountability in the implementation of said measures. As one interviewee put it, 'If heads don't roll when targets are not met, the targets are just lip service and the time for that is long gone.' A diversity and inclusion lead from the technology industry agreed, 'Somehow you have to make it more imperative than it is today.' Firms need to be clear in terms of their gender goals at various organizational levels and functions and have clear and committed plans to achieve them.

Lack of Disclosure in terms of transparency on diversity statistics, board pipelines, incentives and targets, etc. As with other aspects of ESG reporting, the guidelines on what should be reported on DEI are still being defined. In the meanwhile, it behoves organizations to act as good stewards and voluntarily disclose all relevant and material

DEI statistics, ideally going one step beyond what their immediate regulations may be insisting upon.

Petrigleiri and Kinias describe a 'systemic web of challenges'[486] that women face in the workplace, including organizational structures and processes; access to resources; psychological experiences; stigmatization of flexible working; small numbers; workplace norms; systemic biases; and access to informal networks. 'All the evidence indicates that increasing gender equality faces a host of interconnected issues, including ones that are societal, structural and psychological.' Given the complexity of the problems, solutions also need to be multi-pronged and involve all genders at all levels and functions of an organization.

Alleviating the 'S.A.D.ness': Recommendations for change

Recognizing that societal norms, regulatory frameworks and infrastructural issues impact the effectiveness of organizational measures to institute cultural change and stringent accountability, it is also up to individuals to act. This includes the marginalized groups seeking equitable opportunities and career progress, their majority-group colleagues who will also benefit from inclusive workplaces and their bosses who are the leaders best-placed to effect change.

Based on inputs from responders across genders and seniority levels, I offer some concrete recommendations that are extendable beyond the gender aspect to support other minority groups:

To established women leaders (marginalized group leaders): Successful women need to spread the success. They have a special responsibility to actively sponsor other women, going a large step beyond mentorship—because women are often over-mentored and under-sponsored[487]. This is especially evident in the higher echelons of organizational hierarchy, which disproportionately low numbers of women manage to reach, often because they do not receive active endorsement from well-placed sponsors who could insist that they get a shot at the challenging and visible roles that are essential for career progress.

To male colleagues and bosses (privileged group colleagues and bosses): Stop pleading 'Unconscious Bias'—as one of our younger responders asked plaintively, 'We do so much unconscious bias training, how can they still be unaware?' The other important aspect to highlight is that male allyship counts. This is especially because so many more men are in positions of authority where they can sponsor actively and demand inclusion across genders. Gender imbalance is not an issue just for any one gender; everyone benefits when it is mitigated, including the currently privileged groups.

To aspiring women leaders (aspiring minority leaders): Be self-aware—know your strengths and weaknesses and be true to yourself. Women do not have to start acting like the men around them to be successful. This also helps to avoid becoming a victim of stereotype threat, where minority groups succumb to stereotypical assumptions about themselves about what they can or cannot do. 'No one was willing to accept that I could be better or even as good as men in the testosterone-filled trading floor and I almost started agreeing with them till my boss reminded me about why I was promoted to that role,' shared one female bank employee. It is also important to optimize all available resources such as the women's networking groups that many companies and industries have developed. Not all are useful and many benefit from the inclusion of other genders, but they can provide the kinds of coalitions of support that men have always enjoyed.

At the same time, I also advise women to not see barriers where they do not exist—that can become a self-fulfilling prophecy. Sometimes, you do not get a promotion because you simply are not the best person for the job and that is okay. One last point that I always add, often surprising corporate audiences in the many seminars that happen especially around International Women's Day every March, is about choosing their long-term personal partners wisely. This can often be the most impactful decision for both personal well-being and professional success, as attested to by no less a successful persona than Warren Buffet himself. 'You want to associate with people who are the kind of person you'd like to be. You'll move in that direction. And the most important person by far in that respect is your spouse. I can't overemphasize how important that is,' he said[488].

Giving disadvantaged groups a 'voice'

In response to the frequent query about what can be done to help marginalized employees find their voice, I always start by pointing out that no one needs assistance with this. The change that is required is not in the excluded individuals and how they use their voices, but rather in their work environment and policies, which need to evolve to allow everyone to feel comfortable in speaking in their authentic voices.

Our survey respondents expressed some reasons why minority groups may not feel comfortable bringing their authentic voices to the workplace. Being different is intimidating, so they are tempted to try to blend in, go with the majority flow and do what is generally expected of them, rather than standing up for what makes them who they truly are. This happens at all organizational levels, not just with the more junior employees. In fact, C-suite executives tell us that it is more difficult when you are the leader because it is a very lonely space anyway. If you are high on affability needs, you want to be part of the team. You do not want one more reason to be separated from them.

In the volatile global context that they work in today, people are making frequent and, often, quite radical changes in the kind of work they do, which may be occasioned by their own evolving preferences or by factors beyond their control. In striving to adapt to the changing dynamics and improve their performance, staying with a fixed conception of who they are can sometimes be an obstacle to progress, the so-called 'authenticity paradox'[489]. However, being authentic does not mean being so anchored in specific beliefs as to refuse to adapt or grow with changing needs and environment. An organizational culture that encourages authenticity of diverse opinions also allows for the flexibility and adaptability of said opinions.

Another consideration that has an expanding impact on authenticity in work contexts is the contemporary reality of being always-on-display. Individuals may feel the need to painstakingly create an image for themselves that they are comfortable sharing with a broad audience, even if this image clashes with their more private self-concept. As several business and political incumbents have realized to their professional detriment, one false foot forward can result in harsh consequences on social media, encouraging people to play it safe, not drawing attention to anything that may differ from the majority view. This is especially true where there is a perception of lack of psychological safety and trust. If people do not feel that the work environment is safe, supportive, collaborative and encouraging of openness and transparency, they will not take the risk of presenting their whole self and being vulnerable in front of others.

An organizational culture that allows for the authentic display of individual beliefs and values, even where they may not 'fit in' with the traditional values of the founders, inspires trust and productivity. Authentic and transparent behaviour from leaders is possibly even more important. Research has shown that employees' perception of their leaders 'authentic leadership' serves as a strong predictor of an employee's job satisfaction, organizational commitment and workplace happiness[490].

Realigning policies for the modern workplace

Firms need to change antiquated policies and procedures to align with contemporary thinking and requirements. For instance, corporate clients striving to create diversity on their boards often express the concern that they are hard-pressed to find suitable candidates to build a sufficient pipeline of minority candidates. I explain that if they are looking for someone who has already held a similar position on another board or at least a C-suite role and has the same profile and experience as their majority candidates, it is hardly surprising that they are not succeeding. They need to revise their parameters, move beyond set templates and bravely go where few boards have gone before. They need to invite candidates based on appropriate aptitude and competency rather than on the kind of prior super senior management or board experience that has been denied to such marginalized candidates before.

Crisis and DEI impact

Covid-19 was a crisis of truly international proportions. Its ramifications were felt all over the world, by all people, but especially by minority groups. In evaluating the evolution of DEI, the watershed moment created by the pandemic for minority groups can provide useful lessons for dealing with future crises. We know that this will not be the last global pandemic. One silver lining of the Covid-19 outbreak was the amount of data that was collated, which will hopefully aid preparedness for the next one.

Continuing with the case study on gender as a key diversity parameter, the following section demonstrates how the pandemic impacted women. In May 2022, when vaccine-readiness meant that the light at the end of the Covid tunnel was becoming visible, a survey by the INSEAD Gender Initiative (IGI) highlighted the disproportionately negative impact of the pandemic on gender balance on business school alumni[491]. Over 6,000 INSEAD alumni responded from every inhabited continent, including 55 per cent respondents from Europe and over 16 per cent from APAC. 23 per cent of the respondents were women, the rest were men, with only twenty respondents identifying as non-binary. Given the statistically small sample, they could not be included in the gender-focused analysis. While having majority of male respondents may have been the unfortunate consequence of fewer women having historically opted for an MBA, it was useful to have the male viewpoint included. The responder group included many in senior management roles, 35 per cent of them served on boards, thus representing a fairly influential group of potential change-agents in their respective organizations.

In response to questions on the impact of the pandemic on their work lives, the men and women reported as follows:

- Jobs eliminated due to budget cuts: More for women (5.3 per cent) than for men (3.6 per cent).
- When looking for new opportunities, the disruption limited options: More for women (14.3 per cent) than for men (11.4 per cent).

It is important to note that this was a relatively privileged group, alumni of a premier business school, many in key decision-making roles. This may explain why the percentages are much lower than statistics reported for broader populations. However, even in this group of highly educated management professionals, the discrepancy between genders was evident.

- Likelihood of scaling back or quitting jobs due to increased family care: More for women (6.4 per cent) than for men (3.7 per cent).

A survey by Deloitte that came out soon after the IGI research showcased similar findings related to women making the choice to take a step back in their careers[492]. Another one by McKinsey indicated that one in four women has voluntarily given up or stepped back from their careers[493]. This is especially worrisome given that we already had the problem of leaky pipeline with women falling off the corporate ladder as the positions become more senior, which the pandemic has exacerbated. Firms that have put in undoubted efforts into building a diverse talent pipeline have learned to their chagrin that hiring stats are no guarantee of retention.

A study of multinational banks in Singapore conducted by INSEAD and the Financial Women's Association in a reasonably stable global period showcased this gender pyramid[494]. While women comprised 67 per cent of their workforce in entry level roles, this fell drastically to 20 per cent by the time they got to the Managing Director level.

The glass ceiling, sticky floor, various conscious and unconscious biases, inequitable work environs and inadequate potential for advancement and development have been blamed for this phenomenon. Covid-19 has made them worse. When minority groups leave a firm at the higher rungs of the corporate ladder, they take with them multiple years of work experience and expensive training, in addition to creating immediate costs of hiring to fill the skills vacuum created.

- Women and men were equivalently called upon with extra work demands: 35 per cent and 36 per cent respectively.

The IGI survey found that while both men and women were almost equally called upon to shoulder extra work demands during the crisis, there was a critical difference in the *kind* of additional work they became responsible for. For men, it was more of direct, actual crisis management responsibilities. For women, it was more of the secondary responsibilities, possibly like filling in for folks who were unable to come to work, thus, more of handling the knock-on effects of disruption. This discrepancy is unfortunately consistent with gender stereotypes in terms of the perception of who is equipped for what kind of top leadership positions. Collaborators in corporate roles have shared anecdotal evidence of how this is exacerbating stereotyping in their organizational contexts. Men who had direct managerial responsibilities for pandemic management acquired the 'hero effect' with a likely positive impact on their future careers. Not so for the women who played equally important and time-consuming secondary activities but are finding it more difficult to have their efforts recognized.

- Likelihood of changing careers due to re-examining priorities: More for women (15.3 per cent) than for men (9.4 per cent).

The pandemic created an opportunity for people to take a step back and evaluate what was most important to them and where their jobs fitted their priorities, especially as the pandemic created new personal and professional challenges. For the women in our sample, a much higher percentage than the men re-evaluated their careers and considered making changes due to the revised priorities, possibly around situations like child or elder care, created by the pandemic.

- Likelihood of needing support due to increased home demands: More for women (34 per cent) than for men (24 per cent).

The dreaded 'second shift' of unpaid labour at home got exacerbated in many households during the pandemic. The study found that for dealing with this, men relied more on domestic partners or spouses and extended family while women ended up needing to find more paid external support. For instance, when schools closed and children had to be supervised during remote learning, the extra burden fell on women in many societal contexts, making their office work more difficult to manage without support. One related positive finding was that the survey found no difference in terms of the support that men and women got from their employers and colleagues.

As these highlights from the IGI survey and other pandemic research since have shown, Covid-19 disproportionately impacted women, as well as other disadvantaged groups. Speedy action is required to avoid losing decades of hard work towards correcting this imbalance and, with it, the associated negative impact on engaging all to achieve sustainable growth.

Who is invested in DEI improvement?

The IGI survey also explored the relative effort that the two genders put into DEI efforts especially during the tumultuous Covid crisis period. When crisis strikes, businesses and individuals struggling for survival may put off 'non-pressing' commitments like DEI measures. The finding was that while both men and women contributed to DEI efforts in the survey period, women did more than men. Women contributed more than men on DEI taskforces, on creating DEI leadership positions, on returner programmes and on developing talent among women and other underrepresented groups. The one area where men contributed more than women was in building parental leave beyond legal mandates. Given the importance of having men actively engaged in the efforts for gender balance, these are important findings. Male allies have a crucial role to play in effecting gender balance, as do other privileged group allies for their marginalized colleagues. The importance of allyship for aiding DEI efforts is becoming more evident in corporate settings.

Allyship: Impact on career progression
of marginalized groups

Continuing with the case study of gender as a key diversity parameter, my study of how male leaders may modify the self-regulating focus of female followers to motivate their pursuit of career progress showcases one mechanism by which allyship can influence success in the workplace[495].

This study conducted in the financial services and technology industries in the Asia-Pacific region demonstrated how male supervisorial advocacy alters the behavioural regulatory focus of female followers. Active sponsorship by male bosses was found to alter the risk-averse and prevention-focused behaviour of aspiring female leaders. Situationally primed by male bosses' allyship, women's behaviour became more promotion-focused, consistent with a motivation to accept risks and take on challenging work responsibilities.

A C-suite executive from the Asian financial services industry explained that besides 'mentorship', where the relationship belongs primarily to the mentee, his bank actively encourages 'advocacy' as a DEI measure. They have formal programmes matching high potential women with senior male leaders who are expected to actively guide and sponsor their development. This action-oriented form of male allyship is being found to yield better and more measurable results. INSEAD Emerging Markets Research on gender disparity in Asian corporate leadership revealed an almost unanimous view, from responders across all genders and generations, that men need to 'lean in' for gender equality. Allyship fosters an organizational culture of authentic inclusivity because everyone, including members of non-minority groups, demonstrate lack of tolerance for discrimination and exclusion.

The most sustainable way for removing unconscious bias is constant engagement and understanding each other's challenges. As they get more engaged in allyship, allies start to better understand their own privilege and biases and feel responsible to use their influence and advantage to correct the imbalance. This also increases their confidence to call them out or seek rectification. One senior male leader highlighted the need for a 'Hall of Fame' and a 'Hall of Shame' to recognize effective allies and to call out those that still 'hide behind unconscious biases'. Allyship helps to take the pressure off the marginalized groups who have traditionally been encouraged to modify their own behaviour, creating the awareness that while change is required, it is not from them but from the other constituents of their work environment.

When members of both the relatively privileged and the marginalized groups work together, they can create a workplace that allows all of them to thrive.

The workplace of the future

The business management students that I work with describe the world that they expect to graduate into as having moved beyond the VUCA (Volatility, Uncertainty, Complexity and Ambiguity) conditions that we used to reference to more graphic acronyms like RUPT (Rapid, Unpredictable, Paradoxical and Tangled), TUNA (Turbulent, Uncertain, Novel, Ambiguous) and BANI (Brittle, Anxious, Non-linear and Incomprehensible). Given a health crisis that decimated millions, a war that brought home the spectre of nuclear annihilation, climate change at unprecedented levels, a planet in peril and thousands of employees continuing to lose their jobs every few weeks, the acronyms seem well justified.

In consultation with HR professionals across Asia in late 2022, I looked at some of the trends that are defining the post-pandemic workplace that these students are taking up jobs in.

(i) **The Great Realization/Reimagination/Reset/Rethink/ Resignation:** The forced isolation of the pandemic afforded many the opportunity to evaluate what was truly meaningful about their work, often reinforcing the desire to engage in work that had purpose beyond monetary implications. For some, it translated into change of jobs and careers, either to follow up on aspirations or to improve their personal or professional circumstances. Others decided to give up on 'traditional' work structures that created restrictions to personal space, time and creativity. These changes continue to influence how the nature of work and the kind of official policies and procedures impact the employer value proposition.

(ii) **Empowered employees:** HR and business leaders must deal with the reality of more empowered employees who want to fit their work around their life instead of the other way around. To increase their engagement at work, employees expressed the need to feel included and valued beyond the pay cheque. They are also less willing to work for organizations that paint them all with the same brush, offering standardized benefits that may not suit their individual preferences. Today, this continues to create some mismatch of expectations between what employers are prepared to offer and what employees deem important. The workplace of the future will likely witness the creation of increasingly customized menus of benefits that employees truly value as well as work models that fit well with their personal lives.

(iii) **Enlightened employers:** As one regional human resources lead put it, 'For the employers who "got it", the writing was on the wall.' HR policies that were created for a work environment that is vastly different from today's tech-enabled modern workplace need to be replaced. The emphasis now needs to be on enhancing trust between employers and employees. Employees want to be treated like rational adults who can behave a certain way without being bound by rules and stringent policies. The famous Netflix culture memo, discussed in Chapter 3, that did away with vacation, dress code and expense policies, among others, provides an excellent example. The focus needs to be on outcomes rather than on processes and on flexible work arrangements rather than on presenteeism. Covid-19 modified mental models around who needs flexibility, moving beyond the traditional assumptions of women with children being the main beneficiaries of flexibility. Men enjoyed flexibility as much as women did and were also unwilling to give it up when pandemic restrictions were lifted. 'Flexify or Fail' became the mantra I espoused, benefitting not just women but even making some HR practices more inclusive towards men than they had been earlier.

(iv) **Evolving expectations from business leaders:** In making choices about where they want to work, people are looking for leaders who make them feel like valued stakeholders whose interests matter to their leaders. Research on what makes people feel included in firms indicates that the mission, policies and practices of the organization and co-worker behaviours all play a role in this. However, at its core, it is down to the leaders. According to one study, what leaders say and do make up to a 70 per cent difference on whether an individual reports feeling included[496]. Also, teams with inclusive leaders have a greater likelihood of reporting that they are high performing (17 per cent more), make better decisions (20 per cent more) and function collaboratively (29 per cent more).

(v) **Enhanced concerns about socioeconomic inequalities and the environment:** The pandemic created an awareness of how suddenly things can go wrong in a fragile and exploited planet and how inequalities of wealth, gender, development levels, healthcare access, etc. can exact harsh penalties on underprivileged people. This feeling of enhanced vulnerability deepened concerns around organizational sustainability and social impact. It increased the expectation for forward-thinking organizations to integrate sustainability and inclusivity into each aspect of their value chains. And it has made people look to business leaders to play a more active role in mitigating the problems of people and planet that they have played a huge role in creating.

The trend of expecting sincere efforts for measurable inclusion and sustainability both within and outside the firm is defining the workplace of the future. Companies are taking notice. 'We believe the most inclusive and diverse culture makes for a better business and a better world,' Diageo sums up nicely[497].

From ESG to ESL

Larcker, Tayan and Watts in their paper, 'Seven Myths of ESG'[498], explain that in linking the achievement of environmental and societal goals with governance, the fallacy is that the necessity of a governance system and the measurement of its quality are largely unrelated to the company's ESG agenda. They are also independent of the non-shareholder stakeholders the company prioritizes. Even organizations that focus solely on Milton Friedman's ideas of shareholder wealth maximization and have no intention of making larger societal or environmental contributions can have excellent governance systems, which are, after all, needed for all firms. Added to this valid argument is the point that creating rules, regulations and measures for environmental and societal metrics is a gargantuan task that may take years to formalize, given the many standards bodies and measures currently in circulation. The current accounting standards took over a century to formalize, so expecting perfect and universally applicable ESG metrics to be developed in a fraction of that time is unrealistic. Even if such metrics are devised and reporting on them is made mandatory, we can be sure that determined greenwashers will find sophisticated loopholes to beat the system.

The survey (see Appendix for details) conducted by the Stewardship Asia Centre in 2023 confirms the above. It revealed that a crisis of confidence prevails in people's trust in the sincerity of corporate efforts to address existential challenges like socioeconomic inequality and climate change. For the companies that do create more positive impact than others in proactively addressing these issues, the primary motivation cited by responders was 'proactive genuine leadership intent to do well by doing good', the premise of steward leadership. Not trusting rules and regulations alone to drive the innovation needed to create long-lasting positive impact on society and environment, 86 per cent felt that steward leadership will fill this gap. 81 per cent felt that business leaders who promote diversity and inclusion as part of their steward leadership efforts help create sustainable impact by involving the entire organization in these efforts.

And here lies the relevance of the radical idea this book proposes—replacing the 'G' of ESG with 'L' for leading inclusively for sustainable growth. The nature of Leadership this will require is 'Steward Leadership', with business leaders working determinedly and sincerely towards a collective better future for all. It creates the expectation that leaders look beyond the metrics and regulations that governance related to environmental and social issues imposes and the incentives that boards and governments may provide to motivate good behaviour. These leaders must be authentic and transparent in their efforts, relying on their internalized moral perspective[499] to behave as they 'ought to' rather than as they 'must'.

Afterword

At the end of the day, steward leadership is a personal choice.

Before one can lead an organization with steward leadership intent, one must decide honestly if steward leadership is for them. In today's highly connected and transparent world, it is nearly impossible to fake it. If one is not genuine about steward leadership, sooner or later the world will find out. Too many corporate bosses are putting out low carbon pledges and other lofty statements of intent these days because society is asking for more responsible behaviour. I wonder how many of them genuinely intend to do something meaningful about them. With CEO and political office tenures getting shorter and shorter, are some of today's long-term pledges sincere?

So, the place to begin the steward leadership journey is honest self-reflection. The best business leaders do not pursue steward leadership because it generates higher returns, though evidence suggests that it is more likely to do so than not. They do so because they want to leave a positive legacy in light of the existential challenges that threaten humanity today. They know fully well that it will not be easy and that there is no guarantee of success. But they firmly believe that their personal success is intertwined with that of others. Based on this, they proactively take ownership to create a collective better future for multiple stakeholders. They take a long-term view on value creation and dig into their creative resilience to find innovative solutions to drive inclusive profitability and growth. In other words, they craft their own personal Steward Leadership Compass first, then use that as a foundation to lead their organizations.

As I mentioned earlier, the challenge of 21st-century business is to drive profitable returns by addressing the very challenges that are threatening us today. To accept this challenge, one will have to choose steward leadership. Will you?

Appendix

Sustainable Sustainability: A Global Survey

This survey aimed to learn how people perceived the private sector's motivations behind their responses to the environmental and social challenges we face in the 21st century.

To ensure data integrity, we outsourced the data collection to CheckMarket by Medallia. Medallia is the pioneer and market leader in customer, employee, citizen and patient experience[1]. CheckMarket is their online survey software platform that helps businesses gain data-driven insights.

In this structured questionnaire, we asked 10,000 individuals—from rank-and-file employees and middle managers to C-suite executives and board directors—across twenty-five countries the following:

1. **What are the top three greatest challenges of the 21st century?**

We wanted to find out which existential threats respondents were most concerned with. We gave respondents a list of challenges humanity faces today, spread across political, social and economic dimensions and asked them to choose the top three greatest challenges of our century.

2. **As a whole, how sincere are the corporate world's efforts to address existential challenges such as climate change and socioeconomic inequality?**

With this question, we aimed to quantify the public's perception of the corporate world's sincerity in addressing these threats.

3. Volkswagen was charged in 2015 for faking emission levels of vehicles it sold between 2006 and 2015. It used a software intended to pass legally required emissions tests, even while the affected engines emitted pollutants up to forty times above permissible limits in the US. Volkswagen admitted that about 11 million cars worldwide were fitted with this software. Subsequently, Nissan (emissions), Boeing (systems malfunction of 737 Max) and several other scandals came to light despite regulations in place. **What do you think was the primary reason for such scandals to happen in the first place?**

4. Patagonia's founder, Yvon Chouinard, gave his company away. Chouinard, his wife and two adult children transferred their ownership of the company, valued at about $3 billion, to a specially designed trust and a non-profit organization. They were created to preserve the company's independence and ensure that all its profits (about $100 million a year) are used to fight climate change and protect undeveloped land around the world. **What do you think was Chouinard's main motivation to do so?**

Q3 and Q4 are contrasting examples of two businesses' manifestations of their ostensible support for the environment. The questions aimed to understand the extent of the public's skepticism towards the companies' intentions.

5. **To what extent do you agree with the following statement? Business leaders who promote diversity and inclusion create greater sustainable impact because they engage all to take action.**

For this question, we wanted to find out if respondents saw a correlation between business leaders' focus on diversity and inclusion and their extent of sustainable impact.

6. **To what extent do you agree that these factors (measurement and reporting, regulation and compliance, tax and compensation incentives, cheaper capital and proactive genuine leadership intent to do well by doing good) influence businesses to address environmental and social challenges?**

7. **Some companies are more sincere than others in proactively addressing environmental and social challenges. What do you think is the primary motivation of the sincerest companies?** (Respondents were given the same factors as Q6 to choose from)

8. **Some companies create more positive impact than others in proactively addressing environmental and social challenges. What do you think is the primary motivation of these companies?** (Respondents were given the same factors as Q6 to choose from)

With Q6, we aimed to find out if the public thought certain factors influenced businesses to address existential challenges. We presented a list of five possible motivators for businesses to tackle environmental and social challenges. This list consists of extrinsic motivators, such as regulation and compliance and cheaper capital and intrinsic motivators, such as the proactive genuine leadership intent to do well by doing good. For each factor, participants indicated the extent to which they agreed it motivated businesses to address existential threats:

- Measurement and reporting
- Regulation and compliance
- Tax and compensation incentives
- Cheaper capital (e.g., from green finance)
- Proactive genuine leadership intent to do well by doing good

We gave the same options for Q7 and Q8, but we asked respondents to choose the factor they thought was the most influential for companies that were the most sincere or impactful.

9. **Rules and regulations are required to minimize further harm to the environment and society, but they do not drive the innovation needed to create long-lasting positive impact on the environment and society. To what extent do you agree with this statement?**

We wanted to find out if the corporate world's predominant response to existential threats—rules and regulations—was perceived as sufficient to drive the innovation needed to create positive and enduring impact on our environment and society.

10. **Steward leadership is the genuine desire and persistence to create a collective better future. Steward leaders create the collective better future by integrating the needs of stakeholders, society, future generations and the environment. To what extent do you agree that steward leadership is essential to drive the innovation needed to create long-lasting positive impact on the environment and society?**

With Q10, we wanted to see if respondents agreed with our proposal that steward leadership is the direction we need to move towards to drive the necessary innovation for a sustainable future.

Sample sizes were chosen based on the statistically significant proportions of each of the twenty-five countries we looked at.

The global results can be found on the pages that follow.

Q1. What are the top three greatest challenges of the 21st century?

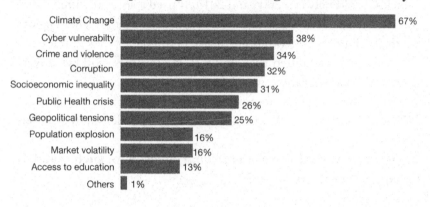

Q2. As a whole, how sincere are the corporate world's efforts to address existential challenges such as climate change and socioeconomic inequality?

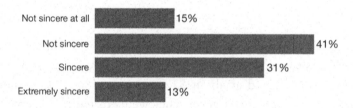

Not sincere at all (e.g., blatant greenwashing and deceiving)

Not sincere (e.g., paying lip service, more form than substance)

Sincere (e.g., playing by the rules, abiding the law, avoiding harmful action)

Extremely sincere (e.g., proactively creating solutions, beyond complying with rules and regulations, to address environmental and social challenges)

Q3. Volkswagen was charged in 2015 for faking emission levels of vehicles it sold between 2006 and 2015. It used a software intended to pass legally required emissions tests, even while the affected engines emitted pollutants up to 40 times above permissible limits in the US.

Volkswagen admitted that about 11 million cars worldwide were fitted with this software.

Subsequently, Nissan (emissions), Boeing (systems malfunction of 737 Max) and several other scandals came to light despite regulations in place.

What do you think was the *primary* reason for such scandals to happen in the first place?

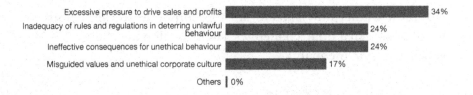

Q4. Patagonia's founder, Yvon Chouinard, gave his company away. Chouinard, his wife and two adult children transferred their ownership of the company, valued at about $3 billion, to a specially designed trust and a non-profit organisation. They were created to preserve the company's independence and ensure that all its profits (about US$100 million a year) are used to fight climate change and protect undeveloped land around the world.

What do you think was Chouinard's *main* motivation to do so?

Q5. To what extent do you agree with the following statement: **Business leaders who promote diversity and inclusion create greater sustainable impact because they engage all to take action.**

Q6. To what extent do you agree that these factors influence businesses to address environmental and social challenges?

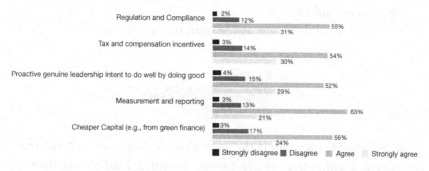

Q7. Some companies are *more sincere* than others in proactively addressing environmental and social challenges.

What do you think is the *primary* motivation of the most sincere companies?

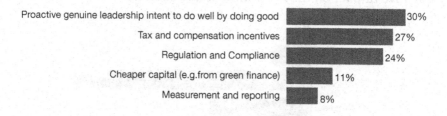

Q8. Some companies *create more positive impact* than others in proactively addressing environmental and social challenges.

What do you think is the *primary* motivation of these companies?

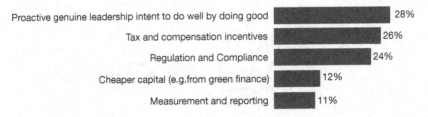

Q9. Rules and regulations are required to minimise further harm to the environment and society, but they do not drive the innovation needed to create long-lasting positive impact on the environment and society.

To what extent do you agree with this statement?

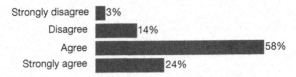

Q10. Steward leadership is the *genuine desire and persistence* to create a collective better future. Steward leaders create the collective better future by integrating the needs of stakeholders, society, future generations and the environment.

To what extent do you agree that steward leadership is essential to drive the innovation needed to create long-lasting positive impact on the environment and society?

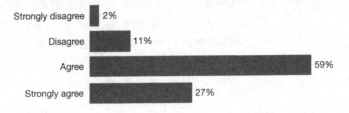

Notes

1   https://www.nytimes.com/2023/07/20/climate/hottest-june-in-history-noaa.html

2   https://www.axios.com/2023/07/20/world-heat-wave-records-us-europe-china

3   https://public.wmo.int/en/media/press-release/past-eight-years-confirmed-be-eight-warmest-record

4   'ESG May Surpass $41 Trillion Assets in 2022, But Not Without Challenges, Finds Bloomberg Intelligence', Jan 24, 2022, Bloomberg, https://www.bloomberg.com/company/press/esg-may-surpass-41-trillion-assets-in-2022-but-not-without-challenges-finds-bloomberg-intelligence/.

5   'The Long View: How will the global economic order change by 2050?', Feb 2017, PwC, https://www.pwc.com/gx/en/world-2050/assets/pwc-the-world-in-2050-full-report-feb-2017.pdf.

6   Budd, Stacey, 'Six scary facts about climate change', Oct 25, 2017, *Ecotricity*, https://www.ecotricity.co.uk/our-news/2017/six-scary-facts-about-climate-change.

7   'Past Earth Overshoot Days', Earth Overshoot Days, https://www.overshootday.org/newsroom/past-earth-overshoot-days/.

8   'Fact Sheet: Global Species Decline', Mar 18, 2022, Earthday.org, https://www.earthday.org/fact-sheet-global-species-decline/.   Budd, Stacey, 'Six scary facts about climate change', Oct 25, 2017, *Ecotricity*, https://www.ecotricity.co.uk/our-news/2017/six-scary-facts-about-climate-change.

9   '5 Climate Change Facts to Scare You into Action This Halloween', Oct 21, 2022, Earthday.org, https://www.earthday.org/5-terrifying-climate-change-facts-scare-halloween/.

10 Whiting, Kate, '5 shocking facts about inequality, according to Oxfam's latest report', Jan 20, 2020, World Economic Forum, https://www.weforum.org/agenda/2020/01/5-shocking-facts-about-inequality-according-to-oxfam-s-latest-report/.

11 Whiting, Kate, '5 shocking facts about inequality, according to Oxfam's latest report', Jan 20, 2020, World Economic Forum, https://www.weforum.org/agenda/2020/01/5-shocking-facts-about-inequality-according-to-oxfam-s-latest-report/.

12 '20 Frightening Cyber Security Facts and Stats', Databasix, https://www.dbxuk.com/statistics/cyber-security.

13 We will discuss Friedman's declaration in more detail in the next chapter.

14 Wong, Christina and Petroy, Erika, 'Rate the Raters 2020', SustainAbility Institute, https://www.sustainability.com/thinking/rate-the-raters-2020/.

15 Pollman, E., *The Making and Meaning of ESG*, 2022, University of Pennsylvania Carey Law School, Institute for Law and Economics Research Paper, 22–23.

16 Annan, Kofi, 'Kofi Annan's address to World Economic Forum in Davos', Feb 1, 1999, United Nations, https://www.un.org/sg/en/content/sg/speeches/1999-02-01/kofi-annans-address-world-economic-forum-davos.

17 You can access the report, titled 'Who Cares Wins', here: https://www.unepfi.org/fileadmin/events/2004/stocks/who_cares_wins_global_compact_2004.pdf.

18 Bushard, Brian, 'Boeing Pleads Not Guilty In 737 Max Crash Fraud Case', Jan 26, 2023, *Forbes*, https://www.forbes.com/sites/brianbushard/2023/01/26/boeing-arraigned-in-court-over-737-max-crashes-two-years-after-25-billion-settlement/?sh=4071c200ad9f.

19 Perkins, Chris, 'VW's Emissions-Cheating Defeat Device Was Developed By Audi In 1999 to Reduce Noise', Jul 19, 2016, *Roadtrack*, https://www.roadandtrack.com/new-cars/car-technology/news/a30029/vw-acoustic-function-defeat-device/.

20 Gardella, Rich and Brunker, Mike, 'VW had previous run-in over "defeat devices"', Sep 23, 2015, *CNBC*, https://www.cnbc.com/2015/09/23/vw-had-previous-run-in-over-defeat-devices.html.

21 Rogers, Christina and Spector, Mike, 'Judge Slaps VW With $2.8 Billion Criminal Fine in Emissions Fraud', Apr 21, 2017, *WSJ*, Judge Slaps VW With $2.8 Billion Criminal Fine in Emissions Fraud - WSJ. Volkswagen

to pay out £193m in 'dieselgate' settlement', May 25, 2022, *BBC*, https://www.bbc.com/news/business-61581251.

22   Metz, Rachel, 'Elizabeth Holmes sentenced to more than 11 years in prison for fraud', Nov 18, 2022, *CNN Business*, https://edition.cnn.com/2022/11/18/tech/elizabeth-holmes-theranos-sentencing/index.html.

23   Khan, Romy, 'Theranos' $9 Billion Evaporated: Stanford Expert Whose Questions Ignited The Unicorn's Trouble', *Forbes*, Feb 17, 2017, https://www.forbes.com/sites/roomykhan/2017/02/17/theranos-9-billion-evaporatedstanford-expert-whose-questions-ignited-the-unicorn-trouble/?sh=7cb14f536be8.

24   Massinon, Stephanie, 'Former Enron CFO: From accounting hero to convict', *UCalgary News*, Apr 16, 2019, https://ucalgary.ca/news/former-enron-cfo-accounting-hero-convict.

25   The detailed article titled 'Sustainable forestry project in Latin America' can be referred to here: https://www.faber-castell.com/corporate/sustainability/sustainable-forestry-projects.

26   More information on the contribution of the Tatas to the community can be found here: https://www.tata.com/community.

27   Kerr, Steven, 'On the Folly of Rewarding A, While Hoping for B', *Academy of Management Journal*, Dec 1975, Vol. 18.4, pp.769–783, https://web.mit.edu/curhan/www/docs/Articles/15341_Readings/Motivation/Kerr_Folly_of_rewarding_A_while_hoping_for_B.pdf.

28   Mulholland, Paul, 'Goldman Sachs Agrees to Pay $4 Million to SEC for ESG Violations', *Chief Investment Officer*, Dec 6, 2022, https://www.ai-cio.com/news/goldman-sachs-agrees-to-pay-4-million-to-sec-for-esg-violations/.

29   Cook, James, 'Amazon, IKEA and Apple exaggerating sustainability claims—can technology solve greenwashing?' Mar 29, 2022, https://www.businessleader.co.uk/amazon-ikea-and-apple-exaggerating-sustainability-claims-can-technology-solve-greenwashing/.

30   The Steward Leadership Summit is an annual conference organized by Stewardship Asia Centre in Singapore to advance the practice of steward leadership and to honour the top 25 true E/S champions, or steward leaders, within Asia-Pacific. More information on the summit and the honouring process called Steward Leadership 25 (SL25) can be obtained at https://www.stewardshipasia.com.sg/what-we-do/engagement-and-outreach/steward-leadership-summit.

31   Horton, Helena, 'Activists accuse drinks firm Innocent of 'greenwashing' with ad', Feb 2, 2022, https://www.theguardian.com/environment/2022/

feb/02/activists-accuse-drinks-firm-innocent-greenwashing-plastics-rebellion-advertising-tv-advert.

32   Peshawaria, Rajeev, *Too Many Bosses, Too Few Leaders: The Three Essential Principles You Need to Become an Extraordinary Leader*, Simon & Schuster, 2011. Peshawaria, Rajeev, *Open Source Leadership*, McGraw-Hill, 2017.

33   Peshawaria, Rajeev, 'How To Develop Your Emotional Integrity', *Forbes*, Nov 17, 2014, https://www.forbes.com/sites/rajeevpeshawaria/2014/11/17/emotional-integrity/?sh=616d8cab37ac.Peshawaria, Rajeev, *Open Source Leadership*, McGraw-Hill, 2017.

34   Khatri, Akanksha, 'A blueprint for business to transition to a nature-positive future', Jul 15, 2020, *World Economic Forum*, https://www.weforum.org/agenda/2020/07/future-nature-business-action-agenda-blueprint-climate-change-biodiversity-loss/.

35   'Unilever Could Use Some Guidance', *Forbes*, Feb 5, 2009, https://www.forbes.com/2009/02/05/unilever-earnings-update-markets-equity-0205_consumers_guidance25.html?sh=6f8dee8c4cc2.

36   Jope, Allan, 'The Unilever Compass: our next game-changer for business', May 12, 2020, Unilever, https://www.unilever.com/news/news-and-features/Feature-article/2020/the-unilever-compass-our-next-game-changer-for-business.html.

37   'Brands with purpose grow—and here's the proof', June 11, 2019, Unilever, https://www.unilever.com/news/news-and-features/Feature-article/2019/brands-with-purpose-grow-and-here-is-the-proof.html.

38   Jope, Allan, 'The Unilever Compass: our next game-changer for business', May 12, 2020, Unilever, https://www.unilever.com/news/news-and-features/Feature-article/2020/the-unilever-compass-our-next-game-changer-for-business.html.

39   George, Bill, Krishna G. Palepu, Carin-Isabel Knoop, and Matthew Preble, 'Unilever's Paul Polman: Developing Global Leaders', Harvard Business School Case 413–097, May 2013, http://store.hbr.org/product/unilever-s-paul-polman-developing-global-leaders/413097.

40   Aziz, Afdhel, 'Paul Polman On Courageous CEOs And How Purpose Is The Growth Story Of The Century (Part 1)', *Forbes*, May 25, 2020, https://www.forbes.com/sites/afdhelaziz/2020/05/25/paul-polman-on-purpose-courageous-ceos-and-the-growth-story-of-the-century-part-1/?sh=26ccbd311dfd.

41 'Unilever, Patagonia, Ikea, Interface, and Natura &Co Most Recognized by Experts as Sustainability Leaders According to 2020 Leaders Survey: Four New Companies Join Ranking', Aug 12, 2020, *Globe Scan*, https://globescan.com/unilever-patagonia-ikea-interface-top-sustainability-leaders-2020/.

42 Todd-Ryan, Samantha, 'Who Are The 100 Most Sustainable Companies Of 2020?', Jan 21, 2020, *Forbes*, https://www.forbes.com/sites/samanthatodd/2020/01/21/who-are-the-100-most-sustainable-companies-of-2020/#4d15c37814a4.

43 Attributed to Nelson Mandela, *Mind Blood*, https://mindblood.com/i-never-lose-i-either-win-or-learn-nelson-mandela-similar-quotes/.

44 Peshawaria, Rajeev, Too Many Bosses, *Too Few Leaders: The Three Essential Principles You Need to Become an Extraordinary Leader*, Simon & Schuster, 2011.

45 'The meaning of emotional intelligence', *Last Eight Percent*, https://www.ihhp.com/meaning-of-emotional-intelligence/.

46 Peshawaria, Rajeev, *Open Source Leadership*, McGraw-Hill, 2017.

47 Peshawaria, Rajeev, 'Boss to Leader to Steward Leader: Three Stages of Leadership Maturity', Sep 13, 2021, *Forbes*, https://www.forbes.com/sites/rajeevpeshawaria/2021/09/13/boss-to-leader-to-steward-leader-three-stages-of-leadership-maturity/?sh=6da4ba6a3c85.

48 Peshawaria, Rajeev, 'Stewardship: The Core Compass of Real Leaders', Sep 22, 2020, *Forbes*, https://www.forbes.com/sites/rajeevpeshawaria/2020/09/22/stewardship-the-core-compass-of-real-leaders/?sh=30be8bbc428a.

49 Friedman, Milton, 'A Friedman doctrine—The Social Responsibility of Business Is to Increase Its Profits', Sep 13, 1970, accessed from *New York Times Archive*. The full text can be found here: https://www.nytimes.com/1970/09/13/archives/a-friedman-doctrine-the-social-responsibility-of-business-is-to.html.

50 Friedman, Milton, 'A Friedman doctrine—The Social Responsibility of Business Is to Increase Its Profits', Sep 13, 1970, accessed from *New York Times Archive*. The full text can be found here: https://www.nytimes.com/1970/09/13/archives/a-friedman-doctrine-the-social-responsibility-of-business-is-to.html.

51 Friedman, Milton, 'A Friedman doctrine—The Social Responsibility of Business Is to Increase Its Profits', Sep 13, 1970, accessed from *New*

York Times Archive. The full text can be found here: https://www. nytimes.com/1970/09/13/archives/a-friedman-doctrine-the-social-responsibility-of-business-is-to.html.

52 Friedman, Milton, 'A Friedman doctrine—The Social Responsibility of Business Is to Increase Its Profits', Sep 13, 1970, accessed from *New York Times Archive.* The full text can be found here: https://www. nytimes.com/1970/09/13/archives/a-friedman-doctrine-the-social-responsibility-of-business-is-to.html.

53 Friedman, Milton, 'A Friedman doctrine—The Social Responsibility of Business Is to Increase Its Profits', Sep 13, 1970, accessed from *New York Times Archive.* The full text can be found here: https://www. nytimes.com/1970/09/13/archives/a-friedman-doctrine-the-social-responsibility-of-business-is-to.html.

54 'Business Roundtable Redefines the Purpose of a Corporation to Promote "An Economy That Serves All Americans"', Aug 19, 2019, *Business Roundtable,* https://www.businessroundtable.org/business-roundtable-redefines-the-purpose-of-a-corporation-to-promote-an-economy-that-serves-all-americans.

55 Friedman, Milton, 'A Friedman doctrine—The Social Responsibility of Business Is to Increase Its Profits', Sep 13, 1970, accessed from New York Times Archive. The full text can be found here: https://www. nytimes.com/1970/09/13/archives/a-friedman-doctrine-the-social-responsibility-of-business-is-to.html.

56 'Internet user growth worldwide from 2018 to 2023', *Statista,* Jan 19, 2023, https://www.statista.com/statistics/1190263/internet-users-worldwide/.

57 A real-time counter of world population can be found here: https://www.worldometers.info/world-population/.

58 Friedman, Milton, 'A Friedman doctrine—The Social Responsibility of Business Is to Increase Its Profits', Sep 13, 1970, accessed from New York Times Archive. The full text can be found here: https://www. nytimes.com/1970/09/13/archives/a-friedman-doctrine-the-social-responsibility-of-business-is-to.html.

59 Henisz, Witold, Koller, Tim, and Nuttall Robin, 'Five ways that ESG creates value', *McKinsey Quarterly,* Nov 2019, https://www.mckinsey.com/~/media/McKinsey/Business Functions/ Strategy and Corporate Finance/Our Insights/Five ways that ESG creates value/Five-ways-that-ESG-creates-value.ashx.

60 McCord, Patty, 'How Netflix Reinvented HR', *Harvard Business Review*, Jan–Feb 2014, https://hbr.org/2014/01/how-netflix-reinvented-hr.

61 Victor, Daniel, Stevens, Matt, 'United Airlines Passenger Is Dragged From an Overbooked Flight', *New York Times*, Apr 10, 2017, https://www.nytimes.com/2017/04/10/business/united-flight-passenger-dragged.html.

62 Definition of 'purpose' as per the *Britannica Dictionary* can be found here: https://www.britannica.com/dictionary/purpose.

63 The entire list of visions and values of Enron can be found here: 'Statement of Human Rights Principles', https://www.csus.edu/indiv/m/merlinos/enron.html.

64 Violo, Marco, '25 companies carrying out corporate social innovation', *SIX*, Feb 1, 2018, https://socialinnovationexchange.org/25-companies-carrying-out-corporate-social-innovation/.

65 More on this can be found here: https://www.faber-castell.com/corporate/sustainability/economic#:~:text=The%20company%20is%20characterized%20by,well%20as%20decorative%20cosmetic%20products.

66 Faber-Castell, *Corporate Kit*, 2011, retrieved May 31, 2023, https://issuu.com/faber-castell/docs/faber-castell_corporate_kit_2011_english.

67 Faber-Castell, *Anniversary Magazine*, 2011, retrieved from https://issuu.com/faber-castell/docs/e-mag_1002.

68 'Limited edition "Polygrades" to mark Lothar von Faber's 200th birthday', Faber-Castell, https://www.faber-castell.com/polygrades.

69 Limited edition "Polygrades" to mark Lothar von Faber's 200th birthday', Faber-Castell, https://www.faber-castell.com/polygrades.

70 'A Brief History of the Pencil', Faber-Castell, https://www.faber-castell.co.uk/~/media/Faber-Castell/brochures/en/Press/A%20-brief-history-of-the-pencil.ashx.

71 'A Brief History of the Pencil', Faber-Castell, https://www.faber-castell.co.uk/~/media/Faber-Castell/brochures/en/Press/A%20-brief-history-of-the-pencil.ashx.

72 'A Brief History of the Pencil', Faber-Castell, https://www.faber-castell.co.uk/~/media/Faber-Castell/brochures/en/Press/A%20-brief-history-of-the-pencil.ashx.

73 'A Brief History of the Pencil', Faber-Castell, https://www.faber-castell.co.uk/~/media/Faber-Castell/brochures/en/Press/A%20-brief-

history-of-the-pencil.ashx. The inflation rate in Germany can be calculated using the calculator here: https://www.lawyerdb.de/Inflationrate.aspx.

74 Vasold, Manfred, 'Mortality in Nuremberg in the 19th century (about 1800 to 1913)', *Pubmed*, National Library of Medicine, 2006, 25:241–338, https://pubmed.ncbi.nlm.nih.gov/17333866/.

75 'Death rate, crude (per 1,000 people) – Germany', World Bank, https://data.worldbank.org/indicator/SP.DYN.CDRT.IN?locations=DE.

76 Faber-Castell, *Anniversary* Magazine, 2011, https://www.tintadlaplastykow.pl/gfx/docs/gitem_16094/fabercastell-anniversary-magazine-engoriginal381.20.pdf.

77 Busse, Reinhard, Blümel, Miriam, Knieps, Franz, Bärnighausen, Till, 'Statutory health insurance in Germany: a health system shaped by 135 years of solidarity, self-governance, and competition', Lancet, 2017, 390: 882–97, https://www.thelancet.com/pdfs/journals/lancet/PIIS0140-6736(17)31280-1.pdf.

78 Faber-Castell, *Anniversary* Magazine, 2011, https://issuu.com/faber-castell/docs/e-mag_1002.

79 In his will, Lothar von Faber stipulated that whichever of his descendants succeeded to his estate should carry on not just the company name but also the Faber name. When his eldest granddaughter married Count Alexander zu Castell-Rüdenhausen, no other member of the Faber family was left, so a new line of Counts von Faber-Castell was established.

80 In his will, Lothar von Faber stipulated that whichever of his descendants succeeded to his estate should carry on not just the company name but also the Faber name. When his eldest granddaughter married Count Alexander zu Castell-Rüdenhausen, no other member of the Faber family was left, so a new line of Counts von Faber-Castell was established.

81 Faber-Castell, *Anniversary* Magazine, 2011, https://issuu.com/faber-castell/docs/e-mag_1002.

82 Sternad, D., Kennelly, J.J., and Bradley, F., *Digging deeper: How purpose-driven enterprises create real value*, Routledge, 2017.

83 *The Honorable Mercahnt*, Nuremberg Chamber of Commerce and Industry, 2018, https://www.ihk-nuernberg.de/de/media/PDF/Publikationen/Hauptgeschaeftsfuehrung/broschuere-the-honorable-merchant-.pdf.

84 *The Honorable Mercahnt*, Nuremberg Chamber of Commerce and Industry, 2018,

https://www.ihk-nuernberg.de/de/media/PDF/Publikationen/Hauptgeschaeftsfuehrung/broschuere-the-honorable-merchant-.pdf.

85 Sternad, D., Kennelly, J.J., & Bradley, F., *Digging deeper: How purpose-driven enterprises create real value*, Routledge, 2017.

86 Woodhead, Michael, 'Pencil tycoon stays at sharp end', *Times*, July 18, 2010, https://www.thetimes.co.uk/article/pencil-tycoon-stays-at-sharp-end-jdpldcztgk2.

87 Faber-Castell, *Anniversary* Magazine, 2011, https://issuu.com/faber-castell/docs/e-mag_1002.

88 Faber-Castell, *Communication on Progress of Faber-Castell*, 2008, https://ungc-production.s3.us-west-2.amazonaws.com/attachments/904/original/COP.pdf?1262614229.

89 Sternad, D., Kennelly, J.J., & Bradley, F., *Digging deeper: How purpose-driven enterprises create real value*, Routledge, 2017.

90 Faber-Castell, 'Corporate Essentials', https://www.faber-castell.com.sg/corporate-essential.

91 De Massis, Alfredo, Audretsch, David, Uhlaner, Lorraine, Kammerlander, Nadine, 'Innovation with Limited Resources: Management Lessons from the German Mittelstand', *Journal of Product Innovation Management*, Mar 10, 2017, https://onlinelibrary.wiley.com/doi/full/10.1111/jpim.12373.

92 'From Pine to Pencil', Faber-Castell, https://www.faber-castell.eu/corporate/magazin/forestry-management-prata.

93 'From Pine to Pencil', Faber-Castell, https://www.faber-castell.eu/corporate/magazin/forestry-management-prata.

94 'Sustainabilioty Factsheets', Faber-Castell, https://www.fabercastell.com/blogs/creativity-for-life/sustainability-fact-sheets.

95 'Faber-Castell Sustainability Fact Sheet 2022', Fabert-Castell, https://issuu.com/faber-castell/docs/sustainability_report_2022_en.

96 Faber-Castell, Anniversary Magazine, 2011, https://issuu.com/faber-castell/docs/e-mag_1002.

97 From Pine to Pencil', Faber-Castell, https://www.faber-castell.eu/corporate/magazin/forestry-management-prata.

98 *Our Global Commitment*, Faber-Castell, 2008.

99 Faber-Castell, Anniversary Magazine, 2011, https://issuu.com/faber-castell/docs/e-mag_1002.

100   Gallon, Vincent, 'Faber-Castell Cosmetics celebrates 40 years and announce new international development plans', *Premium Beauty News*, June 28, 2018, https://www.premiumbeautynews.com/en/faber-castell-cosmetics-celebrates,13606#nb1.

101   Naldi, Samuel, 'The Perfect Pencil, An Icon.' *Inkstable*, Sep 16, 2022, https://inkstable.com/the-perfect-pencil-an-icon/.

102   Olson, Nancy, 'Graf Von Faber-Castell's Pen Of The Year 2022', *Forbes*, May 23, 2022, https://www.forbes.com/sites/nancyolson/2022/05/23/graf-von-faber-castells-pen-of-the-year-2022/?sh=c7dfda839750.

103   'Faber-Castell Malaysia celebrates 40 years of success with extraordinary performance', Faber-Castell, https://www.faber-castell.com.my/corporate/40th-anniversary-malaysia.

104   Diskul na Ayudhya, P., '"It Can Be Done": Economic Forests and Social Entrepreneurship in Doi Tung, Thailand. Knowledge Creation in Community Development,' Hirose Nishihara, A., Matsunaga, M., Nonaka, I., Yokomichi, K. (Eds.), *Knowledge Creation in Community Development*, Palgrave Macmillan, Cham, 2018, https://doi.org/10.1007/978-3-319-57481-3_8, pp. 149–174.

105   Diskul na Ayudhya, P., '"It Can Be Done": Economic Forests and Social Entrepreneurship in Doi Tung, Thailand,' Hirose Nishihara, A., Matsunaga, M., Nonaka, I., Yokomichi, K. (Eds.), *Knowledge Creation in Community Development*, Palgrave Macmillan, Cham, 2018, p.1.

106   Diskul na Ayudhya, P., '"It Can Be Done": Economic Forests and Social Entrepreneurship in Doi Tung, Thailand,' Hirose Nishihara, A., Matsunaga, M., Nonaka, I., Yokomichi, K. (Eds.), *Knowledge Creation in Community Development*, Palgrave Macmillan, Cham, 2018, p.1.

107   'The Mae Fah Luang: The Social Transformation Model for the 21st Century', The Mae Fah Luang Foundation under Royal Patronage, 2010.

108   Diskul na Ayudhya, P., '"It Can Be Done": Economic Forests and Social Entrepreneurship in Doi Tung, Thailand,' Hirose Nishihara, A., Matsunaga, M., Nonaka, I., Yokomichi, K. (Eds.), *Knowledge Creation in Community Development*, Palgrave Macmillan, Cham, 2018, p.1.

109   Diskul na Ayudhya, P., '"It Can Be Done": Economic Forests and Social Entrepreneurship in Doi Tung, Thailand,' Hirose Nishihara, A., Matsunaga, M., Nonaka, I., Yokomichi, K. (Eds.), *Knowledge Creation in Community Development*, Palgrave Macmillan, Cham, 2018, p.1.

110 Diskul na Ayudhya, P., '"It Can Be Done": Economic Forests and Social Entrepreneurship in Doi Tung, Thailand,' Hirose Nishihara, A., Matsunaga, M., Nonaka, I., Yokomichi, K. (Eds.), *Knowledge Creation in Community Development*, Palgrave Macmillan, Cham, 2018, p.1.

111 Diskul na Ayudhya, P., '"It Can Be Done": Economic Forests and Social Entrepreneurship in Doi Tung, Thailand,' Hirose Nishihara, A., Matsunaga, M., Nonaka, I., Yokomichi, K. (Eds.), *Knowledge Creation in Community Development*, Palgrave Macmillan, Cham, 2018, p.1.

112 *Doi Tung: From Opium Poppy Farmers To Social Entrepreneurs*, Global Partnership on Drug Policies and Development (GPDPD), 2018, https://www.gpdpd.org/en/drug-policy/alternative-development/doi-tung-from-opium-poppy-farmers-to-social-entrepreneurs.

113 Diskul na Ayudhya, P., '"It Can Be Done": Economic Forests and Social Entrepreneurship in Doi Tung, Thailand,' Hirose Nishihara, A., Matsunaga, M., Nonaka, I., Yokomichi, K. (Eds.), *Knowledge Creation in Community Development*, Palgrave Macmillan, Cham, 2018, p.1.

114 Diskul na Ayudhya, P., '"It Can Be Done": Economic Forests and Social Entrepreneurship in Doi Tung, Thailand,' Hirose Nishihara, A., Matsunaga, M., Nonaka, I., Yokomichi, K. (Eds.), *Knowledge Creation in Community Development*, Palgrave Macmillan, Cham, 2018, p.1.

115 Diskul, M. R. D., 'Royal Initiatives in the Global Context: The Mae Fah Luang Foundation Under Royal Patronage A Living Example of Sustainable Development', *Sasin Journal of Management*, 2009.

116 'THAI and Doi Tung Launch Black Silk Blend Onboard Premium Drip Coffee', Thai Airways, Mar 14, 2022, https://www.thaiairways.com/en/news/news_announcement/news_detail/blacksilkblend.page.

117 'Global Partnership on Drug Policies and Development', *Doi Tung: From Opium Poppy Farmers to Social Entrepreneurs*, 9.

118 Case Study: Doi Tung Development Project, Japan Research Institute & Multilateral Investment Fund, 2016.
Study of Social Entrepreneurship and Innovation Ecosystems in South East and East Asian Countries, The Mae Fah Luang Foundation, Thailand, Inter-American Development Bank.

119 'Shared meals and local design to create jobs where they are needed', IKEA, February 17, 2021, https://about.ikea.com/en/behind-scenes/products-design/2021/02/17/shared-meals-and-local-design.

120 'IKEA and Doi Tung Development Project Release Allvarlig Tableware Collection', *BK*, Apr 9, 2012, https://bk.asia-city.com/shopping/news/ikea-doi-tung-table-ware-collection.

121 Case Study: Doi Tung Development Project, Japan Research Institute & Multilateral Investment Fund, 2016, The Mae Fah Luang Foundation, Thailand, 12.

122 Case Study: Doi Tung Development Project, Japan Research Institute & Multilateral Investment Fund, 2016, The Mae Fah Luang Foundation, Thailand, 12.

123 Japan Research Institute & Multilateral Investment Fund, 'Case Study: Doi Tung Development Project', The Mae Fah Luang Foundation, Thailand, 2016, 12.

124 Diskul, M.R.D, 'Royal Initiatives in the Global Context: The Mae Fah Luang Foundation Under Royal Patronage A Living Example of Sustainable Development', *Sasin Journal of Management*, 2009, 10.

125 Diskul na Ayudhya, P., '"It Can Be Done": Economic Forests and Social Entrepreneurship in Doi Tung, Thailand,' Hirose Nishihara, A., Matsunaga, M., Nonaka, I., Yokomichi, K. (Eds.), *Knowledge Creation in Community Development*, Palgrave Macmillan, Cham, 2018, p.1.

126 Japan Research Institute & Multilateral Investment Fund, 'Case Study: Doi Tung Development Project', The Mae Fah Luang Foundation), Thailand, 2016, 12.

127 Diskul na Ayudhya, P., '"It Can Be Done": Economic Forests and Social Entrepreneurship in Doi Tung, Thailand,' Hirose Nishihara, A., Matsunaga, M., Nonaka, I., Yokomichi, K. (Eds.), *Knowledge Creation in Community Development*, Palgrave Macmillan, Cham, 2018, p.1.

128 The Mae Fah Luang Foundation under Royal Patronage, 'The Mae Fah Luang: The Social Transformation Model for the 21st Century', *Sasin Journal of Management*, 2010.

129 More about the Tata group can be found here: https://www.tata.com/business/overview.

130 More about the Tata group can be found here: https://www.tata.com/business/overview.

131 More about the Tatas efforts to contribute to the community can be found here: https://www.tata.com/community.

132 More about Tata's efforts to improve labour welfare can be found here: https://www.tata.com/newsroom/people-first-labour-welfare.

133 More about Tata's efforts to improve labour welfare can be found here: https://www.tata.com/newsroom/people-first-labour-welfare.

134 'A Visionary with a Timeless Legacy', Tata Steel, https://www.tatasteel.com/investors/annual-report-2013-14/html/visionary.html.

135 'Corporate Sustainability Report 2003–2004, T'ata Steel, https://www.tatasteel.com/files/csr-2003-04/page_03.htm.

136 'Nerves of Steel', Tata, https://www.tata.com/newsroom/nerves-of-steel#:~:text=Jamsetjipercent20waspercent20inspiredpercent20topercent20set,itspercent20kindpercent20inpercent20thepercent20world.

137 'Nerves of Steel', Tata, https://www.tata.com/newsroom/nerves-of-steel#:~:text=Jamsetjipercent20waspercent20inspiredpercent20topercent20set,itspercent20kindpercent20inpercent20thepercent20world.

138 'The Power of Dreams', Tata, https://www.tata.com/newsroom/the-power-of-dreams-tata-power.

139 'The Power of Dreams', Tata, https://www.tata.com/newsroom/the-power-of-dreams-tata-power.

140 'The Power of Dreams', Tata, https://www.tata.com/newsroom/the-power-of-dreams-tata-power.

141 'The Power of Dreams', Tata, https://www.tata.com/newsroom/the-power-of-dreams-tata-power.

142 'Backing the Brightest', Tata, https://www.tata.com/newsroom/backing-the-brightest-jn-tata-endowment-fund.

143 'Backing the Brightest', Tata, https://www.tata.com/newsroom/backing-the-brightest-jn-tata-endowment-fund.

144 Gautam, Vanya, 'On His 184th Birth Anniversary, Let's Look Back At How Jamsetji Tata Founded The Tata Group', *India Times*, Mar 3, 2023, https://www.indiatimes.com/worth/news/tata-group-founder-jamsetji-tata-184th-birth-anniversary-594789.html.

145 'Backing the Brightest', Tata, https://www.tata.com/newsroom/backing-the-brightest-jn-tata-endowment-fund.

146 'Indian Institute of Science', Tata, https://www.tata.com/community/education/indian-institute-of-science.

147 'Indian Institute of Science', Tata, https://www.tata.com/community/education/indian-institute-of-science.

148 'Indian Institute of Science', Tata, https://www.tata.com/community/education/indian-institute-of-science.

149   'Sir Dorabji Tata', Tata,
       https://www.tata.com/about-us/tata-group-our-heritage/tata-titans/
       sir-dorabji-tata.

150   'Sir Dorabji Tata', Tata,
       https://www.tata.com/about-us/tata-group-our-heritage/tata-titans/
       sir-dorabji-tata.

151   'Sir Ratan Tata', Tata, https://www.tatatrusts.org/about-tatatrusts/sir-
       ratan-tata.

152   'Sir Ratan Tata', Tata, https://www.tatatrusts.org/about-tatatrusts/sir-
       ratan-tata.

153   'Sir Ratan Tata', Tata, https://www.tatatrusts.org/about-tatatrusts/sir-
       ratan-tata.

154   'JRD Tata Birth Anniversary: 10 Interesting Facts About The Great
       Visionary & The Father Of Indian Aviation', Singh, Rity (Ed), *India.
       com*, July 29, 2022, https://www.india.com/news/india/jrd-tata-118th-
       birth-anniversary-10-interesting-facts-about-great-visionary-father-of-
       indian-aviation-5541260/.

155   'Expanding An Empire', Tata, https://www.tata.com/newsroom/
       heritage/expanding-an-empire-jrd-tata.

156   *J.R.D. Tata*, Tata Archives,
       https://www.tatacentralarchives.com/documents/e_book/jrd-tata/E-
       bookpercent20files/mobile/index.html#p=2.

157   '118 years of JRD Tata: Lesser-known facts about the father of Indian
       aviation', *Economic Times*, July 29, 2022, https://economictimes.
       indiatimes.com/news/india/118-years-of-jrd-tata-lesser-known-
       facts-about-the-father-of-indian-aviation/commercial-pilots-license/
       slideshow/93203139.cms.

158   More about this can be found in this post made by Tata Group on
       LinkedIn: https://www.linkedin.com/posts/tata-group_what-did-the-
       first-tata-flight-carry-activity-6901418549483499520-JQNf/.

159   More about this can be found in this post made by Tata Group on
       LinkedIn: https://www.linkedin.com/posts/tata-group_what-did-the-
       first-tata-flight-carry-activity-6901418549483499520-JQNf/.

160   '1953: Air India nationalised', *Hindu*, Aug 11, 2022, https://frontline.
       thehindu.com/the-nation/india-at-75-epochal-moments-1953-air-
       india-nationalised/article65722229.ece.

161   Entry on Air India on Britannica can be found here: https://www.
       britannica.com/topic/Air-India.

162   Aijaz, Basit, 'The Story Of How Tata Airlines Became Air India', Oct 8,
        2021, https://www.indiatimes.com/trending/social-relevance/how-
        tata-airlines-became-air-india-551239.html.

163   Bhat, Harish, 'How Air India topped the list of airlines in the
        world in 1968', *The Hindu Businessline*, Oct 12, 2021, https://www.
        thehindubusinessline.com/books/book-excerpts/how-air-india-
        topped-the-list-of-airlines-in-the-world-in-1968/article36912256.ece.

164   Bhat, Harish, 'How Air India topped the list of airlines in the world in
        1968', *The Hindu Businessline*, Oct 12, 2021,
        https://www.thehindubusinessline.com/books/book-excerpts/
        how-air-india-topped-the-list-of-airlines-in-the-world-in-1968/
        article36912256.ece.

165   Bhat, Harish, 'How Air India topped the list of airlines in the world in
        1968', *The Hindu Businessline*, Oct 12, 2021,
        https://www.thehindubusinessline.com/books/book-excerpts/
        how-air-india-topped-the-list-of-airlines-in-the-world-in-1968/
        article36912256.ece.

166   'J.R.D. Tata and Leadership', Tata, https://www.tata.com/newsroom/
        heritage/jrd-tata-leadership.

167   'Jehangir Ratanji Dadabhoy Tata', Tata Archives,
        https://www.tatacentralarchives.com/documents/e_book/jrd-tata/
        index.html#p=5.

168   More on this can be found here:
        https://www.tatacentralarchives.com/our-collections/memorabilia.
        html.

169   'Jehangir Ratanji Dadabhoy Tata', Tata Archives,
        https://www.tatacentralarchives.com/documents/e_book/jrd-tata/
        index.html#p=5.

170   'Jehangir Ratanji Dadabhoy Tata', Tata Archives, https://www.
        tatacentralarchives.com/documents/e_book/jrd-tata/index.
        html#p=5.

171   'Jehangir Ratanji Dadabhoy Tata', Tata Archives, https://www.
        tatacentralarchives.com/documents/e_book/jrd-tata/index.html#p=5.

172   Lokanathan, P.S., 'The Bombay Plan', *JSTOR*, July, 1945, https://
        www.jstor.org/stable/20029933.

173   'Tata Brand Equity & Business Promotion Agreement', Tata,
        https://www.sec.gov/Archives/edgar/data/926042/
        000119312504156777/dex41.htm.

174   Chatterjee, Dev, 'Tata alters policies to consolidate group operations under one umbrella', *Business Standard*, Sep 1, 2022, https://www.business-standard.com/article/companies/tata-alters-policies-to-consolidate-group-operations-under-one-umbrella-122083100898_1.html.

175   'Corporate Governance', Tata Motors, https://www.tatamotors.com/investors/corporate-governance/.

176   Maheshwari, S.K., Ganesh, M.P., *Ethics in Organizations: The Case of Tata Steel*, *Vikalpa* 31(2). Apr–Jun 2006.

177   Maheshwari, S.K., Ganesh, M.P., *Ethics in Organizations: The Case of Tata Steel*, *Vikalpa* 31(2). Apr–Jun 2006.

178   Biography of Ratan Tata can be found here on Britannica: https://www.britannica.com/biography/Ratan-Tata.

179   Biography of Ratan Tata can be found here on Britannica: https://www.britannica.com/biography/Ratan-Tata.

180   'Tata Motors Completes Acquisition of Jaguar Land Rover', Jaguar-Land Rover, June 2, 2008, https://media.jaguarlandrover.com/node/4917.

181   Garg, Arijit, 'Tata Nano story: Ratan Tata shares the motivation behind launching world's cheapest car', *Zee News*, May 19, 2022, https://zeenews.india.com/auto/for-families-on-scooter-ratan-tata-shares-the-motivation-behind-launching-nano-in-india-2464428.html.

182   Philip, Siddarth Vikram, 'Tata's Nano, the World's Cheapest Car, Is Sputtering', *Bloomberg*, Apr 12, 2013, https://www.bloomberg.com/news/articles/2013-04-11/tatas-nano-the-worlds-cheapest-car-is-sputtering.

183   'Ratan Tata: Marketing Nano as 'cheapest car' was a mistake', *Times of India*, Nov 29, 2013, https://timesofindia.indiatimes.com/business/india-business/ratan-tata-marketing-nano-as-cheapest-car-was-a-mistake/articleshow/26588240.cms.

184   Tiwari, Anuj, '15 Interesting Facts About Ratan Tata Which Prove That He Is The Real "Ratan" Of India', Dec 28, 2021, https://www.indiatimes.com/trending/human-interest/interesting-facts-about-ratan-tata-557828.html#Humble_and_down_to_earth.

185   Walsh, Coleen, 'Business School announces Tata gift; two initiatives', *Harvard Gazette*, Oct 14, 2010, https://news.harvard.edu/gazette/story/2010/10/hbs_gift/.

186   Tata Code of Conduct can be found here: https://www.tata.com/content/dam/tata/pdf/Tatapercent20Codepercent20 Ofpercent20Conduct.pdf.

187   John, Nevin, 'Pivoting Tata', *Fortune*, Feb 14, 2023, https://www.
      fortuneindia.com/long-reads/pivoting-tata/111577.

188   'Tata group aiming at net-zero emission by 2045', *Economic Times*, Mar
      3, 2023, https://economictimes.indiatimes.com/news/company/
      corporate-trends/tata-group-aiming-at-net-zero-emission-by-2045/
      articleshow/98391449.cms.

189   'The Power of Zero', Tata, Dec 2022, https://www.tata.com/
      newsroom/business/tata-power-net-zero-sustainability-aalingana.

190   John, Nevin, 'Pivoting Tata', *Fortune*, Feb 14, 2023, https://www.
      fortuneindia.com/long-reads/pivoting-tata/111577.

191   'The Power of Zero', Tata, Dec 2022, https://www.tata.com/
      newsroom/business/tata-power-net-zero-sustainability-aalingana.

192   More about the Uttar Pradesh Global Investors' Summit can be found
      here: https://upgis2023.in/.'UP Global Investors Summit 2023:
      Tata Group to build integrated multi-modal air cargo in Jewar, says
      N Chandrasekaran', *Times of India*, Feb 10, 2023, https://timesofindia.
      indiatimes.com/videos/business/up-global-investors-summit-2023-
      tata-group-to-build-integrated-multi-modal-air-cargo-in-jewar-says-n-
      chandrasekaran/videoshow/97803666.cms.

193   'Tata Power plans $10 billion renewable outlay in 5 years', *5Paisa*, Dec
      12, 2022, https://www.5paisa.com/news/tata-power-plans-10-billion-
      renewable-outlay-in-5-years.

194   Vijayaraghavan, Kala, Ganguli, Bodhisatva, 'Tata Group set to record
      highest growth in history: Tata Sons chairman N Chandrasekaran',
      Economic Times, Feb 15, 2023, https://economictimes.indiatimes.
      com/news/company/corporate-trends/tata-group-set-to-record-
      highest-growth-in-history-tata-sons-chairman-n-chandrasekaran/
      articleshow/97850230.cms?from=mdr.

195   Carey, Nick, Ravikumar, Sachin, 'Jaguar Land Rover boosts investment
      to catch up in EV race', *Reuters*, Apr 19, 2023,
      https://www.reuters.com/business/autos-transportation/jaguar-land-
      rover-plans-invest-15-bln-pounds-electric-push-2023-04-19/.

196   Vijayaraghavan, Kala, Ganguli, Bodhisatva, 'Tata Group set to record
      highest growth in history: Tata Sons chairman N Chandrasekaran',
      Economic Times, Feb 15, 2023,
      https://economictimes.indiatimes.com/news/company/corporate-
      trends/tata-group-set-to-record-highest-growth-in-history-tata-sons-
      chairman-n-chandrasekaran/articleshow/97850230.cms?from=mdr.

197   'The Chocolate Dynasty', *Creaghan McConnell Group*, Apr 13, 2013, https://cmgpartners.ca/the-mars-family-mars-inc/.

198   Mainwaring, Simon, 'Purpose At Work: How Mars Is Scaling Sustainability Goals Across Generations', *Forbes*, Feb 12, 2020, https://www.forbes.com/sites/simonmainwaring/2020/02/12/purpose-at-work-how-mars-is-scaling-sustainability-goals-across-generations/?sh=1dd10ff42ee7.

199   More about Mars, Inc can be found here: https://www.mars.com/about.

200   'The Chocolate Dynasty', *Creaghan McConnell Group*, Apr 13, 2013, https://cmgpartners.ca/the-mars-family-mars-inc/.'Mars and Good Management Make for Long-Lasting Success', *Prosperity*, https://www.prosperity.net/mars-bar/.

201   Brenner, Joel Glenn, 'Life on Mars: The Mars family saga has all the classic elements', *Independent*, Jul 26, 1992, https://www.independent.co.uk/arts-entertainment/life-on-mars-the-mars-family-saga-has-all-the-classic-elements-1535722.html.

202   More about Mars, Inc can be found here: https://www.mars.com/about/history.   'The Chocolate Dynasty', *Creaghan McConnell Group*, Apr 13, 2013, https://cmgpartners.ca/the-mars-family-mars-inc/.

203   'The Chocolate Dynasty', *Creaghan McConnell Group*, Apr 13, 2013, https://cmgpartnersca/the-mars-family-mars-inc/.

204   Jakub, Jay, 'The Roots of the Economics of Mutuality', *Putting Purpose into Practice: The Economics of Mutuality*, Oxford University Press, 2021, https://purposeintopractice.org/chapter-4-the-roots-of-the-economics-of-mutuality.

205   'Mars and Good Management Make for Long-Lasting Success', *Prosperity*, https://www.prosperity.net/mars-bar/.

206   Hays, Constance L., 'Forrest Mars, 95, Creator of the M & M and a Candy Empire', *New York Times*, July 3, 1999, https://www.nytimes.com/1999/07/03/business/forrest-mars-95-creator-of-the-m-m-and-a-candy-empire.html.

207   'Mars and Good Management Make for Long-Lasting Success', *Prosperity*, https://www.prosperity.net/mars-bar/

208   Hays, Constance L., 'Forrest Mars, 95, Creator of the M & M and a Candy Empire', *New York Times*, July 3, 1999, https://www.nytimes.com/1999/07/03/business/forrest-mars-95-creator-of-the-m-m-and-a-candy-empire.html.

209 'The Chocolate Dynasty', *Creaghan McConnell Group*, Apr 13, 2013, https://cmgpartners.ca/the-mars-family-mars-inc/.

210 'Defining the role of business in five principles: Victoria Mars, Mars Inc.', *Global Family Business Survey 2018*, PwC, 2018, https://www.pwc.com/gx/en/services/family-business/family-business-survey-2018/mars.html.

211 Langer, Emily, 'Forrest E. Mars Jr., enigmatic steward of family confectionery, dies at 84', *Washington Post*, July 27, 2016, https://www.washingtonpost.com/business/forrest-e-mars-jr-enigmatic-steward-of-family-confectionery-dies-at-84/2016/07/27/0265c442-5400-11e6-b7de-dfe509430c39_story.html.

212 'Goodness, greatness, Mars', London Business School, July 15, 2014, https://www.london.edu/think/goodness-greatness-mars.

213 Langer, Emily, 'Forrest E. Mars Jr., enigmatic steward of family confectionery, dies at 84', *Washington Post*, July 27, 2016, https://www.washingtonpost.com/business/forrest-e-mars-jr-enigmatic-steward-of-family-confectionery-dies-at-84/2016/07/27/0265c442-5400-11e6-b7de-dfe509430c39_story.html.

214 Edgecliffe-Johnson, Evans, Judith, 'Mars reveals bigger revenues than Coca-Cola as it appoints new chief executive', *Financial Times*, Jun 22, 2022,
https://www.ft.com/content/302b67a6-5979-49f6-aa55-f288d5baee60.

215 Hauver, Erica, 'Message from Mars: How to institutionalize sustainability', *GreenBiz*, June 18, 2018, https://www.greenbiz.com/article/message-mars-how-institutionalize-sustainability.

216 'Goodness, greatness, Mars', London Business School, July 15, 2014, https://www.london.edu/think/goodness-greatness-mars.

217 More on Mutuality Principle can be found here:
http://begbert.weebly.com/uploads/2/5/0/1/2501899/mm_booknew.pdf.

218 'Defining the role of business in five principles: Victoria Mars, Mars Inc.', *Global Family Business Survey 2018*, PwC, 2018,
https://www.pwc.com/gx/en/services/family-business/family-business-survey-2018/mars.html.

219 'Goodness, greatness, Mars', London Business School, July 15, 2014, https://www.london.edu/think/goodness-greatness-mars.

220 'Goodness, greatness, Mars', London Business School, July 15, 2014, https://www.london.edu/think/goodness-greatness-mars.

221   'What Are Mars Inc.'s 'Five Principles'?', *CSP*, Apr 14, 2014, https://
       www.cspdailynews.com/snacks-candy/what-are-mars-incs-five-
       principles.

222   Jakub, Jay, 'The Roots of the Economics of Mutuality', *Putting Purpose
       into Practice: The Economics of Mutuality*, Oxford University Press,
       2021, https://purposeintopractice.org/chapter-4-the-roots-of-the-
       economics-of-mutuality.

223   Jakub, Jay, 'The Roots of the Economics of Mutuality', *Putting Purpose
       into Practice: The Economics of Mutuality*, Oxford University Press, 2021,
       https://purposeintopractice.org/chapter-4-the-roots-of-the-
       economics-of-mutuality.

224   Jakub, Jay, 'The Roots of the Economics of Mutuality', *Putting Purpose
       into Practice: The Economics of Mutuality*, Oxford University Press, 2021,
       https://purposeintopractice.org/chapter-4-the-roots-of-the-
       economics-of-mutuality.

225   Jakub, Jay, 'The Roots of the Economics of Mutuality', *Putting Purpose
       into Practice: The Economics of Mutuality*, Oxford University Press, 2021,
       https://purposeintopractice.org/chapter-4-the-roots-of-the-
       economics-of-mutuality.

226   Jakub, Jay, 'The Roots of the Economics of Mutuality', *Putting Purpose
       into Practice: The Economics of Mutuality*, Oxford University Press,
       2021, https://purposeintopractice.org/chapter-4-the-roots-of-the-
       economics-of-mutuality.

227   Hauver, Erica, 'Message from Mars: How to institutionalize
       sustainability', *GreenBiz*, June 18, 2018, https://www.greenbiz.com/
       article/message-mars-how-institutionalize-sustainability.

228   Weber, Joel, 'Mars Inc. CEO Grant Reid Is Thinking a Hundred Years
       Ahead', *Bloomberg*, Jan 23, 2019, https://www.bloomberg.com/news/
       features/2019-01-23/mars-inc-ceo-grant-reid-is-thinking-a-hundred-
       years-ahead#xj4y7vzkg.

229   Weber, Joel, 'Mars Inc. CEO Grant Reid Is Thinking a Hundred Years
       Ahead', *Bloomberg*, Jan 23, 2019, https://www.bloomberg.com/news/
       features/2019-01-23/mars-inc-ceo-grant-reid-is-thinking-a-hundred-
       years-ahead#xj4y7vzkg.

230   Reid, Grant, 'To truly reach net zero emissions, we need to transform
       the business supply chain', *Guardian*, Oct 5, 20121, https://www.
       theguardian.com/commentisfree/2021/oct/05/mars-ceo-grant-reid-
       net-zero-emissions-business.

231 'Mars, Incorporated: Investing In A Sustainable Future', *Eco*, https://www.bluetoad.com/publication/?i=589450&article_id=3386203&view=articleBrowser.

232 More about the efforts of Mars, Inc. to cultivate cocoa in a sustainable manner can be found here: https://www.mars.com/sustainability-plan/cocoa-for-generations/sustainable-cocoa-tomorrow.

233 More about the efforts of Mars, Inc. to rehabilitate coral reefs can be found here: https://www.mars.com/news-and-stories/articles/coral-reef-rehabilitation.
Mars, Incorporated, *Mars Coral Reef Restoration Efforts Show Remarkable Progress* (Video), YouTube, Jun 5, 2020, https://www.youtube.com/watch?v=MKPA3R5izT4.

234 More about the efforts of Mars Petcare to tackle pet homelessness can be found here: https://www.endpethomelessness.com/our-ambition.

235 More about the Mars Compass can be found here: https://www.mars.com/about/mars-compass.

236 'MARS: Balancing profit and purpose in the planning process', *Finance for the Future*, Dec 20, 2021, https://www.financeforthefuture.org/winners/2021-winners/mars.

237 More about the Mars Compass can be found here: https://www.mars.com/about/mars-compass.

238 Endeavour Malaysia, *Blitzscaling Business Strategies: Malaysia's Fresh MilkMan, Loi Tuan Ee from Farm Fresh* (Video), October 1, 2021, https://www.youtube.com/watch?v=PkxbA_ONJFY.

239 'The Cream of The Crop:" How Loi Tuan Ee Pioneered Preservative-Free, Farm Fresh Milk', *The Peak*, October 2, 2017, https://thepeak.com.my/people/cream-crop-loi-tuan-ee-pioneered-preservative-free-farm-fresh-milk/.

240 Izzad, N., 'Milking Generational Change on Health & Managing an IPO With Market Leader Farm Fresh', *Endeavour*, May 30, 2022, https://www.endeavormalaysia.org/post/milking-generational-change-on-health-managing-an-ipo-with-market-leader-farm-fresh.

241 Wong, E.L., 'EY Entrepreneur Of The Year: "Truly natural" the key to Loi's success', *The Edge Markets*, November 30, 2016, https://www.theedgemarkets.com/article/ey-entrepreneur-year-percentE2percent80percent98truly-naturalpercentE2percent80percent99-key-loipercentE2percent80percent99s-success.

242 Farm Fresh Berhad, *Farm Fresh Sustainability Report 2022*, retrieved from

https://www.farmfresh.com.my/wp-content/uploads/2022/11/FARM-FRESH_SUSTAINABILITY-REPORT-2022.pdf.

243 Wong, E.L., 'EY Entrepreneur Of The Year: "Truly natural" the key to Loi's success', *The Edge Markets*, November 30, 2016, https://www.theedgemarkets.com/article/ey-entrepreneur-year-percentE2percent80percent98truly-naturalpercentE2percent80percent99-key-loipercentE2percent80percent99s-success

244 Yusof, A., '"My friends felt I was crazy": From working an office job to running a milk empire in Malaysia', *Channel News Asia*, October 9, 2021, https://www.channelnewsasia.com/asia/malaysia-farm-fresh-founder-milk-empire-johor-2228266.

245 Farm Fresh Berhad, *Farm Fresh Sustainability Report 2020*, retrieved from https://www.farmfresh.com.my/wp-content/uploads/2021/08/FFSB-SR2020-230821.pdf.

246 The Breakfast Grille, hosted by See, P., *Moo-Sic to Investors' Ears: Holstein Milk Company's Extraordina-Diary Journey* (Audio podcast episode), BFM 89.9 The Business Station, April 6, 2021.

247 Farm Fresh, *Sustainability*, https://www.farmfresh.com.my/sustainability/.

248 Farm Fresh Berhad, *Farm Fresh Berhad Annual Report 2022*, retrieved from https://www.farmfresh.com.my/reports-presentations/.

249 Farm Fresh Berhad, *Farm Fresh Berhad Annual Report 2022*, retrieved from https://www.farmfresh.com.my/reports-presentations/.

250 Farm Fresh Berhad, *Farm Fresh Berhad Annual Report 2022*, retrieved from https://www.farmfresh.com.my/reports-presentations/.

251 '"The Cream of The Crop" How Loi Tuan Ee Pioneered Preservative-Free, Farm Fresh Milk', *The Peak*, October 2, 2017, https://thepeak.com.my/people/cream-crop-loi-tuan-ee-pioneered-preservative-free-farm-fresh-milk/.

252 Izzad, N., 'Milking Generational Change on Health & Managing an IPO With Market Leader Farm Fresh', *Endeavour*, May 30, 2022, https://www.endeavormalaysia.org/post/milking-generational-change-on-health-managing-an-ipo-with-market-leader-farm-fresh.

253 Yusof, A., '"My friends felt I was crazy": From working an office job to running a milk empire in Malaysia', *Channel News Asia*, October 9, 2021, https://www.channelnewsasia.com/asia/malaysia-farm-fresh-founder-milk-empire-johor-2228266.

254   Farm Fresh Berhad, *Farm Fresh Berhad Annual Report 2022*, retrieved from https://www.farmfresh.com.my/reports-presentations/.

255   Izzad, N., 'Milking Generational Change on Health & Managing an IPO With Market Leader Farm Fresh', *Endeavour*, May 30, 2022, https://www.endeavormalaysia.org/post/milking-generational-change-on-health-managing-an-ipo-with-market-leader-farm-fresh.

256   Tan, Sumiko, 'Young, fresh-faced and "green", Anderson Tanoto leads the way on sustainability at RGE', *Straits Times*, Aug 15, 2022, https://www.straitstimes.com/singapore/scion-of-rge-on-his-mission-to-lead-groups-sustainability-efforts.

257   Maulia, Erwida, 'Indonesia's APRIL starts work on $2.3bn paperboard facility', *Nikkei Asia*, Mar 30, 2022, https://asia.nikkei.com/Business/Markets/Commodities/Indonesia-s-APRIL-starts-work-on-2.3bn-paperboard-facility.

258   Jong, Hans Nicholas, 'Deforestation of orangutan habitat feeds global palm oil demand: Report ', *Eco-Biusiness*, Jun 25, 2021, https://www.eco-business.com/news/deforestation-of-orangutan-habitat-feeds-global-palm-oil-demand-report/.

259   Petro, Greg, 'Consumers Demand Sustainable Products And Shopping Formats', *Forbes*, Mar 11, 2022, https://www.forbes.com/sites/gregpetro/2022/03/11/consumers-demand-sustainable-products-and-shopping-formats/?sh=416cecfa6a06.

260   'Sustainability', *April Asia*, https://www.aprilasia.com/en/sustainability/eco-restoration.

261   More information about the Biodiversity Survey can be found here: https://www.rekoforest.org/biodiversity/biodiversity-survey/.

262   Holder, Michael, 'Can a tiger change its stripes? Meet the pulp and paper giant bankrolling a huge Sumatran rainforest reserve', *Business Green*, Feb 8, 2023, https://www.businessgreen.com/feature/4073959/tiger-change-stripes-meet-pulp-paper-giant-bankrolling-huge-sumatran-rainforest-reserve.

263   'How does landscape conservation work on the ground, at scale?', Restorasi Ekosistem Riau, Dec 17, 2019, https://www.rekoforest.org/media/how-does-landscape-conservation-work-on-the-ground-at-scale/.

264   Holder, Michael, 'Can a tiger change its stripes? Meet the pulp and paper giant bankrolling a huge Sumatran rainforest reserve', *Business Green*,

Feb 8, 2023, https://www.businessgreen.com/feature/4073959/tiger-change-stripes-meet-pulp-paper-giant-bankrolling-huge-sumatran-rainforest-reserve.

265 'RGE Highlights Path to Sustainability Leadership in Northwestern University Kellogg School of Management Podcast', *Cision*, Dec 12, 2023, https://en.prnasia.com/releases/apac/rge-highlights-path-to-sustainability-leadership-in-northwestern-university-kellogg-school-of-management-podcast-388506.shtml.

266 'Indonesia: What is an Ecosystem Restoration Concession?', WRM Bulletin 249, World Rainforest Movement, May 14, 2020, https://www.wrm.org.uy/bulletin-articles/indonesia-what-is-an-ecosystem-restoration-concession.

267 Harrison, Rhett D., et al., 'Restoration concessions: a second lease on life for beleaguered tropical forests?', *Frontiers in Ecology and the Environment*, ESA: Dec 2020, 18(10), pp.567–575, https://esajournals.onlinelibrary.wiley.com/doi/full/10.1002/fee.2265.

268 'Partner News: APRIL Group announces 2030 commitments to achieve net zero emissions by 2030', Tropical Forest Alliance, Nov 17, 2020,
https://www.tropicalforestalliance.org/en/news-and-events/news/partner-news-the-april-group-announces-april2030-plan-to-achieve-net-zero-emissions-goal-by-2030.

269 Holder, Michael, 'Can a tiger change its stripes? Meet the pulp and paper giant bankrolling a huge Sumatran rainforest reserve', *Business Green*, Feb 8, 2023, https://www.businessgreen.com/feature/4073959/tiger-change-stripes-meet-pulp-paper-giant-bankrolling-huge-sumatran-rainforest-reserve.

270 Holder, Michael, 'Can a tiger change its stripes? Meet the pulp and paper giant bankrolling a huge Sumatran rainforest reserve', *Business Green*, Feb 8, 2023, https://www.businessgreen.com/feature/4073959/tiger-change-stripes-meet-pulp-paper-giant-bankrolling-huge-sumatran-rainforest-reserve.

271 Holder, Michael, 'Can a tiger change its stripes? Meet the pulp and paper giant bankrolling a huge Sumatran rainforest reserve', *Business Green*, Feb 8, 2023, https://www.businessgreen.com/feature/4073959/tiger-change-stripes-meet-pulp-paper-giant-bankrolling-huge-sumatran-rainforest-reserve.

272   'Eco-research Camp', Restorasi Ekosistem Riau,
      https://www.rekoforest.org/programme/eco-research-camp/.

273   'RGE Highlights Path to Sustainability Leadership in Northwestern
      University Kellogg School of Management Podcast', *Cision*, Dec 12,
      2023,
      https://en.prnasia.com/releases/apac/rge-highlights-path-to-
      sustainability-leadership-in-northwestern-university-kellogg-school-of-
      management-podcast-388506.shtml.

274   'KPMG assesses APRIL's forest management', *Jakarta Post*, Aug 30,
      2014,
      https://www.thejakartapost.com/news/2014/08/30/kpmg-assesses-
      april-s-forest-management.html.

275   Jong, Hans Nicholas, 'With FSC rule change, deforesters once blocked
      from certification get a new shot', Mongabay, Oct 24, 2022, https://
      news.mongabay.com/2022/10/with-fsc-rule-change-deforesters-
      once-blocked-from-certification-get-a-new-shot/.

276   Jong, Hans Nicholas, 'With FSC rule change, deforesters once blocked
      from certification get a new shot', Mongabay, Oct 24, 2022, https://
      news.mongabay.com/2022/10/with-fsc-rule-change-deforesters-
      once-blocked-from-certification-get-a-new-shot/.

277   Holder, Michael, 'Can a tiger change its stripes? Meet the pulp and paper
      giant bankrolling a huge Sumatran rainforest reserve', *Business Green*,
      Feb 8, 2023, https://www.businessgreen.com/feature/4073959/tiger-
      change-stripes-meet-pulp-paper-giant-bankrolling-huge-sumatran-
      rainforest-reserve.

278   Carstensen. Kim, 'Public Acknowledgement of FSC Baseline Results',
      Nov 4, 2020, https://fsc.org/sites/default/files/2020-11/APRIL%20
      acknowledgement%20of%20harm%20letter.PDF.

279   Haraito, Gloria, 'RGE invests over $2 billion to open major new
      paperboard plant', *Forbes*, Nov 27, 2022, https://www.forbes.com/
      sites/gloriaharaito/2022/11/27/rges-anderson-tanoto-targets-high-
      growth-and-sustainability/?sh=559ffec27593.

280   Haraito, Gloria, 'RGE invests over $2 billion to open major new
      paperboard plant', *Forbes*, Nov 27, 2022, https://www.forbes.com/
      sites/gloriaharaito/2022/11/27/rges-anderson-tanoto-targets-high-
      growth-and-sustainability/?sh=559ffec27593.

281   Haraito, Gloria, 'RGE invests over $2 billion to open major new
      paperboard plant', *Forbes*, Nov 27, 2022, https://www.forbes.com/

sites/gloriaharaito/2022/11/27/rges-anderson-tanoto-targets-high-growth-and-sustainability/?sh=559ffec27593.

282   More about the Royal Golden Eagle's 2030 targets can be found here: https://www.rgei.com/sustainability/2030-targets.

283   'Partner News: APRIL Group announces 2030 commitments to achieve net zero emissions by 2030', Tropical Forest Alliance, Nov 17, 2020, https://www.tropicalforestalliance.org/en/news-and-events/news/partner-news-the-april-group-announces-april2030-plan-to-achieve-net-zero-emissions-goal-by-2030.

284   Lukman, Josa, 'One year on: APRIL Group records milestones with APRIL2030 commitment', *Jakarta Post*, Dec 1, 2021, https://www.thejakartapost.com/business/2021/12/01/one-year-on-april-group-records-milestones-with-april2030-commitment.html.

285   Tan, Sumiko, 'Young, fresh-faced and "green", Anderson Tanoto leads the way on sustainability at RGE', *Straits Times*, Aug 15, 2022, https://www.straitstimes.com/singapore/scion-of-rge-on-his-mission-to-lead-groups-sustainability-efforts.

286   'Indian pilot Bhavye Suneja captained Indonesian plane Lion Air that crashed into sea', *Hindu*, Oct 29, 2018, https://www.thehindu.com/news/international/indian-pilot-bhavye-suneja-captained-indonesian-plane-lion-air-that-crashed-into-sea/article25359127.ece.

287   Slater, Joanna, Mahtani, Shibani, '"Playing with lives": Widow of pilot on doomed Lion Air flight says direct appeals made to ground Boeing model', *Washington Post*, Mar 30, 2019, https://www.washingtonpost.com/world/asia_pacific/playing-with-lives-widow-of-pilot-on-doomed-lion-air-flight-says-direct-appeals-made-to-ground-boeing-model/2019/03/29/56aa778a-5017-11e9-bdb7-44f948cc0605_story.html.

288   Slater, Joanna, Mahtani, Shibani, '"Playing with lives": Widow of pilot on doomed Lion Air flight says direct appeals made to ground Boeing model', *Washington Post*, Mar 30, 2019, https://www.washingtonpost.com/world/asia_pacific/playing-with-lives-widow-of-pilot-on-doomed-lion-air-flight-says-direct-appeals-made-to-ground-boeing-model/2019/03/29/56aa778a-5017-11e9-bdb7-44f948cc0605_story.html.

289   Slater, Joanna, Mahtani, Shibani, '"Playing with lives": Widow of pilot on doomed Lion Air flight says direct appeals made to ground Boeing model', *Washington Post*, Mar 30, 2019, https://www.

washingtonpost.com/world/asia_pacific/playing-with-lives-widow-of-pilot-on-doomed-lion-air-flight-says-direct-appeals-made-to-ground-boeing-model/2019/03/29/56aa778a-5017-11e9-bdb7-44f948cc0605_story.html.

290 'Boeing 737 Max Lion Air crash caused by series of failures', *BBC*, Oct 25, 2019, https://www.bbc.com/news/business-50177788.

291 Baker, Sinéad, 'This timeline shows exactly what happened on board the Lion Air Boeing 737 Max that crashed in less than 13 minutes, killing 189 people', *Business Insider India*, Oct 29, 2019, https://www.businessinsider.com/lion-air-crash-timeline-boeing-737-max-disaster-killed-189-2019-10.

292 'Information on Lion Air Flight JT-610 Route Soekarno-Hatta, Tangerang to Pangkalpinang', Lion Air, Apr 9, 2019, https://www.lionair.co.id/en/about-us/newsroom/2019/04/09/information-on-lion-air-flight-jt-610-route-soekarno-hatta-tangerang-to-pangkalpinang.

293 Griffiths, James, George, Steve, Quiano, Kathy, ' Lion Air crash: No answers as to cause of jet disaster as bodies pulled from sea', *CNN*, Oct 30, 2018, https://edition.cnn.com/2018/10/29/asia/lion-air-plane-crash-indonesia-intl/index.html.

Rahn, Wesley, 'Does Indonesia have an air safety problem?' *DW*, Nov 2, 2018, https://www.dw.com/en/lion-air-crash-does-indonesia-have-an-air-safety-problem/a-46138013.

294 Taddonio, Patrice, 'In 737 Max Crashes, Boeing Pointed to Pilot Error—Despite a Fatal Design Flaw', *Frontline*, Sep 14, 2021, https://www.pbs.org/wgbh/frontline/article/video-clip-boeing-737-max-crashes-fatal-design-flaw-documentary/.

Gates, Dominic, 'How much was pilot error a factor in the Boeing 737 MAX crashes?', *Washington Post*, May 15, 2019, https://www.seattletimes.com/business/boeing-aerospace/how-much-was-pilot-error-a-factor-in-the-boeing-737-max-crashes/.

Devine, Curt, Cooper, Aaron, Griffin, Drew, 'Pilots union to Boeing: "Inexcusable" to blame pilots for 737 Max crashes', *CNN*, May 23, 2019, https://edition.cnn.com/2019/05/23/business/american-airlines-boeing-pilots-union/index.html.

295 Langewiesche, William, 'What Really Brought Down the Boeing 737 Max?' *New York Times Magazine*, Jul 2, 2021, https://www.nytimes.com/2019/09/18/magazine/boeing-737-max-crashes.html.

296   'Indonesian officials: Problems with sensor found on crashed Lion Air jet', *CGTN*, Nov 9, 2018, https://news.cgtn.com/news/   3d3d674e3163444e30457a633356 6d54/share_p.html.

297   Ostrower, John, 'Boeing issues 737 Max fleet bulletin on AoA warning after Lion Air Crash', *Air Current*, Nov 7, 2018, https://theaircurrent. com/aviation-safety/boeing-nearing-737-max-fleet-bulletin-on-aoa-warning-after-lion-air-crash/.

298   Winsor, Morgan, 'Boeing CEO admits faulty sensor triggered automatic flight control system in deadly crashes', *ABC News*, Apr 5, 2019, https://abcnews.go.com/International/boeing-ceo-admits-faulty-sensor-triggered-automatic-flight/story?id=62191006.

299   Gollom, Mark, Shprintsen, Alex, Zalac, Frédéric, '737 Max flight manual may have left MCAS information on "Cutting room floor"', *CBC*, Mar 26, 2019, https://www.cbc.ca/news/business/boeing-737-manual-mcas-system-plane-crash-1.5065842#:~:text=The%20operating%20manual%20 mentions%20the,planes%20in%20Indonesia%20and%20Ethiopia%2C

300   Gajanan, Mahita, 'American Airlines Pilots Confronted Boeing About Safety Issues Before Ethiopia Crash', *Time*, May 15, 2019, https://time. com/5589547/pilots-boeing-737-max-safety/.

301   Kennedy, Rory, dir. *Downfall: The Case Against Boeing*, Netflix, https:// www.netflix.com/sg/title/81272421.

302   Newburger, Emma, 'Audio recording reveals Boeing resisted angry calls from pilots for 737 Max fix in November', *CNBC*, May 15, 2019, https://www.cnbc.com/2019/05/15/boeing-reportedly-resisted-pilots-angry-calls-for-737-max-fix-last-fall.html.

303   Kennedy, Rory, dir. *Downfall: The Case Against Boeing*, Netflix, https:// www.netflix.com/sg/title/81272421.

304   DiFurio, Dom, Aspinwall, Cary, 'Newly surfaced recording details how pilots pressed Boeing after Lion Air crash, requested FAA records', *Dallas Morning News*, May 13, 2019, https://www.dallasnews.com/ business/airlines/2019/05/13/newly-surfaced-recording-details-how-pilots-pressed-boeing-after-lion-air-crash-requested-faa-records/.

305   Newburger, Emma, 'Audio recording reveals Boeing resisted angry calls from pilots for 737 Max fix in November', *CNBC*, May 15, 2019, https://www.cnbc.com/2019/05/15/boeing-reportedly-resisted-pilots-angry-calls-for-737-max-fix-last-fall.html.

306 Robinson, Peter, 'Boeing Built an Unsafe Plane, and Blamed the Pilots When It Crashed', Nov 16, 2021, *Bloomberg*, https://www.bloomberg.com/news/features/2021-11-16/are-boeing-planes-unsafe-pilots-blamed-for-corporate-errors-in-max-737-crash.

307 Kitroeff, Natalie, et al., 'Ethiopian Crash Report Indicates Pilots Followed Boeing's Emergency Procedures', *New York Times*, Apr 4, 2019, https://www.nytimes.com/2019/04/04/business/boeing-737-ethiopian-airlines.html.

308 6 Minutes of Terror: What Passengers and Crew Experienced Aboard Ethiopian Airlines Flight 302', *Intelligencer*, Apr 9, 2019, https://nymag.com/intelligencer/2019/04/what-passengers-experienced-on-the-ethiopian-airlines-flight.html.

309 6 Minutes of Terror: What Passengers and Crew Experienced Aboard Ethiopian Airlines Flight 302', *Intelligencer*, Apr 9, 2019, https://nymag.com/intelligencer/2019/04/what-passengers-experienced-on-the-ethiopian-airlines-flight.html.

310 'Excavators may be damaging Ethiopia crash site: diplomats', *Reuters*, Mar 15, 2019, https://www.reuters.com/article/us-ethiopia-airplane-site-idUSKCN1QW2AD.

311 'China taking lead to ground Boeing 737 MAX 8 signals challenge to US authority in worldwide civil aviation', *SCMP*, May 13, 2019, https://www.scmp.com/news/china/article/3001428/china-taking-lead-ground-boeing-737-max-signals-challenge-us-authority.

312 Liptak, Kevin, 'Trump administration grounds Boeing 737 Max planes', *CNN*, Mar 13, 2019, https://edition.cnn.com/2019/03/13/politics/donald-trump-boeing-faa/index.html.

313 Liptak, Kevin, 'Trump administration grounds Boeing 737 Max planes', *CNN*, Mar 13, 2019, https://edition.cnn.com/2019/03/13/politics/donald-trump-boeing-faa/index.html.

314 Tangel, Andrew, Cameron, Doug, 'Boeing Chief Defends 737 MAX Design Work', *Wall Street Journal*, Apr 29, 2019, https://www.wsj.com/articles/boeing-shareholders-reject-splitting-chairman-ceo-roles-11556551056.

315 Josephs, Leslie, 'Boeing employees raised concerns about 737 Max before crashes, documents show', *CNBC*, Oct 30, 2019, https://www.

cnbc.com/2019/10/30/boeing-engineer-raised-concerns-about-737-max-years-before-crashes-documents-show.html.

316 Frost, Natasha, 'The 1997 merger that paved the way for the Boeing 737 Max crisis', *Yahoo! News*, Jan 3, 2020, https://sg.news.yahoo.com/1997-merger-paved-way-boeing-090042193.html.

317 Frost, Natasha, 'The 1997 merger that paved the way for the Boeing 737 Max crisis', *Yahoo! News*, Jan 3, 2020, https://sg.news.yahoo.com/1997-merger-paved-way-boeing-090042193.html.

318 Kennedy, Rory, dir. *Downfall: The Case Against Boeing*, Netflix, https://www.netflix.com/sg/title/81272421.

319 'Boeing to move headquarters from Chicago to Virginia', *Reuters*, May 5, 2022, https://www.cnbc.com/2022/05/05/boeing-to-move-headquarters-from-chicago-to-virginia-.html.

320 Kitroeff, Natalie, Gelles, David, 'Claims of Shoddy Production Draw Scrutiny to a Second Boeing Jet', *New York Times*, Arp 19, 2020, https://www.nytimes.com/2019/04/20/business/boeing-dreamliner-production-problems.html.

321 'Boeing faces accusations of negligence at Dreamliner plant', Apr 20, 2019, https://www.cnet.com/tech/tech-industry/boeing-faces-accusations-of-negligence-at-dreamliner-plant/.

322 Robinson, Peter, 'Former Boeing Engineers Say Relentless Cost-Cutting Sacrificed Safety', *Bloomberg*, May 9, 2019, https://www.bloomberg.com/news/features/2019-05-09/former-boeing-engineers-say-relentless-cost-cutting-sacrificed-safety.

323 Kennedy, Rory, dir. *Downfall: The Case Against Boeing*, Netflix, https://www.netflix.com/sg/title/81272421.

324 Edmondson, Amy C., 'Boeing and the Importance of Encouraging Employees to Speak Up', *Harvard Business review*, May 1, 2019, https://hbr.org/2019/05/boeing-and-the-importance-of-encouraging-employees-to-speak-up.

325 Frost, Natasha, 'The 1997 merger that paved the way for the Boeing 737 Max crisis', *Yahoo! News*, Jan 3, 2020, https://sg.news.yahoo.com/1997-merger-paved-way-boeing-090042193.html.

326 Gelles, David, et al., 'Boeing Was "Go, Go, Go" to Beat Airbus With the 737 Max', *New York Times*, Mar 23, 2019, https://www.nytimes.com/2019/03/23/business/boeing-737-max-crash.html.

327　Gelles, David, et al., 'Boeing Was "Go, Go, Go" to Beat Airbus With the 737 Max', *New York Times*, Mar 23, 2019, https://www.nytimes.com/2019/03/23/business/boeing-737-max-crash.html.

328　Irving, Clive, 'How Boeing's Bean-Counters Courted the 737 MAX Disaster', *Daily Beast*, Jun 9, 2019, https://www.thedailybeast.com/how-boeing-bean-counters-courted-the-737-max-disaster.

329　Gelles, David, et al., 'Boeing Was "Go, Go, Go" to Beat Airbus With the 737 Max', *New York Times*, Mar 23, 2019, https://www.nytimes.com/2019/03/23/business/boeing-737-max-crash.html

330　Gelles, David, et al., 'Boeing Was 'Go, Go, Go' to Beat Airbus With the 737 Max', *New York Times*, Mar 23, 2019, https://www.nytimes.com/2019/03/23/business/boeing-737-max-crash.html.

331　Gelles, David, et al., 'Boeing Was 'Go, Go, Go' to Beat Airbus With the 737 Max', *New York Times*, Mar 23, 2019, https://www.nytimes.com/2019/03/23/business/boeing-737-max-crash.html.

332　Campbell, Darryl, 'Redline: The Many human errors that brought down the Boeing 737 Max', *Verge*, May 2, 2019, https://www.theverge.com/2019/5/2/18518176/boeing-737-max-crash-problems-human-error-mcas-faa.

333　Irving, Clive, 'How Boeing's Bean-Counters Courted the 737 MAX Disaster', *Daily Beast*, Jun 9, 2019, https://www.thedailybeast.com/how-boeing-bean-counters-courted-the-737-max-disaster.

334　Gates, Dominic, Baker, Mike, 'The inside story of MCAS: How Boeing's 737 MAX system gained power and lost safeguards', *Seattle Times*, Jun 22, 2019, https://www.seattletimes.com/seattle-news/times-watchdog/the-inside-story-of-mcas-how-boeings-737-max-system-gained-power-and-lost-safeguards/.

335　Gates, Dominic, Baker, Mike, 'The inside story of MCAS: How Boeing's 737 MAX system gained power and lost safeguards', *Seattle Times*, Jun 22, 2019, https://www.seattletimes.com/seattle-news/times-watchdog/the-inside-story-of-mcas-how-boeings-737-max-system-gained-power-and-lost-safeguards/.

336　Gates, Dominic, Baker, Mike, 'The inside story of MCAS: How Boeing's 737 MAX system gained power and lost safeguards', *Seattle Times*, Jun 22, 2019, https://www.seattletimes.com/seattle-news/times-watchdog/the-inside-story-of-mcas-how-boeings-737-max-system-gained-power-and-lost-safeguards/.

337   Gates, Dominic, Baker, Mike, 'The inside story of MCAS: How Boeing's 737 MAX system gained power and lost safeguards', *Seattle Times*, Jun 22, 2019,
       https://www.seattletimes.com/seattle-news/times-watchdog/the-inside-story-of-mcas-how-boeings-737-max-system-gained-power-and-lost-safeguards/.

338   Gates, Dominic, Baker, Mike, 'The inside story of MCAS: How Boeing's 737 MAX system gained power and lost safeguards', *Seattle Times*, Jun 22, 2019,
       https://www.seattletimes.com/seattle-news/times-watchdog/the-inside-story-of-mcas-how-boeings-737-max-system-gained-power-and-lost-safeguards/.

339   Gates, Dominic, Baker, Mike, 'The inside story of MCAS: How Boeing's 737 MAX system gained power and lost safeguards', *Seattle Times*, Jun 22, 2019,
       https://www.seattletimes.com/seattle-news/times-watchdog/the-inside-story-of-mcas-how-boeings-737-max-system-gained-power-and-lost-safeguards/.

340   Freed, Jamie, Rucinski, 'Factbox: In Boeing internal messages, employees distrust the 737 MAX and mock regulators', Reuters, Jan 10, 2020,   https://www.reuters.com/article/us-boeing-737max-factbox-idUSKBN1Z90NP.

341   'Boeing 737 MAX 8 Earns FAA Certification', Boeing, Mar 9, 2017, https://boeing.mediaroom.com/2017-03-09-Boeing-737-MAX-8-Earns-FAA-Certification.

342   Office of Inspector General, 'Weaknesses in FAA's Certification and Delegation Processes Hindered Its Oversight of the 737 MAX 8', U.S. Department of Transportation, Feb 23, 2021, https://www.oig.dot.gov/sites/default/files/FAA%20Certification%20of%20737%20MAX%20Boeing%20II%20Final%20Report%5E2-23-2021.pdf.

343   Office of Inspector General, 'Weaknesses in FAA's Certification and Delegation Processes Hindered Its Oversight of the 737 MAX 8', U.S. Department of Transportation, Feb 23, 2021, https://www.oig.dot.gov/sites/default/files/FAA%20Certification%20of%20737%20MAX%20Boeing%20II%20Final%20Report%5E2-23-2021.pdf.

344   Office of Inspector General, 'Weaknesses in FAA's Certification and Delegation Processes Hindered Its Oversight of the 737 MAX 8',

U.S. Department of Transportation, Feb 23, 2021, https://www.oig.dot.gov/sites/default/files/FAA%20Certification%20of%20737%20MAX%20Boeing%20II%20Final%20Report%5E2-23-2021.pdf.

345   Schacter, Joanna, 'Delegating Safety: Boeing and the Problem of Self-Regulation', *Cornell Journal of Law and Public Policy*, 30:637, https://community.lawschool.cornell.edu/wp-content/uploads/2021/11/Schacter-final-1.pdf.

346   Cassidy, John, 'How Boeing and the F.A.A. Created the 737 MAX Catastrophe', *New Yorker*, Sep 17, 2020, https://www.newyorker.com/news/our-columnists/how-boeing-and-the-faa-created-the-737-max-catastrophe.

347   Schneider, Avie, 'Boeing Lands 1st 737 Max Order Since Troubled Plane Was Cleared To Fly Again', *NPR*, Dec 3, 2020, https://www.npr.org/2020/12/03/942133229/boeing-lands-1st-737-max-order-since-troubled-plane-was-cleared-to-fly.

348   Freed, Jamie, Rucinski, 'Factbox: In Boeing internal messages, employees distrust the 737 MAX and mock regulators', Reuters, Jan 10, 2020,
https://www.reuters.com/article/us-boeing-737max-factbox-idUSKBN1Z90NP.

349   Freed, Jamie, Rucinski, 'Factbox: In Boeing internal messages, employees distrust the 737 MAX and mock regulators', Reuters, Jan 10, 2020,   https://www.reuters.com/article/us-boeing-737max-factbox-idUSKBN1Z90NP.

350   Tkacik, Maureen, 'Crash Course: How Boeing's managerial revolution created the 737 MAX disaster', *TNR*, Sep 18, 2019, https://newrepublic.com/article/154944/boeing-737-max-investigation-indonesia-lion-air-ethiopian-airlines-managerial-revolution.

351   Beene, Ryan, Suhartono, Harry, Bloomberg, 'Boeing mocked Lion Air for requesting extra 737 Max pilot training year before crash', *Fortune*, Jan 14, 2020, https://fortune.com/2020/01/14/boeing-lion-air-extra-737-max-pilot-training-simulator-crash/.

352   Beene, Ryan, Suhartono, Harry, Bloomberg, 'Boeing mocked Lion Air for requesting extra 737 Max pilot training year before crash', *Fortune*, Jan 14, 2020, https://fortune.com/2020/01/14/boeing-lion-air-extra-737-max-pilot-training-simulator-crash/.

353   Joesph, Leslie, Lucas, Amelia, 'Boeing fires CEO Dennis Muilenburg, as the company struggles with 737 Max crisis', *CNBC*, Dec 23, 2019,

https://www.cnbc.com/2019/12/23/boeing-stock-halted-pending-news-company-battles-fallout-737-max-crisis.html.

354   Josephs, Leslie, 'Boeing's fired CEO Muilenburg walks away with more than $60 million', *CNBC*, Jan 10, 2020, https://www.cnbc.com/2020/01/10/ex-boeing-ceo-dennis-muilenburg-will-not-get-severance-payment-in-departure.html.

355   Gates, Dominic, 'Boeing gears up to renew its safety culture after 737 MAX crashes', *Seattle Times*, May 24, 2022, https://www.seattletimes.com/business/boeing-aerospace/after-the-737-max-crashes-boeing-gears-up-to-renew-its-safety-culture/.

356   Gates, Dominic, 'Boeing gears up to renew its safety culture after 737 MAX crashes', *Seattle Times*, May 24, 2022, https://www.seattletimes.com/business/boeing-aerospace/after-the-737-max-crashes-boeing-gears-up-to-renew-its-safety-culture/.

357   Oehmke, Philipp, 'The Three Students Who Uncovered 'Dieselgate', *Spiegel International*, Oct 23, 2017, https://www.spiegel.de/international/business/the-three-students-who-discovered-dieselgate-a-1173686.html.

358   Alter, Charlotte, 'Meet the Man Who Brought Down Volkswagen', *Time*, Nov 19, 2015, https://time.com/4119981/the-man-who-brought-down-volkswagen/.

359   More information on the ICCT can be found here: https://climateinitiativesplatform.org/index.php/International_Council_on_Clean_Transportation_(ICCT).

360   Oehmke, Philipp, 'The Three Students Who Uncovered "Dieselgate"', *Spiegel International*, Oct 23, 2017, https://www.spiegel.de/international/business/the-three-students-who-discovered-dieselgate-a-1173686.html.

361   'EPA's Notice of Violation of the Clean Air Act to Volkswagen', ICCT, Sep 18, 2015, https://theicct.org/epas-notice-of-violation-of-the-clean-air-act-to-volkswagen-press-statement/.

362   McGee, P., 'How VW's cheating on emissions was exposed', *Financial Times*, Jan 12, 2017, https://www.ft.com/content/103dbe6a-d7a6-11e6-944b-e7eb37a6aa8e.

363   More about the differences between EU and US car emission regulations can be found here: https://www.europarl.europa.eu/RegData/etudes/ATAG/2017/595363/IPOL_ATA(2017)595363_EN.pdf.

364   Epstein, Richard, 'The Role of Defeat Devices in Environmental Protection: Beyond The VW Scandal', *Forbes*, Sep 27, 2017, https://www.forbes.com/sites/richardepstein/2017/09/27/the-role-of-defeat-devices-in-environmental-protection-beyond-the-vw-scandal/?sh=7a0d0e1652c1.

365   Thiruvengadam, Arvind, 'How We Do It: The Cafee Team on the Volkswagen Scandal and What's Up Next', Roads Scholar Academy, West Virginia University, https://roadsscholaracademy.wvu.edu/speakersandsessionoverviews/arvind-thiruvengadam.

366   'EPA's Notice of Violation of the Clean Air Act to Volkswagen', ICCT, Sep 18, 2015, https://theicct.org/epas-notice-of-violation-of-the-clean-air-act-to-volkswagen-press-statement/.

367   'EPA's Notice of Violation of the Clean Air Act to Volkswagen', ICCT, Sep 18, 2015, https://theicct.org/epas-notice-of-violation-of-the-clean-air-act-to-volkswagen-press-statement/.

368   Glinton, Sonari, 'How A Little Lab In West Virginia Caught Volkswagen's Big Cheat', *NPR*, Sep 24, 2015, https://www.npr.org/2015/09/24/443053672/how-a-little-lab-in-west-virginia-caught-volkswagens-big-cheat.

369   'Defeat device car owners can claim damages—EU court adviser', *Reuters*, Jun 2, 2022, https://www.reuters.com/business/autos-transportation/defeat-device-car-owners-entitled-damages-eu-court-adviser-2022-06-02/.

370   Gardella, Rich, Brunker, Mike, 'VW had previous run-in over "defeat devices"', *CNBC*, Sep 23, 2015, https://www.cnbc.com/2015/09/23/vw-had-previous-run-in-over-defeat-devices.html.

371   Gardella, Rich, Brunker, Mike, 'VW had previous run-in over "defeat devices"', *CNBC*, Sep 23, 2015, https://www.cnbc.com/2015/09/23/vw-had-previous-run-in-over-defeat-devices.html.

372   Gardella, Rich, Brunker, Mike, 'VW had previous run-in over "defeat devices"', *CNBC*, Sep 23, 2015, https://www.cnbc.com/2015/09/23/vw-had-previous-run-in-over-defeat-devices.html.

373   Perkins, Chris, 'VW's Emissions-Cheating Defeat Device Was Developed By Audi In 1999 to Reduce Noise', Jul 19, 2016, https://www.roadandtrack.com/new-cars/car-technology/news/a30029/vw-acoustic-function-defeat-device/.

374   Perkins, Chris, 'VW's Emissions-Cheating Defeat Device Was Developed By Audi In 1999 to Reduce Noise', Jul 19, 2016, https://

www.roadandtrack.com/new-cars/car-technology/news/a30029/vw-acoustic-function-defeat-device/.

375 'Timeline of Major Accomplishments in Transportation, Air Pollution, and Climate Change', USEPA, https://www.epa.gov/transportation-air-pollution-and-climate-change/timeline-major-accomplishments-transportation-air#2000.

376 Goodman, Leah McGrath, 'Why Volkswagen Cheated', *Newsweek*, Dec 15, 2015, https://www.newsweek.com/2015/12/25/why-volkswagen-cheated-404891.html.

377 Rothfeder, Jeffrey, 'The Volkswagen Settlement: How Bad Management Leads to Big Punishment', Jul 1, 2016, https://www.newyorker.com/business/currency/the-volkswagen-settlement-how-bad-management-leads-to-big-punishment.

378 Ewing, Jack, 'Engineering a Deception: What Led to Volkswagen's Diesel Scandal', Mar 16, 2017, *New York Times*, https://www.nytimes.com/interactive/2017/business/volkswagen-diesel-emissions-timeline.html. Goodman, Leah McGrath, 'Why Volkswagen Cheated', *Newsweek*, Dec 15, 2015, https://www.newsweek.com/2015/12/25/why-volkswagen-cheated-404891.html.

379 Rauwald, Christoph, 'VW's Piech Isolated After CEO Slight as End of Era Looms', *Bloomberg*, Apr 12, 2015, https://www.bloomberg.com/news/articles/2015-04-12/vw-chairman-piech-isolated-after-ceo-slight-as-end-of-era-looms#xj4y7vzkg. Dahl, Peter, 'Winterkorn struggling for survival', *DW*, Sep 23, 2015, https://www.dw.com/en/winterkorn-struggling-for-survival-as-vw-board-meets/a-18731369.

380 Taylor, Edward, Schwartz, Jan, 'Ferdinand Piech, architect of Volkswagen's global expansion, dies aged 82', *Reuters*, Aug 27, 2019, https://www.reuters.com/article/us-volkswagen-piech-death-idUSKCN1VG26I.

381 Taylor, Edward, Schwartz, Jan, 'Ferdinand Piech, architect of Volkswagen's global expansion, dies aged 82', *Reuters*, Aug 27, 2019, https://www.reuters.com/article/us-volkswagen-piech-death-idUSKCN1VG26I.

382 Hawranek, Dietmar, Kurbjuweit, Dirk, 'Wolfsburg Empire', *Spiegel Politics*, Aug 18, 2013, https://www.spiegel.de/politik/wolfsburger-weltreich-a-d5d979b0-0002-0001-0000-000107728908.

383   'Piech protege Winterkorn Volkswagen CEO at last', *Reuters*, Jan 20, 2007, https://www.reuters.com/article/newsmaker-vw-idUKNOA93943720061109.

384   Ewing, J., Bowley, G., 'The Engineering of Volkswagen's Aggressive Ambition', Dec 13, 2015, *New York Times*, https://www.nytimes.com/2015/12/14/business/the-engineering-of-volkswagens-aggressive-ambition.html.

385   Ewing, J., Bowley, G., 'The Engineering of Volkswagen's Aggressive Ambition', Dec 13, 2015, *New York Times*, https://www.nytimes.com/2015/12/14/business/the-engineering-of-volkswagens-aggressive-ambition.html.

386   Blackwelder, Britt, et al., 'The Volkswagen Scandal', Robins Achool of Business, 2016, https://scholarship.richmond.edu/cgi/viewcontent.cgi?article=1016&context=robins-case-network.

387   Muller, Joann, 'How Volkswagen Will Rule The World', Forbes, Apr 17, 2013, https://www.forbes.com/sites/joannmuller/2013/04/17/volkswagens-mission-to-dominate-global-auto-industry-gets-noticeably-harder/?sh=60f8e3553c46.
       Schäfer, D., 'VW unveils management reshuffle', *Jul 6, 2010, Financial Times*, https://www.ft.com/content/ebf0a2f4-88fe-11df-8925-00144feab49a.

388   Goodman, Leah McGrath, 'Why Volkswagen Cheated', *Newsweek*, Dec 15, 2015, https://www.newsweek.com/2015/12/25/why-volkswagen-cheated-404891.html.

389   Goodman, Leah McGrath, 'Why Volkswagen Cheated', *Newsweek*, Dec 15, 2015, https://www.newsweek.com/2015/12/25/why-volkswagen-cheated-404891.html.

390   'FTC Charges Volkswagen Deceived Consumers with Its "Clean Diesel" Campaign', Federal Trade Commission, Mar 29, 2016, https://www.ftc.gov/news-events/news/press-releases/2016/03/ftc-charges-volkswagen-deceived-consumers-its-clean-diesel-campaign.

391   Lynch, Luann J., Santos, Carlos, 'VW Emissions and the 3 Factors That Drive Ethical Breakdown', *UVA Darden*, Oct 17, 2016, https://ideas.darden.virginia.edu/vw-emissions-and-the-3-factors-that-drive-ethical-breakdown.
       Smith, Geoffrey, Parloff, Roger, 'Hoaxwagen, *Fortune*, Mar 7, 2016, https://fortune.com/longform/inside-volkswagen-emissions-scandal/.

392   'Fear and respect: VW's culture under Winterkorn', *Reuters*, Oct 11, 2015, https://www.reuters.com/article/volkswagen-emissions-culture/fear-and-respect-vws-culture-under-winterkorn-idUSL8N12A0QZ20151011.

393   Smith, Geoffrey, Parloff, Roger, 'Hoaxwagen, *Fortune*, Mar 7, 2016, https://fortune.com/longform/inside-volkswagen-emissions-scandal/.

394   'VW emissions cheat software came from Audi – report', Guardian,Apr 20, 2016, https://www.theguardian.com/business/2016/apr/20/vw-emissions-software-came-from-audi-report.

395   'Volkswagen: The scandal explained', *BBC*, Dec 10, 2015, https://www.bbc.com/news/business-34324772.

396   Groom, Nichola, Krolicki, Kevin, 'Volkswagen diesel car wins "Green Car of the Year"', *Reuters*, Nov 21, 2008, https://www.reuters.com/article/us-autos-greencar-idUSTRE4AJ7S120081120.

397   'Volkswagen Group deliveries', Volkswagen, 2014, https://annualreport2014.volkswagenag.com/group-management-report/business-development/deliveries.html.

398   Lienert, Paul, Gardner, Timothy, 'Volkswagen's 'clean diesel' strategy unraveled by outside emissions tests', *Reuters*, Sep 22, 2015, https://www.reuters.com/article/us-usa-volkswagen-emission-idUSKCN0RL2EI20150922.

399   Lienert, Paul, Gardner, Timothy, 'Volkswagen's 'clean diesel' strategy unraveled by outside emissions tests', *Reuters*, Sep 22, 2015, https://www.reuters.com/article/us-usa-volkswagen-emission-idUSKCN0RL2EI20150922.

400   Blackwelder, Britt, Coleman, Katherine, Colunga-Santoyo, Sara, Harrison, Jeffrey S., and Wozniak, Danielle, 'The Volkswagen Scandal', Case Study, University of Richmond: Robins School of Business, 2016.

401   Lienert, Paul, Gardner, Timothy, 'Volkswagen's 'clean diesel' strategy unraveled by outside emissions tests', *Reuters*, Sep 22, 2015, https://www.reuters.com/article/us-usa-volkswagen-emission-idUSKCN0RL2EI20150922.

402   Lienert, Paul, Gardner, Timothy, 'Volkswagen's 'clean diesel' strategy unraveled by outside emissions tests', *Reuters*, Sep 22, 2015, https://www.reuters.com/article/us-usa-volkswagen-emission-idUSKCN0RL2EI20150922.

403 'EUROPE NEWS After a year of stonewalling, Volkswagen finally came clean', *Reuters*, Sep 24, 2015, https://www.cnbc.com/2015/09/24/how-volkswagen-fought-epa-on-emissions-cheating-claims.html.

404 Atiyeh, Clifford, 'U.S. Charges Former VW CEO Martin Winterkorn with Four Felonies', *Yahoo! News*, May 4, 2018, https://sg.news.yahoo.com/u-charges-former-vw-ceo-220700159.html.

405 Parloff, Roger, 'How VW Paid $25 Billion for Dieselgate—And Got Off Easy', *ProPublica*, Feb 6, 2018, https://www.propublica.org/article/how-vw-paid-25-billion-for-dieselgate-and-got-off-easy.
Rawlinson, Kevin, 'Six Volkswagen executives charged with fraud over emissions cheating', *Guardian,* Jan 11, 2017, https://www.theguardian.com/business/2017/jan/11/six-volkswagen-executives-charged-with-over-emissions-cheating.

406 'Former CEO of Volkswagen AG Charged with Conspiracy and Wire Fraud in Diesel Emissions Scandal', USEPA, May 3, 2018, https://www.epa.gov/archive/epa/newsreleases/former-ceo-volkswagen-ag-charged-conspiracy-and-wire-fraud-diesel-emissions-scandal-0.html.

407 Ewing, J., 'Volkswagen Says 11 Million Cars Worldwide Are Affected in Diesel Deception', Sep 22, 2015, *New York Times*, https://www.nytimes.com/2015/09/23/business/international/volkswagen-diesel-car-scandal.html.

408 Kresge, Naomi, Weiss, Richard, 'Volkswagen Drops 23% After Admitting Diesel Emissions Cheat', *Bloomberg,* Sep 21, 2015, https://www.bloomberg.com/news/articles/2015-09-21/volkswagen-drops-15-after-admitting-u-s-diesel-emissions-cheat#:~:text=Volkswagen%20plunged%20as%20much%20as,in%20more%20than%20three%20years.

409 Farrell, Sean, Ruddick, Graham, 'Volkswagen CEO Martin Winterkorn quits over diesel emissions scandal', *Guardian*, Sep 23, 2015, https://www.theguardian.com/business/2015/sep/23/volkswagen-ceo-martin-winterkorn-quits-over-diesel-emissions-scandal.

410 Kottasová, Ivana, 'German prosecutors charge former Volkswagen CEO Martin Winterkorn with fraud', *CNN Business*, Apr 15, 2019, https://edition.cnn.com/2019/04/15/business/winterkorn-volkswagen-diesel-fraud-charges/index.html.

411   'Former Volkswagen CEO charged in U.S. over diesel emissions cheating', *CBC*, May 3, 2018, https://www.cbc.ca/news/business/volkswagen-martin-winterkorn-charged-1.4647233.

412   Kottasová, Ivana, 'German prosecutors charge former Volkswagen CEO Martin Winterkorn with fraud', *CNN Business*, Apr 15, 2019, https://edition.cnn.com/2019/04/15/business/winterkorn-volkswagen-diesel-fraud-charges/index.html.

413   Milne, R., 'Volkswagen: System Failure', Nov 5, 2015, *Financial Times*, https://www.ft.com/content/47f233f0-816b-11e5-a01c-8650859a4767.

414   Sharpe, Nicola Faith, 'Volkswagen's Bad Decisions & Harmful Emissions: How Poor Process Corrupted Codetermination in Germany's Dual Board Structure', *Michigan Business & Entrepreneurial Law Review*, 2017, 7(1), https://repository.law.umich.edu/cgi/viewcontent.cgi?article=1065&context=mbelr.

415   Sharpe, Nicola Faith, 'Volkswagen's Bad Decisions & Harmful Emissions: How Poor Process Corrupted Codetermination in Germany's Dual Board Structure', *Michigan Business & Entrepreneurial Law Review*, 2017, 7(1), https://repository.law.umich.edu/cgi/viewcontent.cgi?article=1065&context=mbelr.

416   Stewart, James, B., 'Problems at Volkswagen Start in the Boardroom', *New York Times*, Sep 25, 2015, https://www.nytimes.com/2015/09/25/business/international/problems-at-volkswagen-start-in-the-boardroom.html.

417   Milne, R., 'Volkswagen: System Failure', Nov 5, 2015, *Financial Times*, https://www.ft.com/content/47f233f0-816b-11e5-a01c-8650859a4767.

418   Parloff, Roger, 'How VW Paid $25 Billion for Dieselgate—And Got Off Easy', *ProPublica*, Feb 6, 2018, https://www.propublica.org/article/how-vw-paid-25-billion-for-dieselgate-and-got-off-easy.

419   Riley, Chris, 'Volkswagen's diesel scandal costs hit $30 billion', *CNN Business*, *CNN Business*, Sep 29, 2017, https://money.cnn.com/2017/09/29/investing/volkswagen-diesel-cost-30-billion/index.html.

420   'Volkswagen AG Agrees to Plead Guilty and Pay $4.3 Billion in Criminal and Civil Penalties; Six Volkswagen Executives and Employees are

Indicted in Connection with Conspiracy to Cheat U.S. Emissions Tests', Jan 11, 2017, Office of Public Affairs, U.S. Dept. of Justice, https://www.justice.gov/opa/pr/volkswagen-ag-agrees-plead-guilty-and-pay-43-billion-criminal-and-civil-penalties-six#:~:text=VW%20 is%20charged%20with%20and,vehicles%20complied%20with%20 U.S.%20emissions.

421   'Volkswagen to pay out £193m in "dieselgate" settlement', *BBC*, May 25, 2022, https://www.bbc.com/news/business-61581251.

422   'Volkswagen to pay out £193m in "dieselgate" settlement', *BBC*, May 25, 2022, https://www.bbc.com/news/business-61581251.

423   Shepardson, David, 'Exclusive: Fiat Chrysler nearing U.S. diesel emissions settlement – source', *Reuters*, Jan 9, 2019, https://www.reuters. com/article/us-fiat-chrysler-emissions-exclusive-idUSKCN1P22AP.

424   Shepardson, David, 'Exclusive: Fiat Chrysler nearing U.S. diesel emissions settlement – source', *Reuters*, Jan 9, 2019, https://www.reuters. com/article/us-fiat-chrysler-emissions-exclusive-idUSKCN1P22AP.

425   'Munich prosecutors fine BMW 8.5 million euros for faulty engine software', *Reuters*, Feb 15, 2019, https://www.reuters.com/article/bmw-fine-idINKCN1QE14C. https://uk.finance.yahoo.com/news/vw-dieselgate-fraud-timeline-scandal-044711231.html?guccounter=1&guce_ referrer=aHR0cHM6Ly93d3cuZ29vZ2xlLmNvbS8&guce_referrer_ sig=AQAAABLa-pYx8WoWMSS7lKsmmgI9BxqdUOSN5UnVgoFs enDO2HQF2q8i44bh_CRUWrXm2TjX0w6b8jKytQb92749QM_x9 Zo5azlnhlpowOLIa5Xq7sNutKYJsWLP6-PIgj5XNbDItYZt_2IYwK flvUb93oXBYNWjsuZJY6CjqP1xaZk3.

426   Ewing, Jack, 'Supplier's Role Shows Breadth of VW's Deceit', *New York Times*, Feb 1, 2017, https://www.nytimes.com/2017/02/01/ business/bosch-vw-diesel-settlement.html.

427   Ewing, Jack, 'Supplier's Role Shows Breadth of VW's Deceit', *New York Times*, Feb 1, 2017, https://www.nytimes.com/2017/02/01/business/bosch-vw-diesel-settlement.html.

428   'VW engineer sentenced to 40-month prison term in diesel case', *CNBC*, Aug 26, 2017, https://www.cnbc.com/2017/08/26/vw-engineer-sentenced-to-40-month-prison-term-in-diesel-case.html. Rushe, Dominic, 'Oliver Schmidt jailed for seven years for Volkswagen emissions scam', *Guardian*, Dec 6, 2017,

https://www.theguardian.com/business/2017/dec/06/oliver-schmidt-jailed-volkswagen-emissions-scam-seven-years.

429   Flam, Faye, 'Theranos's empty promise to cure a fake problem', Mar 27, 2019, https://economictimes.indiatimes.com/small-biz/startups/features/theranoss-empty-promise-to-cure-a-fake-problem/articleshow/68590586.cms?from=mdr.

430   Carreyrou, John, 'Hot Startup Theranos Has Struggled With Its Blood-Test Technology', *Wall Street Journal*, Oct 16, 2015, https://www.wsj.com/articles/theranos-has-struggled-with-blood-tests-1444881901.

431   Pierson, Brendan, 'The rise and fall of Theranos founder Elizabeth Holmes', *Reuters*, Jan 4, 2022, https://www.reuters.com/world/us/rise-fall-theranos-founder-elizabeth-holmes-2022-01-04/.

432   Dickler, Jessica, 'Verdict in fraud case of Theranos founder Elizabeth Holmes offers lessons for investors', *CNBC*, Jan 4, 2022, https://www.cnbc.com/2022/01/04/verdict-in-fraud-case-of-theranos-founder-elizabeth-holmes-has-lessons-for-investors.html.

433   Metz, Rachel, 'Elizabeth Holmes sentenced to more than 11 years in prison for fraud', *CNN Business,* Nov 18, 2022, https://edition.cnn.com/2022/11/18/tech/elizabeth-holmes-theranos-sentencing/index.html.

434   Halpert, Madeline, 'Sunny Balwani: Former Theranos executive gets nearly 13 years in prison', *BBC*, Dec 8, 2022, https://www.bbc.com/news/world-us-canada-63895825.

435   Halpert, Madeline, 'Sunny Balwani: Former Theranos executive gets nearly 13 years in prison', *BBC*, Dec 8, 2022, https://www.bbc.com/news/world-us-canada-63895825.

436   Carreyrou, John, 'Hot Startup Theranos Has Struggled With Its Blood-Test Technology', *Wall Street Journal*, Oct 16, 2015, https://www.wsj.com/articles/theranos-has-struggled-with-blood-tests-1444881901.

437   'Young blood', *Economist*, Jun 25, 2015, https://www.economist.com/business/2015/06/25/young-blood.

438   Carreyrou, John, 'Hot Startup Theranos Has Struggled With Its Blood-Test Technology', *Wall Street Journal*, Oct 16, 2015, https://www.wsj.com/articles/theranos-has-struggled-with-blood-tests-1444881901.

439   Carreyrou, John, 'Hot Startup Theranos Has Struggled With Its Blood-Test Technology', *Wall Street Journal*, Oct 16, 2015, https://www.wsj.com/articles/theranos-has-struggled-with-blood-tests-1444881901.

440 Carreyrou, John, 'Hot Startup Theranos Has Struggled With Its Blood-Test Technology', *Wall Street Journal*, Oct 16, 2015, https://www.wsj.com/articles/theranos-has-struggled-with-blood-tests-1444881901.

441 Strand, C.C., 'Christian & Noel Holmes, Elizabeth Holmes' Parents: 5 Fast Facts to Know', *Heavy*, Mar 19, 2019, https://heavy.com/news/2019/03/elizabeth-holme-parents-noel-christian/.

442 Carreyrou, John, *Bad Blood: Secrets and Lies in a Silicon Valley Startup*, Knopf: 2018.

443 Kraus, Rachel, 'Theranos screwed up legit blood test innovations for everybody', *Mashable SE Asia*, Mar 21, 2019, https://sea.mashable.com/tech/2879/theranos-screwed-up-legit-blood-test-innovations-for-everybody.

444 Carreyrou, John, *Bad Blood: Secrets and Lies in a Silicon Valley Startup*, Knopf: 2018.

445 Carreyrou, John, *Bad Blood: Secrets and Lies in a Silicon Valley Startup*, Knopf: 2018.

446 Ramsey, Lydia, 'Controversial health startup Theranos has a board of directors that's anything but medical experts', *Business Insider India*, Oct 16, 2015,
https://www.businessinsider.com/theranos-board-of-directors-2015-10.

447 Carreyrou, John, *Bad Blood: Secrets and Lies in a Silicon Valley Startup*, Knopf: 2018.

448 Carreyrou, John, *Bad Blood: Secrets and Lies in a Silicon Valley Startup*, Knopf: 2018.

449 Siddiqui, Faiz, 'Former Walgreens CFO testifies about pharmacy's troubled partnership with blood-testing start-up Theranos', *Waashington Post*, Oct 13, 2021,
https://www.washingtonpost.com/technology/2021/10/13/theranos-walgreens-holmes/.

450 Carreyrou, John, *Bad Blood: Secrets and Lies in a Silicon Valley Startup*, Knopf: 2018.

451 Khorram, Yasmin, 'Elizabeth Holmes admits she added drugmakers' logos to Theranos reports', *CNBC*, Nov 23, 2021, https://www.cnbc.com/2021/11/23/elizabeth-holmes-admits-she-added-drugmakers-logos-to-theranos-reports.html.

452 Carreyrou, John, *Bad Blood: Secrets and Lies in a Silicon Valley Startup*, Knopf: 2018.

453   Carreyrou, John, *Bad Blood: Secrets and Lies in a Silicon Valley Startup*, Knopf: 2018.

454   Carreyrou, John, *Bad Blood: Secrets and Lies in a Silicon Valley Startup*, Knopf: 2018.

455   Gold, Jenny, 'How Theranos hid its sketchiness from reporters—and helped keep the puff pieces coming', *Vox*, Mar 22, 2018, https://www.vox.com/first-person/2018/3/22/17151906/theranos-controversy-fraud-journalism-holmes-fire-alarm-blood.

456   'Former Employee Says Theranos Cherry-Picked Results From Faulty Machines', *NBC Bay Area*, Sep 15, 2021, https://www.nbcbayarea.com/news/local/elizabeth-holmes-trial/former-employee-says-theranos-cherry-picked-results-from-faulty-machines/2657632/.

457   Carreyrou, John, *Bad Blood: Secrets and Lies in a Silicon Valley Startup*, Knopf: 2018.

458   Carreyrou, John, *Bad Blood: Secrets and Lies in a Silicon Valley Startup*, Knopf: 2018.

459   Stewart, James B, 'David Boies Pleads Not Guilty', *New York Times*, Sep 21, 2018, https://www.nytimes.com/2018/09/21/business/david-boies-pleads-not-guilty.html.

460   Carreyrou, John, *Bad Blood: Secrets and Lies in a Silicon Valley Startup*, Knopf: 2018.

461   Carreyrou, John, *Bad Blood: Secrets and Lies in a Silicon Valley Startup*, Knopf: 2018.

462   Khorram, Yasmin, 'Former Theranos patient testifies that a blood test at Walgreens came back with false positive for HIV', *CNBC*, Nov 17, 2021, https://www.cnbc.com/2021/11/17/theranos-patient-says-blood-test-came-back-with-false-positive-for-hiv.html.

463   Lopatto, Elizabeth, 'The first patient testimony about a Theranos test result: a miscarriage that wasn't', *Verge*, Sep 22, 2021, https://www.theverge.com/2021/9/21/22687026/theranos-patient-bad-test-miscarriage-pregnancy.

464   Khan, Roomy, 'Theranos' $9 Billion Evaporated: Stanford Expert Whose Questions Ignited The Unicorn's Trouble', *Forbes*, Feb 17, 2017, https://www.forbes.com/sites/roomykhan/2017/02/17/theranos-9-billion-evaporatedstanford-expert-whose-questions-ignited-the-unicorn-trouble/?sh=3fe47b376be8.

465   Carreyrou, John, 'Hot Startup Theranos Has Struggled With Its Blood-Test Technology', *Wall Street Journal*, Oct 16, 2015, https://www.wsj.com/articles/theranos-has-struggled-with-blood-tests-1444881901.

466 Huddlestone Jr., Tom, 'Theranos Has Thrown Out Two Years of Blood-Test Results', *Fortune*, May 19, 2016, https://fortune.com/2016/05/19/theranos-void-edison-results/.

467 Pseudonym

468 See for example M. Iansiti and R. Levin, *The Keystone Advantage: What the New Dynamics of Business Ecosystems Mean for Strategy, Innovation, and Sustainability*, Boston: Harvard Business School Press, 2004; Jacobides M.G., C. Cennamo, and A. Gawer, 'Towards a Theory of Ecosystems', *Strategic Management Journal* 39, no. 8, 2018, pp.2255–76; Williamson P.J. and A De Meyer, 'Ecosystem Advantage: How to Successfully Harness the Power of Partners', *California Management Review*, vol. 55, no. 1, 2012, pp.24–46.

469 De Meyer A. and P.J. Williamson, *Ecosystem Edge: Sustaining Competitiveness in the Face of Disruption*, Stanford Business Press, Palo Alto, USA, 2020.

470 RISC: reduced instruction set computing, or a computer architecture designed to simplify the individual instructions given to the computer to accomplish tasks.

471 Williamson, P.J., A. De Meyer and A. Muthirulan, 'ARM Holdings PLC: Ecosystem advantage', Cambridge-310-127-1, 2009, https://www.thecasecentre.org/students/products/view?id=95198.

472 Liu W., A Beltagui, S. Ye and P.W. Williamson, 'Harnessing Expectation and Ecosystem Strategy for Accelerated Innovation: lessons from the VentilatorChallengeUK', *California Management Review*, 64(3), 2022, pp.78–98.

473 De Meyer A. and S. Mitttal, 'Developing the DfMA Ecosystem in Singapore's Construction Industry', SMU case SMU-19-0036, 2019.

474 Moore, J.H., 'Predators and Prey: A New Ecology of Competition', *Harvard Business Review*, May–June, 1993.

475 Williamson P.J. and M. Wang Jingji, 'Alibaba Group: from Intermediary to Ecosystem Enabler', Cambridge Judge Business School Case, 2016.

476 Koh A., R.Speculand, A. Wong, W.K. Lim, 'DBS: digital transformation to best bank in the world', SMU Case study SMU-20-0015, 2020.

477 Iansiti and Levin. 2004. The Keystone Advantage: What the New Dynamics of Business Ecosystems Mean for Strategy, Innovation, and Sustainability. Boston: Harvard Business School Press; Jacobides M.G., C. Cennamo, and A. Gawer 2018. Towards a Theory of Ecosystems. Strategic Management Journal 39, no. 8 p.2255–76; Williamson P.J. and A De Meyer. 2012. Ecosystem Advantage: How to Successfully Harness the Power of Partners, California Management Review, vol. 55, no. 1, pp. 24–46.

478

479   More about the Future of the Corporation programme can be found
      here: https://www.thebritishacademy.ac.uk/programmes/future-of-
      the-corporation/about/.

480   'Business Roundtable Redefines the Purpose of a Corporation to
      Promote 'An Economy That Serves All Americans', *Business Roundtable*,
      Aug   19,   2019,   https://www.businessroundtable.org/business-
      roundtable-redefines-the-purpose-of-a-corporation-to-promote-an-
      economy-that-serves-all-americans.

481   The UN document titled 'Report of the World Commission on
      Environment and Development: Our Common Future' can be found
      here: http://www.un-documents.net/our-common-future.pdf.

482   Hellerstedt, K., Uman, T., & Wennberg, K., 'Fooled by diversity? when
      diversity initiatives exacerbate rather than mitigate inequality', *Academy
      of Management Perspectives*, 2023, doi:10.5465/amp.2021-0206

483   'Gender Equality in Asian Corporate Leadership Is an Achievable Reality',
      INSEAD,   Mar   5,   2018,   https://www.insead.edu/news/2018-new-
      research-insead-emerging-markets-institute-reveals-emergent-themes-and-
      major-implications-for-gender-parity-in-asian-corporate-leadership.
      Burroughes, Tom, 'Asia's Financial, Tech Firms Must Accelerate
      Closure Of Gender Gap', *Wealth Briefing Asia*, Mar 6, 2018,
      https://www.wealthbriefingasia.com/article.php?id=178534#.
      ZEObJXZBzIV.

484   Isabelle Solal, Kaisa Snellman, 'Women Don't Mean Business? Gender
      Penalty in Board Composition', *Organization Science* 30(6):1270–1288,
      2018,
      https://doi.org/10.1287/orsc.2019.1301

485   'Gender Equality in Asian Corporate Leadership Is an Achievable Reality',
      INSEAD,   Mar   5,   2018,   https://www.insead.edu/news/2018-new-
      research-insead-emerging-marketsinstitute-reveals-emergent-themes-and-
      major-implications-for-gender-parity-in-asian-corporate-leadership.
      Burroughes, Tom, 'Asia's Financial, Tech Firms Must Accelerate
      Closure Of Gender Gap', *Wealth Briefing Asia*, Mar 6, 2018, https://www.
      wealthbriefingasia.com/article.php?id=178534#.ZEObJXZBzIV.

486   Kinias, Zoe, Petriglieri, 'Promoting Gender Balance Is Everyone's
      Business', Knowledge, INSEAD, Feb 26, 2019, https://knowledge.
      insead.edu/leadership-organisations/promoting-gender-balance-
      everyones-business.

487   Ibarra, Herminia, 'A Lack of Sponsorship Is Keeping Women from Advancing into Leadership', *Harvard Business Review*, Aug 19, 2019, https://hbr.org/2019/08/a-lack-of-sponsorship-is-keeping-women-from-advancing-into-leadership.

488   Elkins, Kathleen, 'Warren Buffett says the most important decision you'll ever make has nothing to do with your money or career', *CNBC*, May 14, 2018, https://www.cnbc.com/2018/05/14/warren-buffett-says-the-most-important-decision-is-who-you-marry.html.

489   Jacobs, Katie, 'Herminia Ibarra: "Authenticity" not always positive for leaders', *HR Magazine*, Nov 6, 2015, https://www.hrmagazine.co.uk/content/news/herminia-ibarra-authenticity-not-always-positive-for-leaders.

490   Jensen, Susan, Luthans, Fred, 'Entrepreneurs as Authentic Leaders: Impact on Employees' Attitudes', *Leadership & Organization Development Journal*, 2006, 27. 10.1108/01437730610709273.

491   Rao, Vinika D., Trombini, Chiara, Kinias, Zoe, 'DEI When We Need It the Most', *Knowledge*, INSEAD, Apr 27, 2021, https://knowledge.insead.edu/responsibility/dei-when-we-need-it-most.

492   'Deloitte Global research highlights impact of COVID-19 on working women and how employers can prevent a setback in achieving gender parity', Deloitte, https://www2.deloitte.com/cn/en/pages/about-deloitte/articles/pr-understanding-the-pandemics-impact-on-working-women.html.

493   Ellingrud, Kweilin, Segel, Liz Hilton, 'COVID-19 has driven millions of women out of the workforce. Here's how to help them come back', *Fortune*, Feb 13, 2021, https://fortune.com/2021/02/13/covid-19-women-workforce-unemployment-gender-gap-recovery/.

494   Kinias, Z., 'Women in Financial Services: Survey results and next steps', Singapore: INSEAD and FWA, 2016.

495   Rao, Vinika D., *Regulatory focus and female leadership development (5-2019)*, Doctoral dissertation, Singapore Management University, 2019, https://ink.library.smu.edu.sg/cgi/viewcontent.cgi?article=1218&context=etd_coll.

496   Bourke, Juliet, Titus, Andrea, 'Why Inclusive Leaders Are Good for Organizations, and How to Become One', Mar 29, 2019, https://hbr.org/2019/03/why-inclusive-leaders-are-good-for-organizations-and-how-to-become-one.

497   More about Diageo's efforts to promote inclusion and diversity can be found here: https://www.diageo.com/en/esg/champion-inclusion-and-diversity.

498   Larcker, David F., Tayan, Brian, Watts, Edward M., *Seven Myths of ESG*, Stanford: Nov 4, 2021, https://www.gsb.stanford.edu/faculty-research/publications/seven-myths-esg.

499   Boekhorst, Janet A., 'The Role of Authentic Leadership in Fostering Workplace Inclusion: A Social Information Processing Perspective', Wiley: Nov 18, 2014, https://onlinelibrary.wiley.com/doi/abs/10.1002/hrm.21669.